PRAISE FOR *THE BISEXUAL S GUIDE TO THE UNIVERSE*

"A playful, tongue-in-cheek romp that challenges the heterosexual *and* lesbian and gay status quo with gleeful abandon. Jam-packed with juicy tidbits, historical facts, pop quizzes, coming out advice, dating guidelines, personal hygiene tips and sexual relationship strategies, this book puts a new spin on 'bisexuality as a stage' demanding lights, cameras and action!"

—Lani Ka'ahumanu and Loraine Hutchins,
editors of *Bi Any Other Name*

"A thorough, cheeky and celebratory account of what it means to be bi in the modern world. A must-have for anyone straddling the homo/het line."

—Jen Sincero, author of
The Straight Girl's Guide to Sleeping with Chicks

"After reading this book I now believe in my own inner bisexual. I even joined a bi volleyball league. I got to play for both teams."

—ANT, comic and host of VH1's *Celebrity Fit Club*

"An exciting and sexy journey into the vast universe of bisexuality. Fasten your seatbelt and enjoy the ride. You don't even have to be bi to love it. Entertaining, with plenty of food for thought, and some nice fantasy material too."

—Annie Sprinkle, Ph.D., author of *Dr. Sprinkle's
Spectacular Sex: Make Over Your Love Life*

"Sexy, smart and informative. Finally a book that puts the bisexual experience front and center…. I have been waiting for a book like this: a book that will go a long way in taking bisexuality out of the queer ghetto."

—Kyle Schickner, filmmaker, *Rose by Any Other Name*

"Two sexy bisexuals writing about what they know best? It's a must-read, between the sheets and anywhere else."

— Sharon Kane, porn goddess

"Who knew being Bi could be so much fun? Nicole Kristal and Mike Szymanski take a funny look at what it means to be bisexual. This is the definitive guide for bisexuals who are perhaps the most misunderstood sexual-orientation group on the planet. While every bisexual should have *The Bisexual's Guide to the Universe* on their bookshelf, it is also a must for every heterosexual and so-called 'open-minded' homosexual who is confused, enticed and/or envious of their switch-hitter friends."

—Dan Boyle, author of *Huddle*

"Darling, I'm one of those gay people who think you don't exist. I haven't f——d any women lately, but I enjoyed it when I did, I just haven't done it in forever 'cause I like the other stuff better. I really have nothing to say about bisexuality that you want to hear."

— Bruce Vilanch, comedian

"I have always imagined bisexuality to be the greater gift and Nicole Kristal & Mike Szymanski drolly banish any doubt that might have lingered in my one-pointed preference. They gracefully do so like shamans of inclusive fascination! As the book unfolds, following their lead is taking a deep look, not just into 'bi,' but into a prismatic sexuality."

—Mickey Cottrell, actor/publicist/hedonist/mystic

"Can you unlock the truth about your deepest sexual desires by measuring your delight in mochaccino, grapefruit, or extra-cheese pizza? Who knows?! But in-the-know bi folks, metrosexuals, playahs without labels, and the cautiously curious alike will have a blast trying with this breezy read. *The Bisexual's Guide to the Universe* busts bi myths and 'confirms' plenty of them with a wink and a nod in nearly every tongue-in-cheek sentence."

—Robin Renée, singer-songwriter

THE
BISEXUAL'S
GUIDE

TO THE UNIVERSE

QUIPS, TIPS, AND LISTS
FOR THOSE WHO GO
BOTH WAYS

NICOLE KRISTAL AND
MIKE SZYMANSKI

alyson books
NEW YORK

MANUFACTURED IN THE UNITED STATES OF AMERICA.

THIS TRADE PAPERBACK ORIGINAL IS PUBLISHED BY
ALYSON BOOKS
P.O. BOX 1253
OLD CHELSEA STATION
NEW YORK, NEW YORK 10113-1251

DISTRIBUTION IN THE UNITED KINGDOM BY
TURNAROUND PUBLISHER SERVICES LTD.
UNIT 3, OLYMPIA TRADING ESTATE
COBURG ROAD, WOOD GREEN
LONDON N22 6TZ ENGLAND

FIRST EDITION: OCTOBER 2006

06 07 08 09 00 a 10 9 8 7 6 5 4 3 2 1

ISBN 1-55583-650-X
ISBN-13 978-1-55583-650-4

LIBRARY OF CONGRESS
CATALOGING-IN-PUBLICATION DATA
IS ON FILE.

BOOK DESIGN BY VICTOR MINGOVITS.

CONTENTS

PREFACE

GREETINGS, fence-sitters, chameleons, switch-hitters, pansexuals, omnisexuals, bisexuals, whatevers, and all those who loathe labels!

Welcome to the first ever handbook about...well, whatever it is you like to call yourselves. Odds are you're considering reading this book because at one time or another—maybe last night—you realized you go both ways, or at least aspire to.

Separated into handy Beginner, Intermediate, and Advanced sections, this manual to all-things-bisexual will carefully guide you through the gray areas of your hyper-sophisticated, deliciously misunderstood sexuality.

We'll start off gently with the myths and stereotypes surrounding our kind and give you a little lingo, history, and science behind how we came to be so highly evolved, before whisking you off for some hands-on instruction.

We'll tackle the complexities of coming out of two closets with everyone from your conservative father to your hippie mom to your curious coworkers. Just when things start sounding a little too heavy, we'll let you have a long soak in pop culture until you're refreshed and ready to land a date for Saturday night. If you're good, we'll teach you how to navigate a relationship (or that first threesome).

We've got both sides covered by an experienced bi guy and bi gal—at least enough to raise your Bi-Q. Mike came out as gay and then skulked around for years with a girl, went on more than 40 talk shows and became a Baby Boomer bi activist. Nicole came out as bi in college in the mid-nineties and writes articles about the subject and blares her bi-themed songs wherever anyone will listen.

We'll wrap things up with a final exam to ensure you're a card-carrying bisexual and affirm your intense superiority over the entire human race. Bottom line: If you go both ways, or just want to dabble, or need some inside info on that quirky fence-sitter you're dating, this is the only book you'll ever need. But don't take it all so seriously—you may change your mind tomorrow.

Nicole & Mike

INTRODUCTION: MY HIGH SCHOOL SWEETHEART

NICOLE KRISTAL

"JUST TAKE A BIG gulp, then chase it with a piece of sourdough," Julia said as she zipped up the tent and handed me a plastic water bottle filled with the rum stolen from Darla's parents' liquor cabinet.

I was sixteen, and I had never been drunk before. Sure, I'd smoked pot a couple dozen times, but I had principles. Alcohol made you...uninhibited, stupid.

"Come on, just take it," she insisted.

"What if I get sick?" I protested.

"I told you, I won't let you get sick."

"What if I do something really embarrassing?"

"I won't let you," she smiled wickedly. I knew I was in trouble. I lifted the bottle to my lips and took a big swig. The rum stung as it slid down my virgin throat. I grimaced and shoved the hunk of sourdough into my mouth.

"I can't believe we left the soda at the bottom of the fucking hill," she apologized as I chewed the bread. "Now do four more."

"That sounds like a lot."

"No, it's just the right amount. Now go before everyone else gets here and drinks everything."

I placed the bottle to my lips and took a couple more swigs. More sourdough. More burning rum. Finally, Julia was satisfied with my alcohol intake. I leaned back onto my sleeping bag.

Outside, crickets chirped, and the wind rustled through the Marinwood hills. By the time the other campers slogged up the hill, things had grown a bit blurry. As they invaded the tent and dropped their things, they discovered we had already drunk a large portion of the alcohol. Jealous, they quickly caught up, then went outside the tent to look at the stars.

"You guys coming?"

Already completely incapacitated and draped over our sleeping bags, the answer was clear: absolutely not. They exited and sat outside the tent. Within seconds, our lips were locked. We shared drunk, sloppy, teeth-touching kisses. Outside the tent, a fellow camper asked, "You guys OK in there?"

"Oh, yeah, we're good."

Weeks of passing amorous notes in class had culminated in this drunken make-out session. We weren't lesbians—oh, god, no. We were just how friends should be. Good friends. Best friends.

Having a girlfriend in high school is incredibly convenient. You can have sleepovers every Friday night, late-afternoon "study sessions," you name it. We exploited them all. Yes, a few mistakes were made. A note with "I love you!" written in big letters that I somehow forgot on the kitchen counter. A zipper left completely undone and spotted by my mother as I walked through the door one afternoon. All easily explained under the guise of heterosexuality. "Oh, I must have gone to the bathroom and forgot."

Sure, coming out in high school is somewhat accepted now, but in 1994 it was unheard of, especially in a mid-upper-class suburb like Marin County, California. Somehow word leaked out that Julia was fooling around with a girl. The school's biggest gossip, and one of my friends, confronted me over cheeseburgers to see if I knew who it was.

I dipped a french fry in some ketchup, as the Spanish Inquisition began.

"Is it Vanessa?" she pried.

"Nope, I'm pretty sure it's not Vanessa."

"Is it Anna?"

"C'mon, Julia doesn't even know Anna."

"But you know who it is?"

"Yeah, but you have to guess. I won't tell you."

"Um, Karin."

"It's not Karin."

This line of questioning continued for two more hours and cut into the car ride home. Suddenly, a strange look covered my friend's face.

"Is it you?"

"Um hmm."

Dead silence. I had actually rendered the school's biggest gossip speechless. I explained what had happened and made her vow to secrecy. Who knows if she kept the secret. No guys asked me out after that night, but then again, no high school guys asked me out before that night, so it was hard to tell.

After rejecting Julia's invitation to be her date for the senior prom, my "best friend" at the time, who herself was questioning, decided to ask her. Julia, delighted with the opportunity to induce jealousy, purchased a number of prom dresses and then pranced in front of both my friend and myself modeling them. Eventually, they both sat me down to tell me how they both thought I was gay and in denial. I stared at Julia in her stupid flower-coated dress and glowered at my overly insensitive best friend and told them I was bi. They shrugged it off, but I knew they were wrong.

I'd had a boyfriend in seventh grade and didn't exactly mind french-kissing him in front of our other friends. I'd had multiple crushes on all kinds of guys at my school—the hippie hacky-sackers who ignored me, the cocky jock in the remedial English class where I worked as the teacher's assistant. I liked guys. They just never seemed to like me. And the ones who I suspected liked me never had the nerve to ask me out. So I stayed in my holding pattern with Julia, waiting for college to arrive.

Around the same time, I met a thirty-one-year-old satellite designer from Palo Alto while playing guitar on the beach in Capitola (or, as the local Santa Cruz residents like to call the tourist town, Crapitola). At the time, Matt was married to a raven-haired bisexual woman. About six months later, he called me, divorced and overly flirtatious. Sure, he wasn't a high school boy—but he actually dug me and paid for dinners. Taken by his bitchin' Camero and muscular build, we dated behind my parents' back. Knowing I was jailbait, our relationship remained mostly innocent. We never slept together, but enjoyed some intense make-out sessions in his car.

Meanwhile, Julia had taken to dropping acid (though I asked her not to), which evolved into snorting speed and dating a drunken football player. Half the time she'd drive to my house wasted to pick fights with me, and other times call my father to tell him she was "worried" about me. She threatened to tell him our secret. My parents told me they considered Julia deeply troubled and that I should stop spending time with her. But they didn't need to tell me. I already had.

After our graduation ceremony that spring, Julia spotted Matt across the auditorium and told a mutual friend he was "heinous." She was wrong. With chocolate eyes and smooth blond hair, Matt was more attractive than many of the awkward high school boys at my school. From the ceremony, Matt drove my friend and me to the school gymnasium for the all-night postgraduation party. We changed out of our caps and gowns in his cherry-red sports car, and I kissed him goodnight and thanked him for the joint he had shared with us.

I skirted past the parental chaperones and crossed the middle of the gymnasium toward the dance floor. As the disco ball spun, Julia bounced to my side, completely trashed, and grabbed my face and tried to kiss me. "Are you out of your mind? Everyone will see!" I whispered.

"Why do you have to be such a goddamn bitch?" she yelled. She never did care what people thought.

"Just stay the fuck away from me," I said with a shove. That last statement wasn't really necessary because within the next fifteen minutes, she was throwing up outside, and my friends were arguing with the chaperones not to call her parents, a fitting conclusion to the school year and my first relationship.

After my freshman year of college, filled with minirelationships with men and women, I returned home for the summer. An entire school year of freedom disappeared once I moved back into my parents' house. I sank deeply into a depression that evolved into full-fledged panic attacks. A girl with whom I had a relationship in the dorms went home to Chicago and inevitably reunited with her boyfriend. In my nineteen-year-old mind, I knew I had hit rock bottom. I had to alleviate this stress somehow. So as I sobbed on the couch in our family room, I decided to tell my mother.

"I'm bisexual," I sobbed.

My mother paused briefly before blurting, "If I hadn't met your dad, I might have gone the other way."

After stealing my moment, my mother and I gabbed about women and my poorly concealed relationship with Julia, but never once did she question my certainty about my bisexuality. Instead, she shed a disapproving glance. "I always thought something was going on, but I didn't want to admit it to myself because it was her." My mother hated Julia. I couldn't really blame her for loathing the quintessential bad influence of my life. The first time I smoked pot, drank, tried hallucinogens, and had sex all happened as a result of that one person.

Wow, I never did thank her.

INTRODUCTION: THE HOUSE THAT BISEXUALITY BUILT

MIKE SZYMANSKI

I'M SITTING HERE LOOKING out my home office into the famed Hollywood Hills of southern California with flowering trees and grand estates—Bette Davis's old house across the street, Madonna's place just over the hill under the Hollywood sign, Valentino's mansion at the top of the hill—and I hear the symphony across the street from the Hollywood Bowl. The neighborhood is rife with bisexual history—they say Garbo had an affair with writer Mercedes de Acosta Reynal in a house around the corner, Tyrone Power borrowed a house for secret meetings with William Powell, Maurice Chevalier lived in the area with his male companion while still thanking heaven for little girls. Bi surrealist painter Edward James, bi composer Leonard Bernstein, and bi screenwriter Ben Hecht all lived on the hill. And I own my piece of it: a five-level Mediterranean-style 1920s house that snakes high above the thirty-nine geranium-lined steps to my front door, passing both male and female nude statues. Sure, it seems lucky for a guy in his early forties who merely writes for a living to own such a place, but the way I paid for this house is a painful story.

I got this house because I came out as bisexual. Those in-the-know call it "The House That Bisexuality Built."

It was on my birthday, September 1, that my dad told me he didn't think I was his son. Dad declared, "You don't look like me, you don't act like me. I want you to take a blood test to prove that you're not my son." Being gay, he says, is bad enough. But bisexual?! That's absurd, that's confusing, that's freak-show material. Anyway, it got me on talk shows—more than forty to date.

My dad wouldn't even watch a tape of my best appearances. In one of the last seasons of his famous talk show, Phil Donahue proclaimed, "Bisexuals have problems, they're not accepted by the straight community, and they're shunned by gays and lesbians," then Phil mentioned my full name. Dad ejected the tape. He could watch no more.

When I came out to him as gay years before, Dad seemed to take it in stride. I thought we were long over all the anger, blame, embarrassment, and tears. The anger and hurt flushed into me this time.

"I'll give you money to take the test," he said.

"You think you can buy me? I'm insulted that you want to prove that I'm not part of your family!" I shouted.

"I'll give you ten thousand dollars," he said soberly. I hesitated.

Until that moment, I had always felt accepted and part of our family—there was no choice, after all. But now he seemed to be bribing my way out of the family because I was going public as a bisexual. If I wasn't biologically his son, he could explain that to his friends and save face.

My mom—who came with me to the 1993 March on

Washington and lectured with me at the Parents and Friends of Lesbians and Gays' national conference—excused my dad's concerns. "If you're born that way and you can't choose, that's something we can accept, but if you like both, then you do have a choice, and he takes it personally if you choose a guy."

My dad was more succinct, "If you can choose, why would you choose the wrong way?"

When I came out as gay, he hung his head in faux despair and told neighbors it was something I couldn't help. It was as if I had lost a leg.

My dad was an ultra-Republican, religiously Catholic, second-generation immigrant, proud Pole, and is one of the people who really meant to vote for Pat Buchanan in the controversial 2000 Florida election. He always pointed out that I am the last one to carry on our family name.

My dad was an accountant and a miser, and he's not wealthy enough to be throwing around ten grand, so I knew he must really want me to be tested. I also knew that I had to make a point with him. Hitting him in the wallet would definitely hurt.

"You're still my son no matter what the outcome," Dad assured me months after the initial request when I began talking to him again. "I just need to know."

"You'll have to pay," I warned. "You won't get this easily."

"Twenty grand?" he offered.

"Fifty," I countered. "I'll take your stupid blood test if you pay the down payment of my house."

The bottom line for Dad's irrational attitude toward me is the very same reason I'm criticized by friends in the homosexual community—my chosen "family." My gay friends complain, "You're embarrassing (or diluting) 'the family'" or say, "Being bi is fine with me, but don't tell anyone else if you expect to get a date."

It's true, for a group that's stereotyped as being so promiscuous, my dating life has hit the skids since I've been openly bi. Straight women don't dare touch me, and gay men shun me because they think I'll eventually leave them for the "easy" relationship. Truth is, I've always sought a monogamous relationship with either a man or a woman and have wanted to raise children with that partner no matter what they have or don't have between their legs.

I was no less heterosexual when I came out as gay, and I was no less gay when I finally realized what it meant to be bisexual. It's simple: I recognize my physical and emotional attractions toward people of either sex, and I don't have to have them at the same time. I always figured when I settled on one partner that I'd prefer to be with whomever he or she is—even though my eye may wander—and I won't feel like I'm missing out. That is, not any more than any married guy who settles on one gal.

Sure, for a lot of people, labeling themselves as bisexual is a stepping-stone to understanding they are gay. For me, being gay was a stepping-stone to feeling comfortable with my bisexuality. So when I'm in an opposite-sex relationship, I'm just as gay, and I'm not betraying any "family." And when I'm with a guy, I'm not just getting even with my dad.

I wish both my families—my biological one and my chosen one—could just settle down and let me be. Being out doesn't mean wearing a "Bi & Proud" button all the time. It simply means that when I'm home for Christmas I want to be able to freely talk about the girls and guys I'm dating. When I'm at a gay club, I want to be able to mention a cute woman who turns my head.

Bisexuals rarely feel fully out in either family, but that's the fault of the family. Thank goodness a younger generation is adding "bisexual" to the names of their clubs in colleges and high schools. Hurrah for all the centers, publications, parades, and groups that are including "Bi" along with "Gay and Lesbian." Only then can we truly belong.

I cried after I signed my "contract" with my father to take the blood and genetics tests. I knew no matter what the outcome, nothing could ever be the same between us.

People who hear this story mistakenly think my father and

I are estranged. No, even after my TV appearances we talked at least every other day. But we never mentioned the "B-word." Dad heard me talking about "The House That Bisexuality Built" with Marilyn Kagan and Leeza Gibbons and on other talk shows. What he doesn't know is that this house has become a symbol: a haven for bisexual activists who traveled through Los Angeles—bi authors, activists, psychologists, teachers, couples, grandmothers, youths, friends. I had a bisexual roommate upstairs and a bi couple renting downstairs. Bi groups meet regularly in my living room, and much of the bi writing I do is from this office overlooking the hills.

And then, something unexpected happened. A stranger who had read my story left tulips and a letter at my front door. He said he used to be married and had been in a relationship with a man. "I would like to get involved in the bisexual movement, and I would like to meet you," he wrote.

Another crackpot, a stalker, I thought. The story of my hassles with my father touched a lot of people, many who wrote love notes, so I was wary. I was ending a relationship with a girl and had pretty much resigned myself to being alone. But I decided to meet this guy.

Now, John and I have been together more than a decade, and I don't think I ever want to be with anyone else, ever. We're both bisexual, we're both monogamous, and nobody gets it. He has a beautiful baby boy with my sister who lives with us, and we're raising him and my sister's ten-year-old son.

I've not said it since my very public "second coming out," but my dad liked my partner John.

Yep, he never liked any guy I ever dated before: the soap opera actor, the rock musician, the Jewish intellectual, none of them, and when I look back, he didn't like many of the women either. But it's easy to like John. They talked about stocks and politics, and Dad told him secrets he never told any of us. Dad even invited John to his home in Florida, and even allowed us to sleep in the same bed under his roof. You may say he came a long way. But I think I have too.

And you know that blood test? It never happened. Dad was in and out of the hospital with surgeries and illnesses, and he wasn't well enough to give blood. He died just before Christmas 2005, and we said everything we needed to say to each other. John wrote the eulogy. Anyway, I have no doubt I'm his son. Without ever saying so, it's become obvious to me that my dad perhaps just wanted me to be with someone who really cared about me—the right person. Though he never said it, I know he thought that being open about my bisexuality could hurt me in my career, or perhaps even in finding a good relationship.

At the end, we were all at Dad's bedside, even the strawberry-haired four-year-old that he wasn't sure he should acknowledge as a real grandson when he was first born. Dad could communicate by moving his left foot and blinking, and when I held Donovan up to him, he forced a smile, and a tear fell from his eye. "Here's your other grandson," I said. He acknowledged him with two wriggles of his foot, which meant "yes."

Donovan jumped up on the hospital bed, crawled on his chest, and Dad didn't seem to mind. Donovan whispered, "It's OK, Dzia Dzia, you can go to heaven now." Not long after, he did. And some of his ashes are sprinkled in the plants along the steps of the place he helped me buy—The House That Bisexuality Built.

BEGINNER

CHAPTER 1

THE B WORD

WE'D LIKE TO TELL you that being a beginner is easy, but given that there's absolutely nothing about sexuality that we've found to be simple, we won't feed you lies. From the complications of flip-flopping to trying not to fulfill the stereotype to figuring out if you even are bisexual, you've got a lot on your plate. What are you doing reading this introduction?

THE FLIP-FLOP

YOUR MOM'S TELLING YOU you're straight. Your gay buddy's telling you you're gay. You feel sexually schizophrenic. Just when you feel confident enough to tell the world you're gay, poof! Your desire betrays you, and you get hot for the opposite sex. We like to call this dilemma "the flip-flop." (And it has nothing to do with whom you vote for or what you're wearing on your feet.) Don't be fooled. The fact that you flip-flop at all means only one thing: you're bi. Yup, that's right, a minority within a minority. You can keep trying and keep hoping gay-dom or hetero-hood will stick, but don't hold your breath. We bisexuals—excuse us, "label-free," "fluid," "whatevers,"—don't necessarily have to choose. Just go with it.

"I SWEAR TO GOD, SOMETIMES I'M GAY . . . "

SOUND FAMILIAR? ALL OF us have gay days, weeks, months . . . even years. Just 'cause we're leaning to one side for a while doesn't mean we'll stay there. All right, it's true: many of us have a preference for men or women, but unlike those boring monosexuals (people who date only one sex), our preference doesn't define us. We're honest about what we do, at least more so than those in the gay and straight communities who dabble with members of the opposite or same sex and conceal their behavior. We know better than to claim it will never happen again. That doesn't mean we don't on occasion question our sexual identity when we flip-flop between cravings.

Case in point—here's an e-mail from a married bi gal friend: "Some days I really ponder my sexuality. I often am battling against myself trying to figure out if I am 'gay' or not. There are times when I just feel appalled when my husband is touching me and 'poking' me...I just feel disgusted. So, at times that leads me to think that I can't even stand a man so much that I must be gay. But then there are nights like last night where I had multiple orgasms and earth-shattering sex with my husband, and I am reminded I am so not gay."

So don't be a dork. Enjoy your gay phases instead of freaking out about them because, yes, you are kinda gay. Congratulations: you're less boring than most people.

"I'M SO *NOT* GAY!"

THIS PHRASE HAS PROBABLY danced through your head a few times as well. At least, it dances through ours, usually when we're flat on our backs with a member of the opposite sex who really knows what he or she is doing in bed. But it's easy to get lost and focus too much on the gay side. Why? Because it demands so much attention, always reminding us of what sexual deviants we are.

We hear the words *gay, queer, lesbo,* and *fag* in the office or the supermarket and turn to see who's talking. We stare into the vehicles of people with rainbow flags to reassure ourselves that, yep, gay people look just as boring as straight people. In the midst of facing challenging decisions such as, "Should I really order Showtime for the gay programming?" we often forget that straight sex can be kinda fun. Seriously, there must be something to it—just look at how many people swear by it and commit entire books, poems, movies, soap operas, television networks, companies, and lives to it.

True, most women can't have orgasms from the penis, but hey, the penis part doesn't altogether suck. And guys, let's be frank: some women really know how to work it. Though images of hetero love have been beaten to death by the media to the point of actual boredom, once in a very blue moon we notice a straight couple making out in public or catch a TBS showing of *Unfaithful* or *Body Heat* that reminds us of how hot straight sex can be. So next time you're digging the het action, or sitting at a table of straight people, hiding behind heterosexual privilege, don't feel so guilty. Your straight side has feelings too.

YOU'RE PROBABLY BISEXUAL IF . . .

1. You feel unfulfilled spending time in just the gay scene or just the straight scene.
2. You admire someone from the back, it turns out to be a different gender than you expected, and you don't mind.
3. You've defended or made excuses for bisexual celebrities who see spaceships, do drugs until they're arrested, or wear vials of blood around their necks.
4. You enjoy watching both men and women during sex scenes in movies.
5. You've been naked with two or more people and liked it.
6. You follow all the sex scandals in the news involving outed politicians, then yell at the screen when they declare themselves gay despite their wives and children.
7. When you masturbate, both men and women pop into your fantasies.
8. You get depressed when you don't have any bisexual or gay friends.

9. You went to the midnight showing of *The Rocky Horror Picture Show* more than three times in college.
10. You've rented or purchased a gay or bi porno and felt turned on despite the fake boobs, abnormally large erections, and the creepy people.
11. You spell *women* with a *y* or *girl* with extra *rs*—or know someone who does.
12. You don't care whether Gia labeled herself a lesbian or bisexual, just that Angelina played her in the movie, which you own.
13. You think the word *polyamory* sounds practical, not offensive.
14. You never bought that the character Jenny on *The L Word* was gay.
15. You enjoy hugging your same-sex friends more than you should at times.
16. You started watching *The O.C.*, *Six Feet Under*, and *Buffy the Vampire Slayer* box sets because you heard characters had gone bi, but upon watching lamented how all of them said they were gay or "experimenting."
17. You read all of Anne Rice's books until 2005 when she declared herself born-again, blaming her flagrantly bisexual novels on spiritual unrest.
18. You watch bad foreign and straight-to-video films because the back of the box boasts of love triangles.
19. You argued with all of your friends about how 2005's *Brokeback Mountain* wasn't a gay cowboy movie, but a love story about two extremely hot bisexuals.
20. You tell your friends that you're dating somebody, and they have to ask what gender the person is.

If you've checked off five or more, you're bi. Your membership card will be sent in the mail.

BISEXUAL MYTHS WE WISH WERE TRUE

1. **EVERYONE'S BISEXUAL.** Contrary to Freud's famous proclamation, quite a few people actually identify as straight or gay. We know—it's news to us too.

2. **OVERLY SEXUAL PEOPLE ARE USUALLY BISEXUAL.** Many really sexual people are willing to experiment because of their exaggerated sex drives. Although they might like the idea of bisexuality and consider it a good fit, many find to their dismay that they are just straight or gay. Bummer.

3. **STRAIGHT OR GAY PEOPLE WILL GO BI FOR REALLY HOT PEOPLE.** Your gay friends guarantee you that they'd do Kylie. Your lesbian friends swear they'd slip between the covers for Jude. Are they for real? You'll never know. But everyone has someone they'd go bi for.

4. **EVERYONE'S BISEXUAL WHEN THEY'RE DRUNK.** Maybe not everyone, but women and men do have a tendency to go bi once they set their inhibitions free . . . oh, except for that football-watching, Republican guy with the beer gut. Not him.

5. **BISEXUALS MAKE BETTER LOVERS.** Oops, this doesn't belong in the myth section. How'd that get here?

6. **BISEXUALS ARE MYSTERIOUS.** They are! Just look at Sharon Stone in *Basic Instinct*. Did we mention we can wield an ice pick, too?

7. **BISEXUALS ARE COOLER THAN GAY PEOPLE.** Nope. A lot of us can't dress for shit and have no social skills. Then again, most of us are vampires from the fourteenth century, so can you blame us?

8. **BI GUYS ARE MORE SENSITIVE.** Hmm, this is a toughie because so many bi men we've met are sweet, sensitive, and caring . . . equally in touch with their masculine and feminine sides. Then again, there are the bastards who shoot and run and cheat on their wives.

9. **BISEXUALS LIKE KINKY SEX.** Plenty of bisexuals are having boring-ass sex as you read this. We just don't know any of them.
10. **BISEXUALS GET LOTS OF ACTION.** Believe it or not, some of us can't get laid. (Just kidding.)
11. **BISEXUALS NEED A MAN AND WOMAN TO BE SATISFIED.** Gosh, it sounds good, but just finding one decent relationship is hard enough.
12 **BISEXUALS ARE HOT.** Hmm, we really need to check this list again and weed out the nonmyths.

HOW TO FULFILL THE STEREOTYPE

1. Come out as bi, then act really gay or straight.
2. Deny that you're gay, then actually be gay.
3. Get a lot of sexually transmitted diseases, then share them with all your friends.
4. Cheat on your partner every chance you get.
5. Act indecisive and confused about your sexuality at all times.
6. Bi women: leave your female lovers for men.
7. Bi men: never date women. Period.
8. Hide in the straight community like a chameleon.
9. Camp it up in a gay bar on weeknights and then go home to your straight spouse.
10. Tell all your friends that homophobia applies only to gay people and never hurts you.
11. Look at your watch halfway through sex with your partner and say you're yearning for the other sex.
12. Sleep with everybody—and record it all on your blog or live, streaming Web cam.

LABELS THAT REALLY MEAN BI

THE IDEA OF SEXUAL orientation and labels didn't actually exist until the nineteenth century, so we all pretty much still suck at the whole thing. It's hard not to suck at something that's so idiotic. In the 1960s and '70s, baby boomers overintellectualized sexual identity, slathering us with incomprehensible academic jargon, whereas today's teenagers and college kids have pretty much decided to make up their own words in some sort of unspoken battle for individuality and vagueness. We don't care what you call yourselves, as long as it's not evangelical.

FLUID: a word commonly used by trendy twenty-somethings to define their ebbing and flowing desires for both sexes

GIRLFAG: a straight, bi, or lesbian woman who is extremely attracted to bisexual or gay men and considers herself a gay man trapped in a woman's body

GUYDYKE: a straight, bi, or gay guy who is extremely attracted to bisexual or gay women and considers himself a lesbian trapped in a man's body

HALF-DYKE: a bisexual girl who leans more toward women than men

HETERO-FLEXIBLE: a straight person open to having relationships with members of the same sex

"I DON'T LIKE TO LABEL MYSELF": the antilabel label adopted by many true fence-sitters unwilling to take on the stigma and stereotypes of a label

OMNISEXUAL: Latin for someone who will do anyone

PANSEXUAL: one who is attracted to people of multiple genders, exhibiting a sexuality that has many different forms, objects, and outlets—and perhaps kitchen utensils

QUEER: someone who isn't heterosexual but identifies more with the gay community than the straight community

TRISEXUAL: arguably coined by the character Samantha on *Sex in the City* this term means someone who will try anything, that is, a woman or man willing to experiment repeatedly with members of the same sex but who is primarily attracted to the opposite sex

What I don't like about the word "bisexual" is that it sets up an either/or paradigm. Ideally we'd all be sexual. Because, who cares? Why do we have to put labels on it? We live in a world where categories make people feel safer.

—LANI KA'AHUMANU, activist and author

ORIGIN OF THE B-WORD

NOBODY LIKES TO USE "the B-word." Nobody likes to say it. Nobody likes to acknowledge it exists. Even those comfortable with calling themselves bi are constantly searching for a better word. So really, where did that pesky label come from, and why are we stuck with it? Here's a brief history that's likely to frustrate you even more.

1892

The year that *bisexuality* first appeared in the dictionary (don't ask us which dictionary because it was way too long ago), defined as an "attraction to both sexes."

1914

The year the word weaseled its way into the *Journal of the American Medical Association* with a rather progressive definition: "By nature all human beings are psychically bisexual—capable of loving a person of either sex." Wow, where's our time machine?

1924

The year some unknown genius proposed changing the word *bisexual* to *ambisexual*. Unfortunately, it never caught on, and we've been expected to do both sexes simultaneously ever since.

1956

Nobody really used the label *bisexual* until the 1950s. The abbreviation *bi* didn't exist until 1956. How they came up with that abbreviation, we're still researching. We think it may be an acronym for "blithering idiot," coined by a '50s housewife after listening to her husband try to explain why he was sucking face with the pool boy.

SOME PATHETIC DEFINITIONS

CURIOUS AS TO WHY so many people avoid calling themselves bisexual? Perhaps because no one can agree on a clear-cut definition of the damn word. Here are a few pathetic stabs from various sources of the word, which will only confuse you further.

Webster's Unabridged Dictionary in 2006 and the *Merriam-Webster Online Edition* still call us hermaphrodites, listing the primary definition of *bisexual* as "possessing characters of both sexes" and "of both sexes, combining male and female organs in one individual."

At least *Webster's* didn't liken us to foliage, like the biological definition for *bisexual* from the Brooklyn Botanic Garden in 2003: "Having both stamens (male parts) and pistils (female parts); a perfect flower." Well, we are perfect flowers . . . but still.

Though Freud said all people were born bisexual until culture and society forced them to choose, goofy psychologists today (like those who wrote the latest definition of the word for the *Gale Encyclopedia of Psychology*) still expect us to be doing both sexes at all times: "Sexual orientation defined as sexual involvement with members of both sexes concurrently within the period of one year." But what if we had sex with a different gender on day 366? Aw, come on. Can't the rules be bent just a little?

Hmm, maybe the Religious Right can give us some insight. In 1996, Republican senator Don Nickles said, "Bisexual by definition means promiscuous, having relations with both male and female." Senator Nickles, here's a new word for you to define: bigot.

Other religious leaders think we're just gay as hell, especially later in life. Just ask the former pope. "The bisexual term suggests a sort of equivalence for people between homosexuality and heterosexuality, but the homosexual tendency actually predominates (or does so with the passage of time). The individual sometimes presents himself as bisexual for fear of being regarded as homosexual," said John Paul II at the Institute for Studies on Marriage and Family in 1997. Hey, it's not our fault all those gay people lie.

Let's give those goofy psychologists another try. Try the latest definition from the American Psychological Association: "Bisexual persons can experience sexual, emotional and affectional attraction to both their own sex and the opposite sex." Much better. Did some queer write this one? Sounds like Dr. Phil to me.

Crap, we forgot we're all still just in transition, at least according to the British National Survey of Sexual Attitudes and Lifestyles in 2002: "A form of bisexuality prevalent in early adulthood may represent a transitional phase in which preferences are tested through experimentation with different lifestyles and relationships." Who took this survey? Elton John? Or was it the other British former bisexual, George Michael?

Screw all this. Let's just meditate. Heighten our awareness, and maybe the definition will just come to us. Or at least that must have been what the Gay and Lesbian Center (gee, is there a word missing?) in Hollywood advised in 2006 when they concocted this vague description: "One's own awareness of one's own capacity to be attracted to other individuals regardless of gender." So one is not bi if one isn't "aware" that one is bi?

Surely, BiNet USA, the only national bisexual organization in the country, will have a better explanation: "Bisexuals can choose to be open to the full range of possibilities, but our bisexuality is the potential, not the requirement, for involvement with more than one gender. Some bisexual people choose to be in committed monogamous relationships; some choose other forms of relationships and commitments. Heterosexual and homosexual people also make these choices." Oops—never mind.

Let's try the former bi magazine *Anything That Moves*: "Bisexuality is a whole, fluid identity. Do not assume that bisexuality is binary or duogamous in nature: that we have 'two' sides or that we must be involved simultaneously with both genders to be fulfilled human beings. In fact, don't assume that there are only two genders. Do not mistake our fluidity for confusion, irresponsibility, or an inability to commit." Er, duo-whagamous?

Then again, maybe definitions are cultural—at least they are according to Dr. Ruth's *Encyclopedia of Sex:* "While persons who engage in bisexual behavior may describe themselves as bisexual, many identify themselves as heterosexual or homosexual—particularly African-American and Latino bisexual men and African-American women."

Here's the definition we'd select, if we had to. Which we don't. But if we did, we'd choose this one from a small bi group in Milwaukee: "The potential for physical, romantic, or emotional attraction to more than one gender." Leave it to a bunch of queers in the Midwest to actually get it right.

But then again, maybe everyone should just adopt our definition . . .

"*Bisexual* (noun, adj.): the most evolved sexual orientation on the planet that many straight and gay people hesitate to explore or admit because mainstream society, their friends, and the world at large deny its obvious existence."

You have just completed Chapter 1. Take a deep breath. Now, as you exhale, breathe out every ridiculous word you just read and forget them all. As you inhale, be grateful you're not a boring monosexual. Exhale. Meditate on how you will avoid fulfilling the stereotype. Inhale. Ponder how you will seduce that hot gay or straight person in your life. Now slowly open your eyes a little bit wider, lower your hands to your side, and flip to the next chapter.

CHAPTER 2

MEASURING SEX

FOR THOSE OF YOU with dirty minds, this chapter is not about measuring certain body parts beneath your waist. It's about measuring sexuality. Now we know you're thinking, "Wait a second. I want to know whether I'm bi." Let us answer that for you—yes, you are totally bi. Now you just need to figure out how bi you are. We've included some academic and scientific tools for you to use in order to assess the extent of your sexual flexibility.

WAYS TO DETERMINE BISEXUALITY

WE KNOW YOU'RE BI. You know you're bi. Here are some of the most popular methods for determining your fluidity.

> **KINSEY SCALE:** Grades experience and psychological reactions with 0 being entirely hetero, 6 entirely homo, and 3 equally attracted. Most people fall between 1 and 5, revealing some level of bisexuality.
> **KLEIN SEXUAL ORIENTATION GRID:** Created by noted bisexual psychiatrist Dr. Fritz Klein, the grid measures seven elements of sexuality based on the past, present, and future.
> **DUAL ATTRACTION:** In their book, Martin S. Weinberg, Colin J. Williams, and Douglas W. Pryor simplified Dr. Klein's grid by using three variables: sexual feelings,

sexual activities, and romantic feelings, allowing bisexuals to fall into the homo or hetero category.

MULTIDIMENSIONAL SCALE OF SEXUALITY: Developed in the 1980s, this behavioral and cognitive scale measures levels of hetero, homo, and asexual feelings and contains six bisexual categories.

SONEMPORARY FEMALE BISEXUALITY: Writer J. R. Little's thirteen categories of bisexuality just for the gals.

THE THREE-CIRCLE GRAPH: Antonio Galarza has come up with three intersecting circles to show sexuality that includes concepts like hetero-romantic and homo-platonic, but ultimately it shows 70–80 percent of all males are bi.

THE KINSEY SCALE

For those of you who haven't heard, or rented the DVD, Alfred Kinsey was the first scientist to thoroughly examine sex and sexual behavior. Credited with the creation of the field of study known as "sexology," this pioneer founded the controversial Institute of Sex Research in 1947 with his wife, Clara. Kinsey himself maintained many male lovers (many of whom were his graduate students). One biographer claims that Kinsey enjoyed group sex and S&M and encouraged his staff to engage in group sex. His wife, Clara, who had sex with other men, remained his life partner as they explored why people didn't always tell the truth about their sexual behavior. To address this reality, Kinsey and Clara developed a scale that addressed the different degrees of one's sexuality. The couple discovered that 37 percent of men and 13 percent of women had an orgasm at some point in their lives with a person of the same sex. And their conclusion, frightening to many, is that most people's sexuality falls somewhere in between heterosexual and homosexual, which ultimately means most people are fence-sitters.

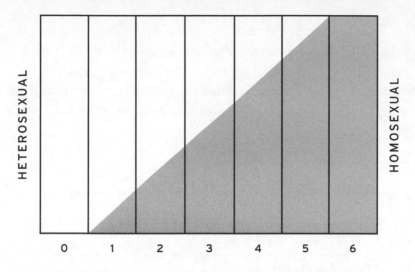

HETEROSEXUAL-HOMOSEXUAL RATING SCALE

0: EXCLUSIVELY HETEROSEXUAL, WITH NO HOMOSEXUAL

1: PREDOMINANTLY HETEROSEXUAL, ONLY INCIDENTALLY HOMOSEXUAL

2: PREDOMINANTLY HETEROSEXUAL, BUT MORE THAN INCIDENTALLY HOMOSEXUAL

3: EQUALLY HETEROSEXUAL AND HOMOSEXUAL

4: PREDOMINANTLY HOMOSEXUAL, BUT MORE THAN INCIDENTALLY HETEROSEXUAL

5: PREDOMINANTLY HOMOSEXUAL, ONLY INCIDENTALLY HETEROSEXUAL

6: EXCLUSIVELY HOMOSEXUAL

DR. KLEIN'S SEXUAL ORIENTATION GRID

Dr. Fritz Klein, an established and well-respected bisexual professor, activist, psychiatrist, and sexologist, took the Kinsey scale and created a more intricate grid to address the complexities of sexuality. Klein's Sexual Orientation Grid analyzes seven parts of your sexual orientation, listed as A through G down the left-hand column. The three columns to the right indicate the person's past, present, and ideal feelings about both sexes. The person then receives a rating from 1 to 7 for each of the twenty-one resulting combinations, one rating for each empty box in the chart below. The meanings of the ratings are indicated below the grid itself.

	VARIABLE	PAST	PRESENT	IDEAL
A	SEXUAL ATTRACTION			
B	SEXUAL BEHAVIOR			
C	SEXUAL FANTASIES			
D	EMOTIONAL PREFERENCE			
E	SOCIAL PREFERENCE			
F	HETEROSEXUAL / HOMOSEXUAL LIFESTYLE			
G	SELF-IDENTIFICATION			

FOR VARIABLES A TO E

1: OTHER SEX ONLY
2: OTHER SEX MOSTLY
3: OTHER SEX SOMEWHAT MORE
4: BOTH SEXES
5: SAME SEX SOMEWHAT MORE
6: SAME SEX MOSTLY
7: SAME SEX ONLY

FOR VARIABLES F AND G

1: HETEROSEXUAL ONLY
2: HETEROSEXUAL MOSTLY
3: HETEROSEXUAL SOMEWHAT MORE
4: HETERO/GAY-LESBIAN EQUALLY
5: GAY/LESBIAN SOMEWHAT MORE
6: GAY/LESBIAN MOSTLY
7: GAY/LESBIAN ONLY

Klein's grid reveals what a person desires for him- or herself and also takes into account actual behavior, but the grid also shows that people can change. Klein wisely defines sexuality as "an ongoing dynamic process."

THE R-U-BI? TEST

1. Have you had sex with both sexes?
   a. Yes
   b. No
   c. I think I did, but I was drunk

2. About that one night in college:
   a. I was drunk, no, really, I was
   b. Which one?
   c. I posted pictures on my Web site

3. When you first heard the word *bisexual*, you:
   a. thought it was something you could ride
   b. thought it was something really trendy and cool
   c. thought that you could have sex only twice

4. AC/DC refers to:
   a. alternate current/direct current
   b. someone who goes both ways
   c. a lame band from the '70s

5. A switch-hitter is:
   a. a baseball player who can bat equally well right- or left-handed
   b. an S&M dom who alternately uses a paddle and a baton
   c. someone who is going to leave me to live a "normal life"

6. The Kinsey Scale proves that:
   a. all sexuality is fluid
   b. if you lay off the carbs, you can really shed those pounds
   c. I'm more gay than you

7. A bonobo is:
   a. a trendy Asian beverage
   b. a species of monkey
   c. the illegitimate love child of Chastity Bono and Bono

8. There's a dog-eared book on your shelf authored by:
   a. Michael Crichton
   b. Danielle Steele
   c. Anne Rice
   d. Madonna

9. Sandra Bernhard is:
   a. an early-twentieth-century stage actress
   b. a man-hating comedienne
   c. the woman who said she slept with Madonna

10. The last time you saw a gay person was:
    a. on a *Will and Grace* rerun
    b. when you woke up, turned over, and said, "Who are you?"
    c. when they ditched you because you weren't butch enough

11. What do you do about unwanted body hair?
    a. I wax every day
    b. I shave only when I might get laid
    c. I don't have any unwanted body hair

12. An "innocent bi-stander" is:
    a. on the sidelines
    b. misspelled
    c. a voyeur

13. Heterosexuals are:
    a. in denial
    b. dull
    c. conquests
    d. all of the above
    e. none of the above

14. Biannual means:
    a. occurring every two years
    b. occurring two times a year
    c. I'm always confused about this

15. Tantric sex is:
    a. something Sting did in the '90s
    b. something hippies do
    c. frustrating
    d. prolonging intercourse to channel orgasmic energy
       and raise consciousness

ANSWER KEY AND SCORE

1. a = 3; b = 0; c = 2
2. a = 1; b = 3; c = 2
3. a = 3; b = 2; c = 1
4. a = 3; b = 1; c = 2
   (nobody calls bisexuals "AC/DC" anymore)
5. a = 3; b = 3; c = 0
6. a = 3; b =0; c = 0
7. a = 1; b = 3; c = 2 (bonobos are bisexual monkeys)

8.   a = 0; b =1; c = 3; d = 2 (Anne Rice = bi vampires, duh!)
9.   a = 0 (Bernhard, not Bernhardt); b = 0; c = 3
10. a = 1; b =2; c = 3
     (don't worry, they weren't right for you anyway)
11. a = 1; b = 3; c = 0 (remember: less is more)
12. a = 1; b = 3; c = 2 (tame that dirty mind!)
13. a = 3; b = 3; c = 3; d = 3; e = 0
14. a = 2; b = 1; c = 3
     (you're bi, so of course you're confused!)
15. a = 1; b = 2; c = 2; d = 3
     (you're bi, so naturally you know everything about sex)

BI, THANK YOU! If you scored 30–45 points, go out and have yourself an orgy. You're a certifiable bisexual.

POTENTIAL FENCE-SITTER If you scored 10–29, time to hop on that fence and see a shrink. You've got tendencies, honey.

STOP READING THIS BOOK If you scored 0–9, do just that.

Now that you've decided where you land on the Kinsey scale or the Klein grid and/or decided that rating your sexuality is a load of crap, you can now move on to read about the tepid job scientists have done at explaining your sexuality. (Psst: If the next chapter arouses bad associations from your college statistics course, by all means skip to Chapter 4 and start agonizing about coming out.)

CHAPTER 3

WEIRD SCIENCE

Even a superficial look at other societies and some groups in our own society should be enough to convince us that a very large number of human beings—probably a majority—are bisexual in their potential capacity for love.

—MARGARET MEAD, cultural anthropologist, *Redbook*, January 1975

NEITHER ACADEMICS NOR SCIENTISTS have ever adequately explained how many bisexuals there are, how our dual attraction works, or even why some scientists are dense enough to think male bisexuals don't even exist. Any way you spin it, the numbers just don't match up. Except when it comes to animals. Plenty of evidence there. Perhaps we should join the bonobos. Hey, it's just a suggestion.

BI CENSUS: JUST HOW MANY ARE OUT THERE?

NO WONDER WE BISEXUALS feel so alone—we don't even know how many of us exist. Estimates range from zero to tens of millions in the United States alone, depending on which study you believe. Here's the bisexual breakdown:

→ 0.3 percent of women and 0.7 percent of men engaged in sexual activity with both males and females within the previous year —SEX IN AMERICA, *University of Chicago, 1992*

→ 0.3 percent of the men and 8 percent of the women study show attraction to the same sex. —*Dr. Richard Lippa of California State University, 2006*

→ 1.5 percent of women and 0 percent of men defined as bisexual based on sexual and romantic attraction. —*National Institutes of Health, 2002*

→ 5 percent of women and 10 percent of men fall solidly into a middle level of the Kinsey scale of sexual preferences. However, when accounting for people's actions and attractions, as many as 25 percent of women and 46 percent of men could be labeled as bisexual. —*Dr. Wardell Pomeroy, director of field research for the Institute for Sex Research*

→ 15 percent to 25 percent of women and 33 percent to 46 percent of men are bisexual, based on activities or attractions. —*Alfred Kinsey, 1950s*

→ 18 percent of women and 21 percent of men admit to some sort of same-sex behavior in their lives. —*Harvard School of Public Health, 1994*

→ 60 percent of women and 50 percent of men reported having partners of both sexes in the past five years, from more than three thousand interviewed by the Social Organization of Sexuality, 1994

→ "About 80 percent of the population could be bisexual if we acknowledge our fantasies, our dreams, our interests, our crushes. If normal curves hold true 10 percent of the population is totally gay and lesbian and 10 percent is totally heterosexual and everybody else is potentially bisexual." —*Institute for Advanced Study of Human Sexuality, San Francisco, 1982*

→ A Zogby poll released in February 2006 says 53 percent of the general population believes "a straight person may occasionally experience sexual attraction to individuals of the same sex."

CONCLUSION/CONFUSION: Even best approximations of 13–20 percent with bi tendencies would mean 40–60 million people. So where are the bi-gentrified neighborhoods with those cool coffee shops and art-house theaters?

BI FIGURES

IT'S TOUGH TO BE bisexual—even in studies. But for the studies that do mention us, here is where we stand:

→ A 2006 California State University study shows that women are 27 percent more likely than men to be attracted to the same sex.

→ Extensive Kinsey studies show that 37 percent of American men have achieved orgasm with other men, yet only 4 percent identify as gay. Hmm, guess circle jerks are done with closed eyes.

→ A large 2002 study in the *Advocate*, reveals that 40 percent of gay men at some point identify as bisexual.

→ 33 percent of bisexuals are in hetero relationships, 20 percent are in homosexual relationships, 25 percent are in no relationship, 10 percent are with a man and woman at the same time, and 10 percent are in multiple relationships of all kinds at the same time. In addition, 35 percent of bisexuals previously considered themselves gay or lesbian. —*Ron C. Fox, psychotherapist, San Francisco*

→ Most bisexuals understood their opposite-gender

attraction at a prepubescent age and about three years later became aware of a same-sex attraction. —*California Institute of Integral Studies in San Francisco*

→ 40 percent of gay men have had sex with women, and almost half still engage in sex with women as well as men, but don't call themselves bisexual. —*James Spada, author of The Spada Report, a 1979 survey of gay male sexuality*

→ 20 percent of the general population experiences same-sex attraction some time in their lives. —*Janus Report on Sexual Behavior, 1993*

→ Of two hundred people who went through the Christian, antigay Exodus reprogramming, 66 percent of the men and 44 percent of the women achieved "good heterosexual functioning," but Columbia University professor Robert Spitzer said he didn't consider them bi "because there's no accepted definition of what bisexuality is." And 9 percent became, essentially, eunuchs.

→ 41.6 percent of the girls and 36.4 percent of the boys ages twelve to nineteen reported fantasizing about sex with both genders, according to a 1987 Minnesota Adolescent Health Survey.

THE SURVEY SAYS . . .

→ Bisexuals were mostly intimate with members of the opposite sex; more than a third were married. Bisexual women described themselves as the happiest group in the sample (compared with straights, gays, and lesbians). Bisexual men voiced the most dissatisfaction. Bi women had sex more than any other group and engaged in more acts of masturbation than other women. —PLAYBOY *survey, 1982*

→ Masters and Johnson in 1979 announced a 60 percent conversion of homosexuals to heterosexuality for a period of five years after treatment; however, it was later found that 93 percent of the subjects weren't homosexual but bisexual.

→ 35 percent of lesbians and 17 percent of gay men report some sexual attraction to the opposite sex, whereas 39 percent of lesbians and 15 percent of gay men had sexual fantasies about the opposite sex in the past year. Even more dramatic, 75 percent of lesbians and 50 percent of gay men had had vaginal intercourse at some point in their lives. —ADVOCATE *survey, 2002*

→ Syndicated columnist Dan Savage's 2001 Big Trouble Sex Survey found: Bi women and gay men were the most likely to cheat on their partners. Bi women were twice as likely to be drunk during sex than their straight or lesbian counterparts. Bi men were more likely to rat out a friend than their gay or straight counterparts. Bi men and women when asked to pick between Kenny G or Linda Tripp to sleep with picked Kenny G by 70 percent.

DEPRESSING BI STATS

BI'S DON'T ALWAYS COME out on top—especially in studies. Here are a few sobering stats that may even get those on the down-low a bit down.

→ Bi men are five times more likely to have used crystal meth than the general population. —*University of California at San Francisco, 1998*

→ The 1.7 percent of the population openly identifying themselves as bi actually show physical attraction patterns "substantially different" from their professed desires—Sexual Practices in the United States, 1994

→ People who said they were abused as children are six times more likely to become bi than anyone else. —*Johnson and Shrier, 1985*

→ In a 2002 survey of heterosexuals at the University of Iowa's nursing school, 61 percent found bi men unacceptable, and 50 percent found bi women unacceptable. For gays and lesbians, the number was 40 percent. Bi's ranked lower than intravenous-drug users.

→ 54 percent of homophobic men showed definite signs of sexual arousal when shown pictures of naked men, suggesting that they may be closet bisexuals. —*Kinsey, 1948*

→ A suicide-prevention study in Australia in 2004 found that self-labeled bi women and bi men were the highest percentages of suicide attempts (35 percent and 29 percent, respectively).

→ Bi youth between the ages of fourteen and twenty-one are more likely to be suicidal than any other sexually identified group. —*University of Minnesota, 2003*

→ "Women who have sex with women and men are at significantly increased risk of bacterial vaginosis, breast cancer and ovarian cancer than are heterosexual women." —*L. A. Valleroy, Ph.D., an affiliate at the Centers for Disease Control and Prevention*

→ "If the same pattern of mortality were to continue, we estimate that nearly half of gay and bisexual men currently aged 20 years will not reach their 65th birthday." —*Medical Institute of Sexual Health, 1999*

→ One out of three lesbians believes that bisexuality does not exist, giving responses like: "I was born [homosexual]; some are born heterosexual. I find it hard to believe that people can be bisexual." —*survey of four hundred participants at a woman's event conducted by bi author and researcher Paula Rust*

→ A 1998 study by the Centers for Disease Control of about thirty-five hundred gay and bi men fifteen to twenty-two years old in seven cities showed that one in six guys had had sex with women recently, and one-fourth of them had unprotected sex with men and women, confirming young bi men as a bridge for HIV transmission to hetero women. (Nothing like emphasizing a stereotype.)

→ 60 percent of those identifying themselves as bisexual do not fit the definition of bi behavior. —*Dr. Fritz Klein, bi psychiatrist and sexologist, 1985*

STATISTICALLY, GAY GUYS GO FOR MARRIED BI GUYS

WE KNOW WHAT YOU'RE thinking: gay guys won't go near a breeder. You're wrong . . . or at least according to a survey in gay mag *Genre*. For starters, 51 percent of respondents said they had done it with women, which means they just might understand the attraction (though only 5 percent of respondents called themselves bisexual. Yeah, right!). But get this: almost 25 percent of respondents said that they liked "the marrying kind," and 31 percent said they would be down for a married breeder if "he made the first move." So make it. Just make sure you have your wife's approval first.

STATISTICALLY, ALL WOMEN ARE BI

A BRILLIANT GROUP OF scientists at Northwestern University decided to study female sexual-arousal patterns in response to male and female erotica in June 2003. "Sex Difference in Sexual Arousal" was the first one to examine what sort of visual erotica gets girls wet, and guess what? All straight and gay women in the study were sexually aroused by male and female erotica. That's right: the straight women in the study were just as aroused by watching two women together as the lesbians in the study. The coolest part of the study revealed that these women weren't just sexually aroused but were psychologically aroused as well. J. Michael Bailey, an author of the study, asked, "Since most women seem capable of sexual arousal to both sexes, why do they choose one or the other? Probably for reasons other than sexual arousal." So go out there and arouse her. It's a biological imperative.

I have been with men. I like sex. I like beautiful people, men and women. And I'm not ashamed of it. Besides, a lot of women like that because they like to see a man in touch with his feminine side—to be able to be with men and not be embarrassed about it.

—ANDY DICK, *TV Guide*, October 11, 1997

STATISTICALLY, BI MEN DON'T EXIST

THAT SAME DR. BAILEY is the knucklehead who was widely discredited when his studies showing male responses to bisexuality proved that guys who said they were bi were really gay. Applying a sensor to the guys' privates, sexual arousal was measured by having the guys watch porn—some with just men, some women, some both. Most of the guys identifying as bi, 75 percent, showed they were reacting the same as gay guys, while the rest reacted the same as het guys. "I'm not denying that bisexual behavior exists," said Dr. Bailey, "but I am saying that in men there's no hint that true bisexual arousal exists, and that for men arousal is orientation." The big question in all this is what kind of crappy porn were they watching?

BI PLANTS, CAN YOU DIG IT?

THE WORD *BISEXUAL* WAS created by botanists, and about 90 percent of all flowering plants have bi characteristics of both a male stamen and a female pistil. The hibiscus flowers are bi, and in the early morning the female parts stick out beyond the stamens to be pollinated from some other plant, and if it doesn't happen, it curls up. Papayas have three sex types: male, female, and bisexual. The bi plants are best for home growing. In the botany world, a flower with male and female parts, like an orchid, is considered "perfect." And maybe the biggest surprise is that one special plant is famous for changing from male to hermaphroditic to female before becoming parthenocarpic, which means "virgin." That's the cucumber.

THE TASTE TEST–THE SUSHI OR HOT DOG DILEMMA

JUST LIKE YOUR TASTE buds, we believe that your sexuality is fluid. So, quickly mark the things on the list below that you want to put in your mouth right now, and then determine what that means as far as your sexuality at the moment. Pick only one that you'd prefer in each category, even if you don't like any of them—and if you're that picky an eater, then maybe you should just be home alone.

1. Vegetable
   a. Cucumber
   b. Broccoli
   c. Onion
   d. Cauliflower
   e. Eggplant

2. Breakfast
   a. Eggs
   b. Sausage
   c. Bacon
   d. Grits
   e. Pancakes

3. Fruit
   a. Banana
   b. Watermelon
   c. Raspberry
   d. Boysenberry
   e. Peach

4. Juice
   a. Wheat grass
   b. Orange
   c. Apple
   d. Grapefruit
   e. Kiwi

5. Fast food
   a. Vegan burger
   b. Charbroiled
   c. Cheeseburger
   d. Mushroom burger
   e. Hot dog

6. Potatoes
   a. Curly fries
   b. French fries
   c. Baked potato
   d. Mashed potato
   e. Scalloped potato

7. Coffee
   a. Decaf
   b. Mochaccino
   c. Nonfat latte
   d. Colombian
   e. Cappuccino

8. Coffee mixer
    a. Creamer
    b. Half and half
    c. Milk
    d. French vanilla
    e. Black

9. Chicken
    a. Tenders
    b. Fingers
    c. Nuggets
    d. Legs
    e. Strips

10. Water
    a. Crystal Geyser
    b. Evian
    c. Perrier
    d. Arrowhead
    e. Tap

11. Salad
    a. Caesar
    b. Cobb
    c. Mixed green
    d. Coleslaw
    e. Chinese chicken

12. Salad dressing
    a. Thousand Island
    b. Oil and vinegar
    c. Raspberry vinaigrette
    d. French
    e. Ranch

13. Mixed drink
    a. Cosmopolitan
    b. Jack Daniels and Coke
    c. White russian
    d. Gin and tonic
    e. Apple martini

14. Beer
    a. Pete's Wicked Ale
    b. Heineken
    c. Coors
    d. Miller Lite
    e. Guinness Stout

15. Pizza topping
    a. Pineapple
    b. Pepperoni
    c. Anchovy
    d. Extra cheese
    e. Green pepper

16. Fish
    a. Smoked salmon
    b. Fish sticks
    c. Sardines
    d. Lox
    e. Whitefish

17. Snacks
    a. Potato chips
    b. Pretzels
    c. Wheat Thins
    d. Mixed nuts
    e. Sunflower seeds

18. Candy
    a. Milk Duds
    b. Marshmallows
    c. Licorice
    d. Good 'N Plenty
    e. Milky Way

19. Mexican food
    a. Burrito
    b. Tamale
    c. Taco
    d. Enchilada
    e. Taquito

20. Sushi
    a. Sea urchin
    b. Salmon roe
    c. Unagi
    d. Tuna
    e. California roll

21. Pasta
    a. Farfalle
    b. Gnocchetti
    c. Campanelle
    d. Fusilli
    e. Spaghetti

22. Greek
    a. Souvlaki
    b. Moussaka
    c. Gyro
    d. Falafel
    e. Hummus

23. Ice-cream flavors
    a. Rocky Road
    b. Tutti Fruity
    c. Pistachio
    d. Vanilla
    e. Chocolate

24. How you like your ice cream
    a. Cone
    b. Cup
    c. Sundae
    d. Dish
    e. Boat

25. Diet
    a. Zone
    b. Weight Watchers
    c. Atkins
    d. South Beach
    e. What diet?

SCORING: USE THE SCORING SYSTEM BELOW TO FIND OUT WHERE YOU FALL.

1. a = 5; b = 2; c = 4; d = 1; e = 3
2. a = 1; b = 2; c = 5; d = 4; e = 3
3. a = 5; b = 4; c = 3; d = 2; e = 1
4. a = 1; b = 2; c = 3; d = 4; e = 5
5. a = 1; b = 4; c = 2; d = 3; e = 5
6. a = 5; b = 4; c = 1; d = 2; e = 3
7. a = 1; b = 3; c = 5; d = 4; e = 2
8. a = 2; b = 3; c = 1; d = 5; e = 4
9. a = 5; b = 2; c = 1; d = 4; e = 3
10. a = 3; b = 1; c = 5; d = 2; e = 4

11. a = 1; b = 2; c = 3; d = 4; e = 5
12. a = 4; b = 3; c = 5; d = 2; e = 1
13. a = 2; b = 3; c = 1; d = 4; e = 5
14. a = 3; b = 1; c = 4; d = 2; e = 5
15. a = 5; b = 1; c = 4; d = 3; e = 2
16. a = 3; b = 1; c = 4; d = 5; e = 2
17. a = 4; b = 2; c = 1; d = 3; e = 5
18. a = 4; b = 5; c = 1; d = 3; e = 2
19. a = 4; b = 1; c = 2; d = 3; e = 5
20. a = 1; b = 5; c = 2; d = 4; e = 3
21. a = 5; b = 2; c = 1; d = 3; e = 4
22. a = 3; b = 1; c = 4; d = 5; e = 2
23. a = 3; b = 5; c = 1; d = 2; e = 4
24. a = 4; b = 2; c = 3; d = 5; e = 1
25. a = 5; b = 2; c = 1; d = 3; e = 4

RESULTS

25-39 Lesbian
40-55 Straight woman
56-95 Bisexual
96-110 Straight man
111-125 Gay man

WAYWARD ANIMALS

SCIENTISTS HAVE LONG BEEN aware of bi behavior in the animal world—at least 450 species and counting. Small wonder that some of the observers are called bi-ologists. The scientific community has been voyeuristically noting both same-sex and opposite-sex behavior in species ranging from the lowly, slimy flatworm to huge, humping whales. Bisexual tendencies have been seen in sheep, caribou, the red-necked wallaby, the golden plover, and the black-rumped flameback. (Heck, we don't even know what some of those animals are, but don't they sound kinky?) Guinea pigs and geese have been known to pair off in threes (not with each other, get your mind out of the gutter), male monkeys have masturbated each other before going off with their mates, and African hunting dogs have been observed mounting anything that moves.

Here are some of the best bi observations found in this truly wild kingdom:

YEASTS. Even the lowest form of life, the saccharomyces yeast, has displayed distinct bisexual behavior. The big question is whether they worry about getting a yeast infection.

BEDBUGS. There's a reason your mom told you not to let them bite. These guys have warped large penises that stab another bedbug's backside, whether there's a vagina there or not. Then the sperm breaks into the body cavity and migrates via special pouches to the bug's ovaries. Some species of bedbugs have special organs that allow them to receive the sperm of another male, and he can later ejaculate both his own and his former lover's sperm into a female.

FLIES. Don't call these guys fruit flies, but one type of fly identified as Voila 1 shows strong bi behavior, particularly in males, and particularly when they are in their second larva or late pupa stages (teen years). These guys rarely make it to adulthood, so it seems like they're getting all they can while they can, especially when they're in a perfect mushroom-shaped form.

EARTHWORMS. All earthworms are easy. They don't even need to check each other out before they go at it. They simply lay side by side, head to tail, and secrete a mucus pool around them as they drive hairlike spines into each other's bodies. Because both worms have the ability to make eggs and sperm, both of them spill their seeds over the other, and they twist and writhe a lot together before they compose themselves and go their separate ways.

FLATWORMS. A certain species of worm, *Cotylea feint*, has an unusual mating ritual of "penis fencing," as described in *Science News* (the Valentine's Day edition, 1998), in which a male flatworm tries to stab his penis into the exposed flesh of his partner. At that point, the stabber's sperm may find its way to its partner's eggs for fertilization, but scientists note that most of the sperm goes straight to the partner's gut, allowing for the stabber to go out and find more partners. Once the battle for being the top is lost, the worm settles in its role as mom, and also nurses the new holes in her body. The whole thing lasts about twenty minutes—an enviable period of time for sexual interaction in the animal world.

SNAILS. Who'd have thought they're the party animals of the wild kingdom? They are known to have rather raucous orgies, with copulation going on in long chains simultaneously. Another interesting fact is that their sex organs are in their head, so they can never be blamed for thinking with the wrong one.

OYSTERS. Not known for their particularly pretty appearance, these slippery characters do have bisexual tendencies and can morph into a different sex if it suits them. Sounds handy, doesn't it? Well, it's true. Depending on how aggressively the suitor knocks at their thick shell, they can then decide whether they're going to be a male or female. Although not scientifically proven, the oyster is also known to be a good natural source for a Viagra-like effect in both male and female humans and has enhanced the swallowing abilities of both.

FISH. The Caribbean bluehead wrasse, a coral reef fish, is distinguished by the ability of females to change into males when males are lacking. The females can become more masculine than even their male counterparts and

become "supermales"—and these changes occur even
when the gonads are removed.

CARP. Fish were found to have abnormal sex in eleven rivers
around the country in 1996, showing increased amounts
of bi behavior. It turns out it was linked to polluted sewage.

SEAHORSES. Those horselike water creatures with the long
tails are often difficult to tell apart, male from female, but
it makes no difference. Their courtship dance is a raucous
show of head-tossing and tail-wagging, as the male
convinces the female to accept his seed. Then she pushes
her bright-orange penislike probe into his pouch and can
insert about six hundred eggs into him. A male seahorse
can actually give birth in his pouch fifty days later if
the lady of the house decides to go out and be the food
hunter, and the male then become the nurturer.

FROGS. Most types of frogs are unaware of what their
sexual role will be until they have reached adulthood.
Genitalia and the types of sexual orientation these green
amphibians adopt often depend on their environments—
and no, there's nothing that correlates which sex a frog
adopts and the time spent around pink lily pads.

RATS. In a surprising test of Roman rats, same-sex behavior
was displayed after otherwise "normal" rats were
given Ethanol and made drunk. As in humans, those
tendencies seemed to wear off as the hangover set in.

BIRDS. Scientific observers have noticed the fowl effects of
bi behavior, and lifelong ménage-à-trois relationships,
in many species of birds, especially raptors, eagles,
shorebirds, Harris hawks, acorn woodpeckers, spotted
sandpipers, red-necked phalaropes, little stints, mountain
plovers, sanderlings, Japanese macaques, zebra finches,
and other types of feathered friends detailed below. The
birds-do-it and birds-of-a-feather slogans seem to take
on whole new meanings.

GULLS. The state bird of Utah, home to polygamy-practicing Mormons, exhibits occasional bisexual behavior and sometimes mates for life in three-way pairings. After two decades of research, it was found that 5 percent of the ring-billed gull and 2 percent of the California gull (no surprise there) are inseminated by male gulls who have male mates. Sometimes, all three nest together, and sometimes after insemination the female goes off with another girl gull to do the child rearing together. This phenomenon also brings up the question of nature versus nurture and whether humans have unduly influenced the behavior of their birds.

FLAMINGOS. Male flamingos pair, have sex, build nests, and rear foster chicks together.

OSTRICHES. Two percent of boy ostriches completely ignore female ostriches—at least for a time—and court other males with a lively dance that involves darting toward their partner at thirty miles per hour, skidding to a stop in front of him, doing a sort of pirouette, and then puffing out his throat and twisting his neck like a corkscrew while fluffing up his feathers. These drama queens don't do the same with the women.

SWANS. Male black swans form stable pairs and even steal eggs to raise as their own. They tend to fend off more territory for themselves, proving that in the animal kingdom, at least some same-sex parents can provide better homes.

PORCUPINES. It's a prickly matter, but these guys will masturbate each other, very carefully, and then go find a girl to stick it to.

FOXES. One study has shown a commonplace practice of homosexual incest among some species of foxes to show dominance.

MONKEYS. Primates have been observed monkeying around

with every sex possible in the wild, particularly cottontop tamarins, common marmosets, golden tamarins, orangutans, saddleback tamarins, callitrichids, mountain gorillas, other great apes, and a few listed below.

CHIMPANZEES. Seemingly perpetually horny, the younger monkeys have been known to cop a feel from their same-sex friends—guys rub each other in chimp circle jerks, and gals finger each other's red swollen areas. Then they go off to breed.

BONOBO. Only five thousand of this species of monkey exist, and perhaps one of the problems is their passion for simply fooling around rather than reproducing. There's sex between females, between males, and with juveniles. Sex is frequently used during moments of tension or competition. Females tend to dominate this species, and two female leaders often develop a strong sexual "sisterhood" of sorts that can last a lifetime.

BIGHORN RAMS. Both in the wild and domesticity, about 16 percent of rams tend to ignore a ewe, and instead prefer fellow rams—bighorns, of course.

DOGS. African hunting dogs and Alaskan sled dogs are also known for mating with the same sex, if a good bitch isn't available. And face it: you've seen all kinds of dogs, from dachshunds to Great Danes, humping and sniffing at anything that comes their way.

GRIZZLY BEARS. Female grizzlies link up together, fight for each other, and raise cubs as a pair, as well as cuddle up for long hibernations.

LIONS. Female lions can take over a pride and hook up for a while, but it comes with a cost—often at the expense of the new significant other's cubs.

DOLPHINS. The bottlenose dolphin doesn't form male/female couplings, but males with their swiveling penises have formed lifelong buddy pairings. Some are interested only in other males, and others are bisexual but indulge in a lot of beak-genital propulsion with males and females alike.

WHALES. Small wonder that fishermen nicknamed female humpbacks "the whores of the sea" because they will rub up against anything that will satisfy them. And if size is important, this is the species to flaunt it, and they don't have to lie about it. Whale penises stand a full ten feet long when erect and one foot thick, while a female's hymen is a full five inches long.

You have now completed Chapter 3. Can you believe whales have bigger penises than you? Oh, we're sorry, did you get something more out of this chapter? Come on, you know that at the end of the day, that's probably the most important thing you'll retain . . . that and that all women are sexually bisexual. Funny how one scientist can completely piss us off by dismissing the male half of our kind as nonexistent yet validate the other half— all with a silly little study that centered around porn. Well, Dr. Bailey, you're going to have to do a little better than that. If you can't, we suggest you study yeast.

INTERMEDIATE

CHAPTER 4

TWO CLOSETS

SOME PEOPLE LIKE CHOCOLATE. Some people like vanilla. Some people like chocolate and vanilla. Some people prefer chocolate, but get bored every once in a while and crave some vanilla, and vice versa. Same goes for sexual preference. You can be behaviorally bi, eating all different flavors of ice cream, or emotionally bi, loving aspects of both, but necessarily feeling the need to hit your grocer's freezer. You can be experimentally bi and bravely order vanilla, although you know you're more comfortable with the chocolate; or transitionally bi, throwing out the French vanilla once and for all one day and insisting chocolate's really the only flavor for you.

Bottom line: you know what you've eaten and what you crave. Just don't wait around and let it all melt before you taste any of it.

COMING OUT WITHOUT COMING OUT

MANY PEOPLE CREATE A genuine air of mystery around themselves by making comments alluding to their nonheterosexuality without spelling it out. For instance, when the issue of dating or past relationships comes up at a party or with a friend, they nonchalantly drop a comment about past male or female lovers or mention their willingness to explore. Eyebrows raise, yet they don't explain themselves. They don't feel the need to because, quite frankly, their sexuality is nobody's business but their own. Odds are, the folks around them won't have the chutzpah to ask.

But when they do pry, feel free to respond in an even more noncommittal way by saying, "I don't like to label myself." That will really get their heads spinning. They won't know whether you're gay or bi or just plain experimental, whether you're still up for some same sex or just plain over it. If you feel like really coming out as bi without saying the B-word, offer an innocent comment like, "I go out with girls and guys." From there, just keep dropping vague hints about your preferences, experiences, or whatever until somebody gets it. It might take a while for all the monosexuals to understand, so don't be disappointed if no one catches on right away. They all can't be as highly evolved as you are.

COMING OUT TO YOUR RADICAL-RIGHT DAD

→ Do consider not telling him at all.
→ Don't tell him when he's watching his favorite minister on *Praise the Lord*.
→ Do stand a safe distance when you utter any word or phrase containing *sexual*.
→ Don't breathe a word while he's cleaning his guns, holding a power tool, or sharpening a kitchen knife.
→ Do tell him Arnold Schwarzenegger says he doesn't have "any problem" with gay people
→ Don't tell him that Schwarzenegger vetoed gay marriage.
→ Do explain that staunch right-wingers like Terry Dolan, David Dreier, and Ken Mehlman were closet cases.
→ Don't tell him during Monday Night Football or before he's had his evening scotch.
→ Do have a PFLAG brochure handy.
→ Don't be surprised when he asks you to change your mind.

COMING OUT TO YOUR CONSERVATIVE MOM

→ Do use television to your advantage and tell her after she watches her favorite talk show, *Ellen*.

→ Don't let her think your upbringing was to blame, or the media, or your gym teacher.

→ Do remind her that you got your genes from her (they're Levis).

→ Don't let her compare you to the misbehaving bi celeb who just appeared on the *Barbara Walters Special*.

→ Do mention that Leviticus, aside from condemning homosexuality, also supports the notion of selling women into slave labor.

→ Don't let her talk you into an emergency meeting with your local minister.

→ Do let her know that grandchildren aren't entirely out of the question, but not to get her hopes up.

→ Don't let her mention "hell" and your name in the same sentence.

COMING OUT TO YOUR HIPPIE MOM

→ Do tell her anytime, anyplace, any day.

→ Don't expect her to be surprised.

→ Do tell her this isn't an open invitation to discuss her love life.

→ Don't be surprised when she tells you about her sex life anyway.

→ Do resist giving her details about your sexual exploits.

→ Don't be shocked when she tries to live vicariously through you.

→ Do accept the free pot that she gives you to celebrate.

→ Don't whine when she complains that "your generation can't roll a decent joint."

COMING OUT TO YOUR SOCIALIST FATHER

→ Do tell him your sexuality is just another by-product of his progressive upbringing.

→ Don't let him attribute it to existentialism.

→ Do mention that being bisexual stands in opposition to the oppressive power structures undermining our society today.

→ Don't let him recommend you as a topic to his anarchist book club.

→ Do remind him that the FBI isn't any more likely to tap your phone now than before.

→ Don't remind him that many greedy corporations are run by gay men.

COMING OUT TO YOUR
STRAIGHT-BUT-NOT-NARROW SIBLINGS

→ Do use them as a litmus test for your entire family.

→ Don't expect them to keep their mouths shut.

→ Do act surprised when they express envy at how "interesting" your life is.

→ Don't encourage them to experiment because they'll just come crawling back with questions.

→ Do use it as an excuse to keep that Pet Shop Boys or Indigo Girls CD you stole from them in high school.

→ Don't let them borrow your club clothes because, hey, they may never return that hot ribbed tee.

COMING OUT TO YOUR CURIOUS COWORKERS

→ Do avoid telling the office closet case—you'll suddenly find yourself working on those "special" projects alone.

→ Don't breathe a word to the office gossip.

→ Do tell your best friend at work.

→ Don't say anything to the tactless wonder in your department who will loudly ask about your techniques for giving head.

→ Do defend the office queen whom your homophobe coworker always calls "a freak."

→ Don't expect to teach the office homophobe the error of his ways; just avoid him or her.

→ Do admit to your boss why you clocked so many hours surfing BiCafe.com.

→ Don't apologize for it because you got your work done— and besides, now you're in a protected minority that can't be hassled.

ADVANTAGES OF BEING A BI WOMAN

→ You look stunning in high heels and combat boots.

→ You know how to blend lipsticks and change a tire.

→ If you get tired of shaving your legs, you can just date a lesbian.

→ You can cruise women with your guy friends.

→ You can cruise women with your lesbian friends.

→ You can snare hot guys by simply mentioning you're bi.

→ You can scare spineless guys by simply mentioning you're bi.

→ You can land straight, experimental girls because unlike lesbians, you "understand."

→ You can fend off pushy lesbian advances by mentioning you're bi.

→ Your straight male friends will forever set you up with gorgeous women in hopes of a threesome, or at least a chance to watch.

→ You can be a shining example for "questioning" women, help them out of the closet, and be single-handedly responsible for doubling the number of bi women at your local lesbian bar.

ADVANTAGES OF BEING A BI MAN

→ You look great in beige chinos and baggy Levis.

→ You have an excuse for not having any fashion sense, well, at least half the time.

→ If you get tired of shaving your pubes, you can stop dating gay men.

→ You can snare men by simply mentioning your sexuality because they foolishly think you're inexperienced.

→ You can drive women wild by playing the sensitive innocent who's had his heart broken by men.

→ You can tease other guys unmercifully if you give them a look when you're with a girl, or, better yet, your kid.

→ You can dodge unwanted gay attention by simply offering the gory details of your last female conquest.

→ You can snare the straight, experimental girl because she's trying to "save" you.

→ You can scare unwanted advances from either sex by mentioning you're unsure if you're a top or bottom.

→ Your straight girlfriends will forever set you up with gorgeous men in hopes of a threesome or at least a chance to watch.

→ You can be a shining example for "curious" men, help them out of the closet, and be single-handedly responsible for doubling the number of bi men at your local disco.

ADVANTAGES OF BEING A BI MAN
OR BI WOMAN

→ You can quote Ani DiFranco to your dyke friends, Pink to the gay boys, and old Guns 'N' Roses lyrics to your macho older brother.

→ You can throw a football and wear pink on the same day.

→ You don't have to worry about the headings when perusing the personals.

→ Jealousy . . . what's that? (Just kidding.)

→ You actually know what good oral sex is (or you'll learn).

→ You don't have to be embarrassed about that dildo in your nightstand.

→ You don't lament your "experimental" days because you're still living them.

→ You're so open-minded that people have to remind you to be judgmental.

→ You can blame dating failures on your partner's gender and renounce that entire sex for a few months until you get over it . . . and you can keep dating in the meantime!

→ Your friends see you as their most sexually experienced friend. Let them think that.

→ Bisexuals don't exist, so technically, you can't be responsible for hurting anyone during a bad breakup.

→ No one expects you to settle down—ever.

→ You can bitch to straight men about how fucked up women are.

→ You can bitch to straight women about how fucked up men are.

→ You can bitch to bisexuals about everyone.

TELLTALE SIGNS YOUR "STRAIGHT" FEMALE FRIEND IS BI

→ She gives one too many hello and good-bye hugs to her female friends and tries to squeeze in a good-bye kiss . . . on the lips.

→ She touches you emphatically when agreeing with you on something.

→ She always tells you how cute you look.

→ She tags along with you and your bi/lesbian friends to gay bars and gay movies.

→ She owns *The L Word* seasons one and two and a panoply of Angelina Jolie flicks and other queer DVDs.

→ She has at least one piece of art in her apartment that features a scantily dressed woman.

→ She shoots seductive looks at women, and possibly even you.

→ She gets nervous when you are alone together and reins in her affections.

→ She tells you one too many times she wishes you had a dick.

→ She avoids changing clothes in front of you and other girls.

→ She dresses butch one day and femme the next.

→ She says she understands men much better than women.

→ She wears only masculine shoes.

→ She rarely wears a skirt.

→ She holds on to old issues of the Victoria's Secret catalog "for the articles," then challenges you when you say, "What articles?"

TELLTALE SIGNS YOUR "LESBIAN" FRIEND IS BI

→ She says she would sleep with Jude Law.

→ She rides one too many gay man's hips while at the club.

→ She tells you lesbians having sex with gay men is the new thing.

→ She says she fell in love with a man once, but then came to her senses.

→ She tells you lesbians can have occasional sex with men and it doesn't mean they're not gay.

→ She shrugs off the fact that 65 percent of lesbians have slept with men as "inaccurate."

→ She hits on your boyfriend because she thinks she can get away with it.

→ She has condoms in her bedside table . . . for when she runs out of latex gloves.

→ She prefers the strap-on to oral sex.

→ She says she never goes down on women because it's just "too yucky."

→ She admits that "one guy in college" really got her off.

→ She reads *Men's Health* for the "workout tips."

TELLTALE SIGNS YOUR STRAIGHT MALE FRIEND IS BI

→ He isn't awkward about hugging other guys.

→ He loves to wrestle with dudes, but only when he's drunk.

→ He knows who Alexis Arquette is and thinks he looks great in a dress.

→ He explains that his James Dean and Marilyn Monroe posters are on his wall because he likes their movies.

→ He obsesses about whether guys really do give better head than women.

→ He doesn't leave a seat between you when going to a movie together.

→ He really, really argues that Kylie Minogue is the world's best singer next to Barbra Streisand.

→ He really, really believes that Madonna can act.

→ He loves taking you to games and cringes when you squeal over every touchdown, but doesn't mind slapping your butt each time.

→ He actually follows the advice on *Queer Eye for the Straight Guy*.

→ He says he wouldn't mind a camping buddy like Ennis in *Brokeback Mountain*.

→ He owns CDs by Rufus Wainwright, Michael Stipe, Elton John, George Michael, and Rob Halford, but insists he collected them before any of them came out of the closet.

→ He poses in his jockstrap for his guy friends and asks how he looks.

→ He shaves his pubes.

→ He gets manicures.

→ He subscribes to GQ and displays it on his coffee table.

TELLTALE SIGNS YOUR GAY MALE FRIEND IS BI

→ He wears white socks—always.

→ He never saw a musical.

→ He wants a relationship longer than three months.

→ He thinks Anna Kournikova is a great tennis player.

→ He watches Jeff Stryker pornos for the acting.

→ He argues that David Bowie's "Ziggy Stardust" era was just a "phase."

→ He actually changes the oil in his car himself and doesn't understand that a "lube job" could mean something non-car-related.

→ He likes to kiss.

→ He can say *vagina* like it's not a yucky word.

→ He hates cooking and doesn't care if his silverware doesn't match.

→ He insists he's never measured his penis.

→ He doesn't give fashion advice to his female friends.

THE PROFESSIONAL BISEXUAL

pro·fe'·shun·el bi·SEX·you·el adj. 1. a bisexual activist who has profited or profits from being bisexual.

ONCE YOU'VE FULLY ADOPTED your bisexual identity and begin to explore the bi community, you will encounter a "professional bisexual." Professional bisexuals have the noblest intentions: to promote visibility (sorry, visi-BI-lity) about bisexuals around the world and dispel misconceptions about it. They lead support groups, create Web sites, write newsletters, and organize conferences where they sit around and talk about being bi. They've published books, speak at coffee shops, sing at schools, read really funny or heavy poetry, and put it all on their résumés without shame.

Because professional bisexuals have busted their asses to create the floundering, sputtering machine we call the bisexual movement, they also are the most touchy members of the practically invisible bi community. They will insist that *Bisexual* be capitalized, and that there isn't just male or female but many genders. Also look for a button, sticker, or piece of clothing with pink, blue, and purple involved.

Then there's the complicated jargon that is often overwhelming and takes pie charts and diagrams to decipher. These people use (and sometimes coin) nonsensical words such as *pansexual, bi-dyke* and *heteroflexible*. Yep, you got it. The flaw of the professional bisexual is that they're so busy deconstructing the nuances of sexuality that they're liable not to make sense to the mainstream. They deflate the fun out of bisexuality and instead replace it with the biggest turnoff—anger.

Though a "professional" is the most valuable person to have standing next to you while defending your bisexuality, they're also the first group to take offense at any articles published about them and bisexuality in general. Even the hippest queer writer will get something wrong about "the cause" or misquote them. Instead of trying to reappropriate derogatory terms like *fence-sitter*, they write angry letters to the editor when they see a photo of a cute guy and girl sitting on a fence to illustrate a bi article. Or they propagate a flurry of activism against a publication that shows three people together, saying that it emphasizes that bi's are always in threesomes and can't be with one person. The poor editor who dares approve art of a male and female symbol intertwined to symbolize bisexuality will never know what hit him or her (or whatever).

What art screams bisexuality other than a threesome in front of the fence or a cross-gendered person with lots of purple, pink, and blue tattoos? What visual representation of bisexuality is easily accessible? Instead of asking themselves these questions, many professional bisexuals get their panties in a twist and bite the media publications that feed them by trying to change common misconceptions instead of determining how we should visually represent bisexuality. Although most have the purest of intentions and will give any fellow bi a smothering, comforting bear hug (even if they don't want it), most professional bisexuals lose their cool way too much and have forgotten how to play off the positive stereotypes—mainly, that the mainstream perceives bisexuality as incredibly hip, adventurous, and interesting (not to mention hot).

Or maybe that's just our opinion. After all, we're professional bi's too. Mike has written books and columns for more than a decade and lectured at schools and conferences around the world. Nicole has written articles and songs, led school groups, and performed at conferences. So what makes us different? It'd be easy to say we're just laid-back bisexuals who think sexuality is as simple as a tingle between your legs and that professional bisexuals have forgotten how difficult it is for the gay and straight communities to wrap their brains around the concept of bisexuality. But some of our best friends are "professional bisexuals," and we know there's no one better than a "pro bi" to chat with if you're just coming out or are confused about what to do or where to meet like-minded folk.

SUPPORT GROUPS AND WHY THEY SUCK

DON'T GET US WRONG: there's nothing scarier in the world than feeling like you're the only bisexual on the planet—and every fledgling bisexual should attend at least one bi support-group meeting to realize they aren't extremely alone. But after you've made that realization, realize this: if you expect to make bi friends or get some action from other group members, you might hit a snag.

Sure, when you walk in everyone seems normal enough. There's the shy woman in the corner with the deer-in-headlights eyes. The two "alternative" college girls holding hands and smiling. The well-groomed, Republican-looking married guy . . . and that hippie lady with the "Bi-sexual, not Bi-Polar" button leading the group seems really friendly, though her haircut's about thirty years out of style. Everyone knows how hard it is to be told by the world that you don't exist. No one knows whether to tell their coworkers or their grandmother whether they're bi or to blend. And though you don't talk your first time out, you feel like someday if you returned to the group that you would open up. Heck, even that guy who asked for your number as you walked to your car seemed genuinely interested in knowing you.

Then again, there's that weird guy who dominated the entire discussion, tried to pick a fight with everyone, and said he's never had friends. Hmm, it wasn't very fun listening to him. And there isn't really anyone your age and no one you're even remotely attracted to, so you're wondering, "Really, what did I have in common with any of those people besides being bi? Do I really need my sexuality to be my identity because I don't have a personality?" or "Maybe I won't go back. God, I'm such a judgmental ass."

OK, wait, hold it. You're experiencing what we like to call "support-group backlash," and it's extremely common. First thing, you should know why that weird guy who talked too much was sitting right next to you. Many people attend bi support groups and support groups in general because their therapists recommend they do so in order to gain a better understanding of their sexuality. The unfortunate by-product: a number of socially dysfunctional head cases end up in these groups, and there's no screening process. And in the L.A. and New York areas, you might even encounter stand-up comic wannabes testing out their material in the groups. But what about the seemingly nice, quiet people?

First question: did you notice a larger number of men than women in your group? Thought so. That's because a lot of straight men crash bi support groups in hopes of finding two women for sexual adventures. Equally disturbing is that a number of gay men crash the group in order to experiment with women. Wait, it gets worse: lots of lonely women attend support groups to find an easy guy. And it may turn out that one of those women is actually a guy trying to express his kinky side. Bottom line: you don't know why these people are there, so don't let them use you as their personal playground in the meantime.

A ton of married bisexuals attend support groups in search of a quickie, while a ton of adulterers, who can't 'fess up to their partners, attend in order to swap tips on how to deceive their straight spouses. So if you do come back for seconds, don't be surprised if that topic springs into the mix. Topics you can expect include coming out and coming out and coming out. After a hearty chat about, well, coming out, other topics that might emerge include how to tell someone you're dating that you're bi, the discrimination against bi's, how to explain being bi, and why it's easier for women to be bi. If one of these is of greater interest to you than the others, then tough luck. You have no control over which topic gets chosen and, thus, no control over whether that week's session proves to be helpful to you or redundant. Once you've come out and gotten over the squeamishness, hearing the same tired coming-out story will probably grate on you a bit ... if you can understand it at all. The leader of the group may speak in such politically correct jargon you won't even know what he or she is saying half the time. Do you really care what a "gender fag" is? How about a "bisexual-identified lesbian"? Does it matter? Not really, 'cause you know you ain't one of them.

The greatest tragedy about support groups is this: everyone goes in hope of meeting other bi's for friendship or more. In fact, the support group is a place to meet other bi's, just not the kinds of bi's you want to meet. So where do you meet other bisexuals? Good question. So good, there are no concrete answers. If you don't like the people at the support group, you can bet the bar, club, or groups they recommend won't be to your liking either. The only wisdom we have to impart: every lesbian and gay man knows at least one bi person or someone who's "questioning." It's your job to start collecting those people like scratch-'n-sniff stickers or butterflies or stamps because if you don't . . . well, you already know, and do you really want to be the only bi person on the planet?

WACKY CONFERENCES

ONCE YOU'RE SURE ABOUT this bisexuality thing and have been predictably unfulfilled by your local bi support group, you'll probably stumble upon the phenomenon of the bisexual conference. Well established internationally as well as domestically, these conferences are attended by la crème de la crème of bisexual activists and researchers and the occasional weirdo. Fortunately, these conferences cost beaucoups dinero, so you can be assured that the goth couple with multiple piercings who keep hitting on you are at least financially stable. After more than a decade of attending the local, state, regional, national, and international bisexual conferences, we've witnessed a sex therapist talking with vagina and penis puppets, a tribal pagan marriage ceremony, and a group of nearly nude women demonstrating safe sex with dental dams from atop a pack of actual motorcycles. If that shocks you, you ain't heard nothing yet.

Just take a peek at these seminars' names: "Swinging and Polyamory," "Bisexual Masturbation," and "Loving Our Pre- and Postmenopausal Pussies." But don't worry, there's plenty of opportunity to love your twenty-something pussy as well, with seminars taught by younger bi femmes. There's also ample opportunity to catch women with facial hair and men in dresses—and things only get kinkier from there. Check out these lecture topics: "Famous Erotic Triangles," "Forming a Polyfidelitous Triad," . . . some conferences even feature monogamous and polyamorous advice for couples and singles—and that's just the tip of the iceberg. We could go on for pages, detailing just how wacky these conferences can be (and in fact we did until our editor suggested we stop blathering).

The best way to feel out the vibe at one of these things is just to slap down the cash and attend. True, it's intimidating, but being in a hotel filled with bisexuals pretty much rivals any other experience you may have in this lifetime. So take your time, and pick the conference that seems best for you—and that very well might be no conference at all. The best source for any bisexual group from Argentina to Zimbabwe is the Bisexual Resource Guide, http://www.biresource.org, compiled by fellow bi Robyn Ochs. Bisexual.org also usually contains info about upcoming conferences.

You have now completed Chapter 4. We hope that by now you've come out to every personality type known to man, and done it with pride. You've dodged the curious coworker, confided in your trustworthy sibling(s), and explained why you can't just be straight to Mom and Dad. You've realized that support groups aren't the best place to meet potential partners, and you've signed up for the next wacky bi conference coming to a town near you. Wow, we'd say you've earned a slight reprieve . . . a brief moment of fun before you ponder the intricacies of bi dating. Congratulations! You have successfully reached the pop-culture jackpot.

CHAPTER 5

FAMOUS FENCE-SITTERS

GIVEN THAT WE DON'T really have a community that meets in its own nightclubs and wears identifiable stylish clothing (well, not always), we fence-sitters often huddle in our homes feeling a strong connection with the sexually ambiguous or openly queer characters and performers we see in movies, on TV, and in the news or hear on the radio. This chapter captures quite a few bi media moments that you won't want to miss.

CELEBS ON ALL THINGS BI–FROM A TO Z

YOU WOULDN'T BELIEVE HOW much creative people like to gab about bisexuality, especially in gay publications and to bi journalists like Mike. We're not saying they're one of us, but they certainly have a lot of fluidity on the brain. (P.S. We haven't outed anyone who hasn't outed themselves, and many of the quotes were told directly to Mike in interviews.)

A

Actress **JOEY LAUREN ADAMS**, who once dated filmmaker Kevin Smith, played a lesbian who realizes she also likes men in Smith's bi-friendly *Chasing Amy* (1997). "I'm bisexual, and I realized that when I went to Bali where the culture there is very bisexual, and it is the first time I was very attracted to women," she said. "I have a lot of friends who are [that way], in fact, most."

BEN AFFLECK said during interviews for *Chasing Amy*, "I think everyone has the capacity for being bisexual." He added, "I have a lot of close male friendships that are like love relationships; they're close and loyal, and I know that's a risky thing to say in public." Affleck also played a straight guy who turns a lesbian character bi in *Gigli*. Perhaps he's drawn to such bi-friendly films because of his open mind. "I don't believe anyone is exclusively gay or straight, no one is," Affleck said in an interview.

Bi actor **ROSS ALEXANDER** fell in love with Bette Davis and ended up killing himself over her rejection. Davis wasn't comfortable with Errol Flynn's advances either because of his sexual ambiguity.

DANIELLA ALONSO plays a Latina bisexual high schooler on the teen television drama *One Tree Hill*. Her character revealed she swung both ways after kissing a female friend then admitting to her boyfriend she liked them both.

Queer cinema director **GREGG ARAKI** examined sexual ambiguity in today's youth in his 2004 film *Mysterious Skin*. "Young people today don't want labels for their sexuality, who needs it? You're going to see this more and more in movies from now on because that's what's happening out in the real world, whether people want to recognize it or not."

B

BILLY BALDWIN played a character involved with a bi women in the 1993 film *Three of Hearts*. At the premiere he joked, "If you're over 30 and unmarried and in the [entertainment] business, then you're bisexual."

STEPHEN BALDWIN starred in 1994's *Threesome*, in which his character enters a sexy tryst with another man and woman, and later in the bi-themed *Zebra Lounge*.

Spanish actor **JAVIER BARDEM**'s played sexually flexible characters in films like the 2000's Oscar-nominated *Before Night Falls* and in films earlier in his career like 1992's *Jamón, jamón*. In 2004's *The Sea Inside* he played Ramón, a quadriplegic writer loved dearly by men and women. He said of his character, "He attracts everyone, and he invites us to wonder if we're able to love without the need of sex."

Teen queen **MISCHA BARTON** went bi in a story line on *The O.C.* when her character experimented with stereotypical bad girl Alex before returning to her heterosexual ways. Barton also starred in the überlesbian prep-school indie flick *Lost and Delirious* and on ABC's *Once and Again*, where she played the female love interest of Jessie, a teenage girl played by Evan Rachel Wood.

Though she's married, **JENNIFER BEALS** sometimes looks a little too into her love scenes with the ladies on *The L Word*. She told the *Advocate*, "I heard a rumor that somebody—a studio executive in L.A. who saw some of the show—assumed I was bisexual. Which was a huge compliment to me. . . . I feel really proud, actually, that somebody would think that I was bisexual." Jen, if that's acting, you deserve an Emmy.

Comedienne and actress **SANDRA BERNHARD** appeared on *David Letterman* in 1986 with Madonna and said she enjoyed sleeping with the pop star more than sleeping with the pop star's husband at the time, Sean Penn. "I've had long-term sexual relationships with both men and women. If that classifies me as bisexual, then I'm bisexual. I'm very committed to people, so when I'm with somebody, I'm with them," she told the *Advocate* in 1992. "I just think that people connect to people and I don't think that it's necessary to define it. Love is pretty undefinable."

Singer **JON BON JOVI** said, "It used to be cool to be bisexual, but I see it as being more than simply a trendy thing—it's a worldwide change."

In her best-selling autobiography, *Backstage Passes: Life on*

B(ICON)

DREW BARRYMORE has been open about her bisexuality for like forever. "I have always considered myself bisexual . . . I think a woman and a woman together are beautiful, just as a man and a woman together are beautiful," she told *New Woman* magazine in July 2003.

Yet she's honest that her relationship preference lies with men, telling the magazine, "When I was younger I used to go out with a lot of women . . . I don't think I could ever just solely be with a woman...It's just not enough for me." Bi with a boyfriend. Nothing wrong with that. But really, Drew, what gives with all the straight-laced characters? Aside from your performance in *Poison Ivy*, where you psychotically kissed Sarah Gilbert, you've pretty much stuck to straight romantic comedies. Even in the super lesbo flick *Boys on the Side*, you played one of the only straight characters in the entire freakin' flick. What's up with that? And *Bad Girls*? Such squandered possibilities. Drew, we know you have chemistry with Adam Sandler, Sam Rockwell, and Jimmy Fallon, but really, it's time you reexplore your indie roots and let us watch. We wouldn't be opposed to you exploring your crush on Michelle Pfeiffer, which you hinted at in the *My Date with Drew* special features (yes, we noticed). Or perhaps you could star opposite Liv Tyler, whom you kissed so sweetly on the red carpet that one time. Whatever you decide, even if you never play bi again, you still deserve a big bisexual gold star for being so damn forthright.

---

the *Wild Side*, **ANGELA BOWIE** revealed numerous affairs she and her husband, **DAVID**, had with various friends such as Mick Jagger. "David and I may have been the best-known bisexual couple ever," she wrote.

In Gary Carey's biography *The Only Contender,* **MARLON BRANDO** was quoted in 1985 as saying, "Like many men, I, too, have had homosexual experiences and I am not ashamed."

SAFFRON BURROWS played bi in 2000's *Timecode* and said of her own fence-sitting tendencies, "Was I confused? Not at all. I love men, I love women."

C

BRUNO CAMPOS played a creepy, but hot, bisexual surgeon on F/X's *Nip/Tuck,* easily fulfilling the stereotype.

Queer icon comedienne **MARGARET CHO** openly gabs about her attraction to both men and women. In a June 2002 interview, she said, "I've never had any kind of biphobia specifically directed at me, but I won't put it up with it. I don't believe in intolerance in any way."

GEORGE CLOONEY was quoted as saying, "I've no preference toward anyone, ladies or men, Italian or American," on MSNBC, November 7, 2005.

PHIL COLLINS portrayed a bi bathhouse owner in *And the Band Played On* and said in an interview that he has no problem spending time in gay bathhouses. "It's for my voice on the road, I go to a bathhouse or a steamroom every day," he said. "Sometimes it's in a very sleazy gym, sometimes in an old-fashioned bathhouse just like in the Roman days."

ALFONSO CUARON, director of 2001's *Y tu mamá también* said, "Exploring and experimenting with your sexual identity is a rite of passage. The younger generation knows now that bisexuality is one of those identities they can choose, and that is good. They can choose both."

Pansexual actor **ALAN CUMMING** adores his androgynous reputation. "I'm the acceptable face of sexual ambiguity. I'm like a naughty schoolboy. I can get away with stuff that's controversial," he said. He starred on Broadway in *Cabaret* and said during *X-Men 2* interviews that his weird character, Nightcrawler, has something in common with shape-shifter Mystique, played by Rebecca Romijn-Stamos. "We both had sex with John Stamos," he teased.

Actor **TONY CURTIS** played the character Antonius in the 1960's *Spartacus*, which contains one of the most controversial bisexual movie scenes of all time. In the scene, which was cut from the original and later restored, Laurence Olivier's character asks Antonius whether he eats both snails and oysters. Curtis's character says he eats only oysters, but after some prodding says he finds nothing wrong with the consumption of both.

B(ICON)

One could argue that **NEVE CAMPBELL** has played more bi women throughout the course of her career than Angelina Jolie and Drew Barrymore combined. "People can think of me however they want," she says . She has definitely been "bi-typecast." Here's a list of her bi-conquests:

Wild Things: a film on every frat boy's top-ten list, the 1998 film featured a scorcher of a threesome scene with Neve, Denise Richards, and Matt Dillon. This trashy flick also contained a strong bisexual subtext between Kevin Bacon's and Dillon's characters. Naturally, they were stereotypical bisexual crooks.

Party of Five: During the show's final season, Neve's character, Julia, grows bi curious after breaking it off with an abusive boyfriend. She locks lips with a female classmate.

Panic: Neve played a troubled, promiscuous gal who seduces a blonde woman on a couch while wearing leather pants and a hit man played by William H. Macy.

Drowning Mona: In this wacky, tasteless comedy, Neve played yet another sexually adventurous woman, this time whimsically kissing a rather butch female character in a police station.

Investigating Sex: In this period piece, Neve played a stenographer who studies sex, including bi sex.

54: Most of the bi content in the swinging nightclub scene was cut from the final edit, and Neve and Ryan Phillippe blasted filmmakers for it.

Three to Tango: Neve costarred with Matthew Perry in this film in which everyone assumes Perry's character is gay. Neve's character mentions her sexual history with women to Perry's character while shaving her legs in a bathtub.

When Will I Be Loved: Neve's character explores her sexuality with sixty-nine-year-old Count, a wannabe hustler, and an adorable blonde woman all in one day. She said of bisexuality today, "I think it's more accepted. There's a lovely new acceptance [among the younger generation], and certainly it is easier for women than men. Women can be out in this business, but not men."

D

JAMES DEAN had male and female lovers. Some have written books about their encounters. Television writer and journalist William Bast recounted his affair with Dean and detailed Dean's other bisexual affairs in his 2006 book *Surviving James Dean.*

The unbearably stunning **DREA DE MATTEO** of *The Sopranos* and *Joey* declared, "I love men and they're who I go out with, but every now and then—well I can't say I've never been with a woman."

CATHERINE DENEUVE starred as a bisexual vampire alongside David Bowie and Susan Sarandon in 1983's *The Hunger.* In 1996's *Les voleurs,* she played a married college professor who falls for her female student Juliette; in *Zig-Zig* her character was part of a lesbian cabaret act, and in *Ecoute voir,* she portrayed an omnisexual private eye.

MARLENE DIETRICH toyed with gender as much as one could in the 1930s. In the 1930 film *Morocco* she sings a number in male drag, wearing a top hat and tuxedo, and kisses a female audience member on the lips. In real life, she had an affair with Greta Garbo and is quoted by writer Marjorie Rosen as saying, "In Europe it doesn't matter if you're a man or a woman, we make love with anyone we find attractive."

Back in 1987, **ROBERT DOWNEY JR.** played a bisexual drug addict in 1987's *Less than Zero*. He also played pansexual in 2000's *Wonder Boys* and 1999's *Black and White*. In interviews he has openly talked about his sexually ambiguous past and is now a married dad.

ELIZA DUSHKU, who played Faith on *Buffy the Vampire Slayer*, dances with both men and women during a dance scene on the show, while her character in 2001's *Soul Survivors* made out with a hot butch woman.

CLEA DUVALL's no stranger to queer roles. Her character in 1998's *The Faculty* is constantly grilled about her sexual ambiguity, while her role as a lesbian conducting research in a disturbingly homophobic town in 2002's *The Laramie Project* shouldn't go unnoticed either. DuVall also sucks face with her leading lady, Natasha Lyonne, in 1999's over-the-top *But I'm a Cheerleader*. "I hate the term bisexual, and I hate any kind of label, really," DuVall said.

BIcon

ANI DIFRANCO's raw folk-punk/jazz-funk and her openness about her relationships with men and women have attracted legions of devoted queer followers. Ani has always defended her straight and gay sides through her songs, and "In or Out" contains some of the best bisexual lyrics ever written. Worship her.

E

Before their separation, sexually ambiguous rock god Dave Navarro may have had a strong influence on his wife, **CARMEN ELECTRA**—at least when it came to hitting on gorgeous supermodels. Electra swooned, "I fancy Kate Moss. She has the best style. People need to give her a break. I'd love to meet her. You can't deny her beauty and her sexuality." She also declared her first husband, basketball star Dennis Rodman, as "the best bisexual I ever had," and said, "Johnny Depp is hot, and so is Angelina, I'd love to shoot a steamy threesome with them."

MELISSA ETHERIDGE told a gay Los Angeles paper, "I do believe in true bisexuality. We all have the capacity. . . . The more the world understands their bisexuality the better we'll be. I'm attracted to souls. I can be attracted to both."

RUPERT EVERETT hinted at his flirtation with bisexuality to *Out* magazine in 1992: "It's time for people to be honest about what they do." The openly gay actor also played bi in 1998's *B. Monkey* and portrayed a gay man who had sex with Madonna in 2000's *The Next Best Thing.*

F

Bad boy **COLIN FARRELL** played sexually ambiguous characters in 2004's *Alexander* and *A Home at the End of the World.* He said of sexuality in the ancient world: "It was simpler, a time when men and men laid together and they shared knowledge, and they laid together. There was no word for it."

ERROL FLYNN's male lovers included fellow leading man Tyrone Power and writer Truman Capote. One of Flynn's three wives, according to author Boze Hadleigh, also was bisexual.

G

GRETA GARBO had numerous affairs with women, and she dresses in male drag in 1933's *Queen Christina* and plants a kiss on a fellow female costar in the film.

JUDY GARLAND, famous for clicking her heels through the *The Wizard of Oz*, may have took it to heart when the scarecrow told her "some people go both ways" on the yellow brick road. In real life, Garland had a romantic relationship with Betty Asher and was also married to bi director Vincente Minnelli, who was father to Liza Minnelli, who married showman Peter Allen, who had a proclivity for the male sex—well, this could go on forever.

BOY GEORGE told *Details* magazine, "To me, a truly evolved person is bisexual, or at least open to the possibility of being bisexual."

GINA GERSHON has become a "dykon" for her role as lesbian "Corky" in the mob thriller *Bound*. She and Jennifer Tilly "wanted straight girls to want to be gay, we wanted gay girls to want to be us." Gershon played a stereotypical power-hungry bisexual in *Showgirls* then an aging bisexual rock singer in the indie *Prey for Rock & Roll*.

CARY GRANT is rumored to have had an affair with fellow actor Randolph Scott at a time when both men were married. Bisexual Ed Wood, the infamous cult film director, also claimed that Grant was a transvestite. (He should know!)

JAKE GYLLENHAAL received an Oscar nomination for his role as Jack Twist in the love story *Brokeback Mountain*. He told *Details* magazine in November 2005: "You know, it's flattering when there's a rumor that says I'm bisexual. It means I can play more kinds of roles. I'm open to whatever people want to call me. I've never really been attracted to men sexually, but I don't think I would be afraid of it if it happened."

H

"I want to represent bisexuals as well as I want the straight girls on the show to represent lesbians," said **LEISHA HAILEY,** the only out lesbian acting on Showtime's *The L Word* who coincidentally plays the only bi character. "I've really come to learn that bisexuality is a true, legitimate sexual orientation. It's not about crossing over from straight to gay."

ALYSON HANNIGAN played the "lesbian" witch Willow on the cult TV show *Buffy the Vampire Slayer*. In earlier seasons of the show, Willow crushes on the character Xander and has a season-long relationship with Seth Green's character, Oz. But her heterosexual past is forgotten when Willow falls for a lesbian witch played by Tara Maclay. Their relationship lasted for two and a half seasons and marked the longest-running lesbian relationship on a mainstream television network, according to AfterEllen.com.

SALMA HAYEK dances seductively with Ashley Judd and maintains female lovers in her role as the legendary artist Frida Kahlo in *Frida*. When asked at an international press conference if she had any past bi experiences, Hayek said, "No, I feel a sisterhood with all women."

ANNE HECHE played a high-class hooker and locked lips with Asian beauty Joan Chen in 1995's entirely hokey *Wild Side*. But everyone really remembers Heche for her relationship with comedienne Ellen DeGeneres in 1997. The couple split in 2000 after being scrutinized as the first prominently out lesbian couple in Hollywood. Heche married cameraman Coley Laffoon in 2001 after dating him for a year. In an interview, she said, "I hate the label, I hate the word," but said her feelings are the same.

Ultimate Playboy **HUGH HEFNER** talked about his swinger days and described them as "really bisexual."

A hacked photo from **PARIS HILTON**'s cell phone revealed the blonde high school dropout kissing Eglantina Zingg—an MTV Latin America VJ—while topless.

MARIN HINKLE portrays Jon Cryer's bisexual ex-wife in the television show *Two and a Half Men*.

XAVIER HOLLANDER is the infamous Dutch author who wrote the 2002 bestseller *The Happy Hooker*. She has loved multitudes of men and is now living with a female poet.

LAUREL HOLLOMAN, who plays the bisexual character Tina on *The L Word,* also played a teenage lesbian in 1995's *The Incredibly True Adventures of Two Girls in Love.* She told *In the Life,* the gay and lesbian newsmagazine on public television, during the segment *Behind the Scenes of The L Word,* "I always consider myself bisexual; from the minute I was sixteen, I said that in interviews. I said it to *The Advocate.* I've made a commitment. It's to a man. If you want to call me heterosexual, fine. I don't really call myself anything now but 'married.'"

I

Punk rock guru **IGGY POP** played a sexually ambiguous character named Curve in *The Crow: City of Angels,* and wrote music for bi-themed films like *Velvet Goldmine* and *Wonderland.*

Model **IMAN,** wife to bi guy David Bowie, played a shapeshifter in *Star Trek: The Undiscovered Country.* She said, "Everyone should be as open to different experiences and be as versatile as that character."

Director **SAM IRVIN,** once married and now with a longtime male partner (who was also married), directed a few bi-themed films, including *Acting on Impulse,* which involved a lot of bi interplay thanks to actress Linda Fiorentino's character.

J

Handsome director and actor **LANE JANGER** playfully explored triad relationships in his 1999 film *Just One Time.* Janger starred as a rugged fireman who encourages his fiancée into a three-way with another woman, who turns the tables on him. The out gay actor has produced a handful of other indies with bi subplots. "I think that society has mellowed out a lot. I've taken my friends to a straight bar and they've not freaked out, and I've had straight [male] friends want to kiss a guy to see what it feels like."

Director **NEIL JORDAN** has injected gender-bending themes

B(ICON)

ANGELINA JOLIE has become somewhat of a bi-con because of her honesty about her real-life relationship with Jenny Shimizu, her *Foxfire* costar, and for her rendering of the bi/lesbian supermodel title character in *Gia*. Even while playing the sociopath in her Oscar-winning role in *Girl, Interrupted*, Angelina locks lips with Winona Ryder in the backseat of a van. As one of the most honest celebrities of our time, Jolie has supplied us with a panoply of flirty bi quotes:

In response to being voted "The Female Actor Who Makes Your Knees Weak" in *Jane* magazine in February 2000, Jolie said, "They're right to think that about me, because I'm the person most likely to sleep with my female fans. I genuinely love other women. And I think they know that."

In an *Elle* interview in June 2000, she said, "Honestly, I like everything. Boyish girls, girlish boys, the heavy and the skinny.... I am begging for the man that can put me on the bottom. Or the woman. Anybody that can take me down."

Jolie told *Movieline* in July 2001, "When I was 20, I fell in love with somebody who happened to be a woman. I didn't flirt around with girls; I just suddenly noticed this woman's sweater and the way her pants fit and realized, my God! I was noticing things in a sexual way."

Jolie proclaimed to *Talk* magazine in June 2000, "I always play women I would date."

She told the German magazine *Amica* in June 2001, "Can you imagine that, Lara Croft as a lesbian? That would be a shock for the boys playing with their joysticks in their bedrooms around the world. I'd love it if the girls in the cinema watching Lara Croft find me just as hot as their boyfriends do."

Even during her interview with Barbara Walters in 2003, Jolie held her own and said she would be open to falling in love with another woman.

At a Screen Actor's Guild Awards press conference, Jolie acknowledged, "The younger generation is fluid with [its] sexuality."

While doing press for *Alexander*, in which she played the great warrior's mom, she mused about the acceptance of sexuality in ancient times versus today: "Isn't it strange that we haven't evolved that much?" Jolie also noted that bisexuals had it easier during that time period than now and says if her son, Maddox (her only child at the time of the interview), was in fact bi, she'd be more than accepting: "I'd be excited about him being confident about what he was and who he was."

---

in many of his movies, including 1992's *The Crying Game*, 1994's *Interview with a Vampire*, 2002's *The Good Thief*, and 2005's *Breakfast on Pluto*. He also revealed that almost all characters in his movies "have some bisexual side to them."

K

In 1996's *Never Met Picasso*, **MARGOT KIDDER** played a mom with a gay son. Her character also falls in love with a woman. In an interview, Kidder said, "The term bisexual is usually incredibly misleading and demeaning in the sense that it leaves out the social soul of who you are giving a label to and [leaves you] walking into a mess of stereotypes."

MIA KIRSHNER has played bi in Fox's *24*, the 2002 film *New Best Friend*, and most notably in Showtime's *The L Word* in which she plays Jenny, a Jewish bi character loathed by most lesbians. In real life, Kirshner has hinted at going both ways, according to TheLWordOnline.com.

NANCY KULP, that uptight Miss Hathaway from the old *Beverly Hillbillies* series, came out toward the end of her life, saying, "I swing both ways."

L

KRISTANNA LOKEN, the female terminator in *T3*, was caught kissing pop star Pink and told *Curve* magazine, "I have dated and have had sex with men and women and have to say that the relationships I have had with certain women have been much more fulfilling, sexually and emotionally, than of those with certain men."

"I'm all for anything that breaks down categories," **COURTNEY LOVE** said at a film premiere. "Anything that moves, I'm all over that! But I don't know if true bisexuals exist. I've argued with a gay member of my band about it a lot. I understand people can like both." Not only did Love play bi in *The People vs. Larry Flynt, Basquiat,* and *Sid and Nancy,* but she will also play bisexual porn pussycat Linda Lovelace on the big screen. "I have had a lot of gay boyfriends, and you know why? Because they can't top me. After me they turn gay."

M

Aside from the rumors that swirled around her relationship with Sandra Bernhard in the '80s, **MADONNA**'s no stranger to exploiting sexuality for shock value. She locks lips with a butch topless woman dressed as a man in her 1990 "Justify My Love" video. She portrayed kinkiness in all its incarnations in her 1992 book *Sex.* She even dished in an interview about her unhappiness with a scene in *Body of Evidence* in which her character criticizes bisexuality: "Yeah, that annoyed me. I had a conversation about that, but he's the director." Despite going domestic, she doesn't balk at using bisexuality to continue to provoke audiences—for example, the Britney Spears kiss at the MTV Video Music Awards in 2003. Now she explains it differently, or at least she did to daughter Lourdes in an *Out* magazine interview in 2006, explaining that as a mama pop star she had to pass her energy to the baby pop star. (Yeah, that's what they all say.)

JENA MALONE, who played a teenage girl dating a teenage

gay boy in *Saved*, said at the press junket, "Jesus would want you to be open and honest. Labels are for jars. . . . America is more tolerant to female bisexuality and there's this preconceived notion that pop stars are all bi."

Academy Award winner **FRANCES MCDORMAND** smooches with Kate Beckinsale and Allesandro Nivola in a steamy swimming pool threesome scene in *Laurel Canyon*. McDormand said in an interview, "Gosh, I hope everyone is bisexual. Wouldn't it be nice if we all copped to it?"

MALCOLM MCDOWELL, who portrayed a slew of bi characters in films like 1971's *A Clockwork Orange*, 1979's *Caligula*, and 1992's *Chain of Desire*, said in a 1993 newspaper interview, "I don't have any problems dealing with doing a romantic scene with a man. I rather enjoyed it. We're all bisexual anyway, aren't we? That's what I've always believed. Maybe we don't always sleep with members of our sex, but there's an attraction. A lot of my characters in the past are bisexual. I know that all of my characters have crossed over at some point."

Dashing *Rebel without a Cause* star **SAL MINEO,** who played the sexually ambiguous Plato in the 1955 film, once said of bisexuality, "As long as you don't wear a dress or sound like Marilyn Monroe, there's not a problem." He added, "Do I think everybody is bi? Yeah."

MARILYN MONROE's private therapist tapes describe intimate moments with women, including Joan Crawford. Some of those times are in the 2005 book *Marilyn's Last Words: Her Secret Tapes and Mysterious Death,* by author Matthew Smith.

ALANIS MORISSETTE revealed her experimental tendencies to Howard Stern in November 2005: "I experimented with women, but I am heterosexual. I think everyone should do it, I recommend it."

British singer **MORRISSEY** said, "I refuse to recognize the terms hetero, bi and homosexual. Everybody has exactly the same sexual needs. People are just sexual, the prefix is immaterial."

MEGAN MULLALLY of *Will and Grace* told the *Advocate*, "I consider myself bisexual, I just haven't explored it fully ... and my philosophy is, everyone innately is."

N

ME'SHELL NDEGEOCELLO said, "Queer? I'm not feeling that. I can't really embrace that. I can't embrace lesbian either. I hate the way the word sounds; it's not an attractive word. It's hard being bisexual, omnisexual, multisexual, whatever you want to call it, when people have their agenda and expect you to just represent their agenda."

O

SIR LAURENCE OLIVIER not only played a bisexual in *Spartacus* but also enjoyed a ten-year relationship with fellow actor Danny Kaye. One of Olivier's three wives also went both ways.

P

We can learn a lot from the teachings of **PEACHES**. For starters, she boldly sings about sex in songs like "Fuck the Pain Away" and delivers a threesome invitation in the track "I U She." She sports a beard on the cover of her 2003 release, *Fatherfucker*, and doesn't apologize for any of it. We love her. Besides, how can a woman who titled her 2006 release *Impeach My Bush* ever be wrong?

Psycho guy **ANTHONY PERKINS** admitted his numerous affairs with men during his marriage before he died of AIDS in 1992. Perkins had two children with wife Berry Berenson.

RIVER PHOENIX was outed as bisexual in Brian J. Robb's book, *River Phoenix: A Short Life,* and also by a former male lover in a full-page *Variety* ad just after the actor died. Director Gus Van Sant also noted River's unconventional sexuality in interviews. At dinner in Toronto, just before he died, Phoenix said, "If I would sleep with a guy, it'd be someone like Elvis or maybe James Dean." Then he paused and said, "Didn't he have a reputation for being into gay S&M? Maybe that's too kinky. Maybe not. Anyway, it'd have to be with someone who was dead because I wouldn't have to run into them again." Another friend said Phoenix once pounded on the door of a director at the Chateau Marmont one night, "drunk and wanting to talk about his struggles with bisexuality."

"I'm trisexual. I'll try anything once," said singer **PINK**.

Horror film master **VINCENT PRICE** and his wife were both outed as bi in a biography by their daughter, insisting her parents' marriage was quite genuine.

SHAWN PYFROM plays Bree Van De Kamp's wicked teenage bisexual son Andrew on ABC's most popular show, *Desperate Housewives*. Andrew recites lines like: "I'm not confused. I know exactly who I am." Creator Marc Cherry promises more bi antics from Andrew in the future.

Q

QUEEN LATIFAH described her character in 2002's *Chicago*, Mama Morton, as a "lady who was more than interested in the girls behind bars, and liked men, too."

QUEEN PENN, who acted in the film *Colorz of Rage*, is an out bi rapper and discusses her sexuality in her song "Girlfriend."

R

VANESSA REDGRAVE starred as the mother of bi playwright Oscar Wilde in *Wilde*, as an elderly lesbian in *If These Walls Could Talk 2*, as transgender tennis player Renee Richards in *Second Serve*, and as Virginia Woolf's lover in the play *Vita and Virginia* and won an Oscar for *Julia*, playing a bi woman who was playwright Lillian Hellman's companion.

KEANU REEVES played a bisexual hustler opposite River Phoenix in 1991's *My Own Private Idaho* and played the close friend to bi Beat writer Neal Cassady in 1997's *The Last Time I Committed Suicide*. He said, "I've been in plenty of roles with androgyny and bisexuality, yeah sure. There are kids like my sister and her friends talking about not defining their sexuality. I guess it's happening and there's different strokes for different folks."

"I like men and I like women, and if I can have them both at the same time, all the better," said **GABRIEL ROMERO**, star of the Spanish sitcom *Los Beltran*.

"Yes, I have done that," comedienne **ROSEANNE** said about having sex with women. "The way I think about it is that anybody can have sex with anything."

S

SUSAN SARANDON gets seduced by Catherine Deneuve in *The Hunger*, which also starred David Bowie. She recalled, "The director told me maybe I had a little too much to drink before she seduces me. I said, 'Look, no one needs to be drunk to bed Catherine Deneuve.'" Sarandon's characters experiment with various forms of sexuality all the way back to the bi cult classic *The Rocky Horror Picture Show* and she admitted, "It thrills me that one day my grandchildren will see their grandma in half-slip and bra seducing a monster."

Filmmaker **KYLE SCHICKNER** explained bi behavior in his 1997 film *Rose by Any Other Name* in which his main character, Rose, actually attends a BiNet meeting. "There's a blurring of straight and gay and the youth today are breaking down those barriers," said Schickner, who started the nation's first collegiate bi group, at Rutgers University. "Like the people in 'Rose,' young people are finding that their lives are not fitting into categories."

CHLOË SEVIGNY told the *New York Times*, "I've questioned issues of gender and sexuality since I was a teenager, and I did some experimenting." Sevigny played a softhearted, white-trash bi gal in 1999's *Boys Don't Cry* and went butch for 2000's *If These Walls Could Talk 2*, proving she really could go both ways . . . on screen.

DUSTY SPRINGFIELD: "Look, let's say I've experimented with most things in life. And in sex, I suppose you can sum it up that I remain right down the middle."

"It's very simple, everyone is bisexual," smirked **STING,** who in the film *The Grotesque* played a butler who seduces everyone in the household, men and women alike. "It's about time the movies started reflecting that."

R.E.M. singer **MICHAEL STIPE** talked about bi stuff, saying, "It's just another category. No one wants to use the b-word. I understand that things are getting a bit more fluid in the younger generation."

MINK STOLE, the rabid, crazy mainstay of all John Waters's movies, said, "I would be bisexual if I had the energy to be it. We were all bi in the early days."

T

CHARLIZE THERON won an Oscar for playing a bi/lesbian serial killer in 2003's *Monster* and played another sexually ambiguous character opposite Stuart Townsend in 2004's *Head in the Clouds.*

JENNIFER TILLY played the bisexual wife of a mobster and is seduced by the maintenance girl next door, played by Gina Gershon, in *Bound.* "I sure love playing a bisexual, wish I could do it all the time," she giggled.

Described as the tallest dancer in the country, Tony-winning **TOMMY TUNE** is perhaps the most open about being bi. "It's hard to label what I am, but I'd say I'm pansexual. I have never understood why we need to limit ourselves."

U

GEORG UECKER, a German actor, created a stir when his bi character on the German show *Lime Tree Road* kissed a guy fully on the lips.

V

RUDOLPH VALENTINO shared his bed with both men and women. Both his first wife, Jean Acker, and his second wife, Natasha Rambova, had female lovers.

W

MICHELLE WILLIAMS of *Dawson's Creek* fame appeared in 1999's *But I'm a Cheerleader* as a straight girl, but played a shy femme seduced by Chloë Sevigny in 2000's *If These Walls Could Talk 2*. Williams also played a straight yet heartbroken housewife in *Brokeback Mountain*, for which she received an Oscar nomination.

Singer **CARNIE WILSON:** "I was with a woman when I was about 15-16 years old, I was really really horny and I would fantasize about boobs."

X

Xena: Warrior Princess featured an ongoing relationship between Lucy Lawless's character, **XENA**, and Gabrielle. The show broke a number of boundaries, especially boundaries when bi HIV-positive porn star Geoffrey Karen Dior played a guy posing as a girl who kisses Xena, causing a tabloid furor wondering if she would get AIDS. Lawless said, "It was much ado about nothing," and says the end of the show proved that she and Gabrielle were "definitely bisexual, if not married."

Y

MICHAEL YORK has made a career out of playing bisexuals in films like 1970's *Something for Everyone* and 1972's *Cabaret* and once said, "Gosh, I think every character I've played is bisexual."

Z

PIA ZADORA played a bi writer who sleeps her way to the top with members of both sexes in 1983's *The Lonely Lady*. And in

Peter Lefcourt's novel *The Dreyfus Affair*, she tests the bisexuality of a male main character. When he loses interest in fantasizing about Zadora, he knows he's gay.

CATHERINE ZETA-JONES played a predictably narcissistic bisexual in 1999's *The Haunting* and didn't even kiss costar Lili Taylor. Yet Zeta-Jones did snag an Oscar for that gay movie *Chicago*.

BI MOVIE FACTS

FIRST BI CHARACTER IN FILM: The first bisexual characters appeared in a silent film by Sidney Drew in 1914 called *A Florida Enchantment*, according to Wayne Bryant's extraordinary book *Bisexual Characters in Film: From Anaïs to Zee*. Based on the controversial 1896 Broadway play of the same name, in the film a woman is magically turned into the opposite sex—she gets a mustache, and suddenly all the women in the film want to sleep with her.

FIRST WELL-ADJUSTED BI CHARACTER IN FILM: Murray Head played the stud who takes on a doctor (Peter Finch) and his wife (Glenda Jackson) in John Schlesinger's 1971 film *Sunday, Bloody Sunday*.

QUICKEST BISEXUAL BEDDING: *The Rocky Horror Picture Show* (1975). That cheap transvestite from transsexual Transylvania in this late-night classic beds both Brad and Janet individually and successfully in two consecutive scenes.

BEST BI MALE-MALE KISS: *Deathtrap* (1982), featuring Christopher Reeve kissing another man. Runner-up: *Far From Heaven* (2002), featuring Dennis Quaid passionately kissing a man in his office after hours.

BEST BI GIRL-GIRL KISS: Neve Campbell and Denise Richards in *Wild Things* (1998). Runner-up: *Kissing Jessica Stein* (2001).

BI HORROR: Who really was the "bride of Frankenstein"? There are musings that gay director James Whale in his 1935 *Bride of Frankenstein* classic intended for his Henry Frankenstein to be perceived as bisexual and his partner, Dr. Pretorius, as gay, leaving bride Elizabeth in the wings. Perhaps there's some truth to this rumor, for the character Henry would rather spend his honeymoon night with his coworker than his bride.

BEST BI DOCUMENTARY: *Three of Hearts: A Post-Modern Family.* This 2004 documentary shows how two guys and a girl live together and have a family together in a utopic triad, but sadly, it ends with their breakup.

BEST HISTORICAL BI FILM: *Frida* (2002). Salma Hayek's Oscar-nominated portrayal of Frida Kahlo reveals the famous painter's penchant for Diego Rivera, Leon Trotsky, and female photographer Tina Modotti.

BEST BI MURDERER: Played by Sharon Stone in *Basic Instinct* (1992) and more than a decade later in the sequel (2006).

BEST BI SUBTEXT BETWEEN THE UNDEAD: Played by Brad Pitt and Antonio Banderas in *Interview with a Vampire* (1994).

BEST BI SCUMBAG: Dustin Hoffman in *Confidence* (2003) and *Midnight Cowboy* (1969).

BEST MACHO BI MOMENT: *Gladiator* (2000). Russell Crowe's character is asked very casually if he'd rather have a girl or a boy for his pleasure the night before the big battle, implying his bisexuality. Runner-up: *Spartacus* (1960), when Laurence Olivier, playing a Roman general bathing a young slave played by Tony Curtis, utters the restored line, "Do you like snails or oysters?" Second runner-up: Colin Farrell, whose title-role character in *Alexander* (2005) has relationships with both Rosario Dawson and Jared Leto.

BEST BI MONOLOGUE: The scene in *Chasing Amy* (1997) in which Joey Lauren Adams's character tells Ben Affleck's character why she slept with him when she's historically been with women. Her character wisely explains her unwillingness to halve her options of finding her soul mate by simply searching within one gender.

SEXIEST BI AMNESIAC: Laura Harring played the sumptuous bisexual Rita who had amnesia in 2001's *Mulholland Drive*, only later to transform into a conniving, selfish actress who abandons her lesbian lover, played by Naomi Watts, for a director. No matter. The hot sex scene between her and Watts in the middle of the film proved to be one of the most intense woman-woman scenes in history.

BEST FILM WITH A BI CHARACTER WHO FALLS FOR A HETERO GUY WHO HAS SEX WITH GAY MEN FOR MONEY: *The Fluffer* (2001). Actor Michael Cunio played a bi guy who develops an obsession for a gay-for-pay porn star played by Scott Gurney. Cunio's character receives a lap dance from Gurney's character's girlfriend in order to feel closer to him. Runner-up Tie: *Midnight Cowboy* and *My Own Private Idaho*. Dustin Hoffman's character falls for cowboy Jon Voight, as does River Phoenix for fellow male prostitute Keanu Reeves. Second Runner-up: *Speedway Junky* (1999). Jonathan Taylor Thomas played a hustler who does everyone. "He's bisexual," a character in the film says, "if you're buying."

BEST COMEBACK TO BIPHOBIA IN A FILM: The scene in *Bound* when Gina Gershon's character, Corky, attacks Jennifer Tilly's character, Violet, for not being gay enough. Violet responds by saying she doesn't need to tattoo her sexuality on her arm because she knows who she is.

BEST FILM WITH A BI CHARACTER AS A PIVOTAL PLOT

TWIST: *The Crying Game.* Stephen Rea's character, Fergus, follows his desire for a woman who turns out to be a man played by Jaye Davidson. Runner-up: *The Daytrippers* (1996). The Stanley Tucci character in a surprise twist turns out to be bi after his wife's family spends all day searching for him, only to find him with a male lover at a party.

BEST SEDUCTION OF A BI MARRIED WOMAN: In *Aimee & Jaguar* (1999) the wife of a Nazi officer gets love letters from a secret admirer who turns out to be a self-confident girl who initiates a forbidden romance.

BEST SEDUCTION OF A BI MARRIED MAN: Peter Sarsgaard seducing Campbell Scott's bi character in the indie thriller *The Dying Gaul.*

OSCAR-WINNING BEST PICTURES WITH BI SUBTEXTS: *Wings* (1927), *Broadway Melody* (1928), *All About Eve* (1950), *Lawrence of Arabia* (1962), *Midnight Cowboy* (1969), *The Last Emperor* (1987), *Shakespeare in Love* (1998), *American Beauty* (1999), *Gladiator* (2000), *A Beautiful Mind* (2001), and *Chicago* (2002)

BI PERFORMANCES WE DON'T BUY: In 2002's *Femme Fatale* Rebecca Romijn kisses a supermodel-esque beauty in a restroom. Two women sucking face haven't look less into it since Sarah Michelle Gellar and Selma Blair in 1999's *Cruel Intentions,* in which one can practically see Gellar's revulsion as Blair hesitantly pokes her tongue between her unwilling lips. Gellar also reportedly grew very angry on the set during that scene because onlookers in Central Park were watching. And Jennifer Lopez as a bisexual in 2003's *Gigli?* Pleeease! She doesn't even plant a real kiss on her stereotypically suicidal lesbian lover throughout the entire picture. Not to mention all the forced bi woman-to-woman kisses shoved into Hollywood blockbusters for straight men, like Jennifer

Garner and Natassia Malthe's kiss in *Elektra*. True, Malthe's character, Typhoid, literally delivers the kiss of death, but we expected a little more heat.

BEST BISEXUAL PLAYING A BISEXUAL: Angelina Jolie in *Gia* (1998). Runner-up: Alan Cumming in 2001's *The Anniversary Party* and the *Spy Kids* movies.

BEST SURPRISE BISEXUAL: *Some Like It Hot* (1959). At the end of the film, millionaire Joe E. Brown finds out that Jack Lemmon, who is posing as Daphne in an all-girl band, is really a man. He mugs for the camera and says, "Well, nobody's perfect!"

AWARD-WINNING FILMS

IT'D BE EASY TO say that the 2006 Academy Awards marked the bi-est if not gayest Oscars of them all, with films like *Brokeback Mountain* getting nominated alongside films like *Capote* and *Transamerica*. Even one nervous female producer accidentally thanked her "husband and wife" during her acceptance speech. The opening of the show featured host Jon Stewart in bed with Halle Berry and George Clooney. But the most bi Oscar year was 2000, when at least ten of the movies nominated in the various categories contained some element of bisexuality, especially among all the big winners. *American Beauty* featured the next-door neighbor with the big secret, *The Matrix* contained a subtle subplot between two women who were more than just friends and liked men too, and *Topsy-Turvy* featured bisexual women and cross-dressing men.

Other nominated films with bi content that year included *Election; Being John Malkovich; The Talented Mr. Ripley; All about My Mother; Boys Don't Cry; Girl, Interrupted;* and *Magnolia* (this was subtle, but notice the sidelong glances many of the same-sex characters have with each other). Chloë Sevigny was nominated for her bisexual role in *Boys Don't Cry*, and out bi actress Angelina Jolie snagged a statuette for *Girl, Interrupted*.

IF YOU'RE BI, YOU'RE EXPECTED TO HAVE SEEN . . .

→ *Bound (1997)*
→ *Brokeback Mountain (2005)*
→ *Chasing Amy (1997)*
→ *The Crying Game (1992)*
→ *Henry and June (1990)*
→ *Kissing Jessica Stein (2002)*
→ *The Rocky Horror Picture Show (1975)*
→ *Three of Hearts (1993)*
→ *Wild Things (1998)*

IF YOU'RE BI & OVER FIFTY . . .

→ *Carrington (1995)*
→ *The Hours (2002)*
→ *Jules & Jim (1962)*
→ *Making Love (1982)*
→ *Sunday, Bloody Sunday (1971)*

IF YOU'RE BI & ONLY INTO INDIES . . .

→ *Heavenly Creatures (1994)*
→ *High Art (1998)*
→ *The Incredibly True Adventures of Two Girls in Love (1995)*
→ *The Velocity of Gary (1998)*
→ *When Night Is Falling (1995)*

IF YOU'RE BI & YOUR IQ IS OVER ONE HUNDRED . . .

→ *Frida (2002)*
→ *Kinsey (2005)*
→ *Last Time I Committed Suicide (1997)*
→ *Pinero (2001)*
→ *The Sticky Fingers of Time (1997)*

IF YOU'RE BI & YOU DON'T MIND
A LITTLE BLOOD . . .

→ *Doom Generation (1995)*
→ *The Fluffer (2001)*
→ *The Fourth Man (1983)*
→ *The Matador (2005)*
→ *Savage Nights (1992)*

IF YOU'RE BI & YOU DON'T MIND BAD ACTING . . .

→ *Alexander (2004)*
→ *Both (2005)*
→ *Kiss Me Guido (1997)*
→ *Luster (2002)*
→ *Rose by Any Other Name (1997)*

IF YOU'RE BI & YOU DON'T CARE ABOUT PLOT . . .

→ *Basic Instinct 2 (2006)*
→ *Mulholland Drive (2001)*
→ *Nadja (1994)*
→ *Necromania: A Tale of Weird Love (1971)*
→ *The Pillow Book (1996)*

IF YOU'RE BI & YOU LIKE MUSIC . . .

→ *Cabaret (1972)*
→ *De'Lovely (2004)*
→ *Rent (2005)*
→ *Stoned (2006)*
→ *Velvet Goldmine (1998)*

IF YOU'RE BI & YOU DON'T MIND R
EADING SUBTITLES . . .

→ *Bad Education (Spain) (2004)*
→ *Beautiful Women (Germany) (2005)*
→ *Farewell My Concubine (China) (1993)*

→ *Gauzon Maudit (French Twist) (France) (1995)*
→ *Zus & Zo (Holland) (2001)*

IF YOU'RE BI & YOU'RE INTO THREE-WAYS . . .
→ *Head in the Clouds (2004)*
→ *Laurel Canyon (2002)*
→ *Score (1973)*
→ *Threesome (1994)*
→ *Where the Truth Lies (2006)*

I WANT MY BI TV

THOUGH IT FEELS LIKE some of today's shows frequently dabble in bi content, it's nice to note that mainstream shows in the past, such as *Friends, Dawson's Creek, Buffy, Cold Case,* and even *All in the Family* dealt with bi story lines. Today, shows like *Scrubs* deal with three-ways, while shows like *Desperate Housewives* feature a stereotypical but wickedly fun bi teenager. With a show like *The L Word* still going strong, we can only hope even more bi portrayals will leak onto mainstream TV. Here are a few significant moments in bi television:

1. Unless you count Uncle Miltie in drag all the time, Billy Crystal's character on *Soap,* Jodie, in 1979 was the first bi regular on TV, but not on prime time. He first dated a quarterback, then dated two women, then had a sex-change operation to please his man.

2. On prime time in the hit show *Dynasty,* handsome Steve Carrington (Al Corley) had a long-term male lover, then married a woman, and then in the reunion show sneaked off with a man again. Let's see how bi he's going to be in the big-screen version.

3. Tim Bayliss (Kyle Secor) on the crime drama *Homicide* asks Detective Renee Sheppard (played by actress Michael Michele) out on a date. Bayliss says he's "bi

curious," to which Renee answers that she is bi curious as well and has in fact dated "bi guys" before. *Homicide* at the time was the only prime-time television show with bi characters.

4. *Roseanne* featured the character Nancy (Sandra Bernhard) who is openly bi. In a later episode, Roseanne, kisses Mariel Hemingway.

5. In *Sex and the City* Carrie (Sarah Jessica Parker) dates a twenty-six-year-old bi man in the episode "Boy, Girl, Boy Girl," and in the same series the character Samantha has a bisexual relationship with a character played by actress Sonia Braga.

6. C. J. (Amanda Donohoe) on *L.A. Law* initiated the historic first same-sex kiss on network television.

7. *Babylon 5* introduced the tough but sexy bi commander Susan Ivanova.

8. In a bi-phobic *Ally McBeal*, a bi character has to defend himself by insisting he's totally monogamous. In another episode, Ally grapples with whether she can handle dating a bi guy because she might not be able to fulfill his needs. In one episode, Lucy Liu's character, Ling, kisses Ally, but both women decide ultimately they need the penis.

9. Julia, Neve Campbell's character on *Party of Five*, dumps her abusive boyfriend and becomes involved in a lesbian relationship.

10. The British TV show *Gimme Gimme Gimme* shocked audiences when Bob, the gay character, not only falls in love with Rose but also has a lot of indisputably hot hetero sex with her.

11. When macho soccer player Eric Cantona signed to play a gay pirate in the British series *Corto Maltese*, he said, "The character is, well actually bisexual." He had no problem with it, saying, "Some of the greatest gays are the most macho."

12. *Dr. Who* featured a bisexual intergalactic time traveler named Captain Jack Harness.

13. On *Arrested Development*, Lindsay's gay-vague husband, played by actor David Cross, snagged laughs by being constantly unaware of his obvious gay side. The show also toyed with gender, like in the episode in which Lindsay, played by out lesbian Portia de Rossi, hits on her high school daughter's male crushes. In a funny comeback, the daughter tells the teenage boy that her mother is really her dad who had a sex change.

14. The now-deceased *Six Feet Under* featured a number of tasteful bi story lines. The character Claire, played by Lauren Ambrose, experimented with a college friend, played by Mena Suvari, in season four. Instead of going for the usual "experimentation" story line, the show dealt with Claire's inner turmoil as she realizes her sexuality is predominantly straight despite her adoration for her friend. In the same season, the character David is surprised to discover his gay boyfriend, Keith, slept with a teen female pop singer, played by Michelle Trachtenberg, while working as a security guard on her tour. During the same tour, a male security guard who says he likes women solicits Keith for sex.

15. The character Karen, played by bi actress Megan Mullally, on the now-retired *Will and Grace*, went both ways according to Mullally. Karen frequently hit on the ladies and in one episode noticed she was in a room filled with women and suggested they throw on some tunes and remove their tops. Too bad Karen never got any action from Grace.

16. In the late 1990s, *Xena: Warrior Princess* kept viewers captivated with vague allusions and references to Xena and her female companion Gabrielle's sexual relationship. Though hailed for its intense lesbian subtext, both

characters were arguably bisexual, sometimes kissing
male characters and evoking one another's jealousy. The
relationship between the women ended in the finale,
when Xena allowed herself to be beheaded, leaving
Gabrielle to live without her, pissing off many bi and
lesbian fans.

17.   When *The L Word* premiered in January 2004, it posed
an almost immediate bi dilemma for one of its characters
(Jenny), featured another character who was openly
bisexual (Alice), and had an interesting development in
which a straight character (Kit) dated a female drag king.
But during most of season two, bi story lines vanished, as
bi characters went unrealistically gay or virtually ignored
their bi side. Alice injected the occasional line about
being bi, but pretty much stopped dating guys, while
Jenny unrealistically declared herself gay. Fortunately,
for us bisexuals, season three reignited some serious bi
story lines—Bette's partner, Tina, strayed to explore
her sexual cravings for a man. Jenny dated a transman,
and Alan Cumming guest-starred as a bisexual club
promoter. Even the unlikable character Helena Peabody
turned sympathetic through her affair with a bi-curious
straight girl who has a boyfriend. Maybe it's just cheap
melodrama, but in this world it seems no one's ever
permanently gay or permanently straight.

18.   Leave it to MTV, the network that first acclimated
teens to gay and bisexual reality-show stars on *The Real
World*, to introduce 2005's *South of Nowhere*, a show
that integrates bisexual and gay teenagers as regular cast
members. Broadcast on MTV's new teen network, The
N, *South of Nowhere* features Spencer, a teenage girl new
to L.A. who gets close with bisexual Ashley Davies, who
used to date the school's basketball star, but now pretty
much just dates girls. Spencer develops genuine feelings

for Ashley, culminating in a juicy confrontation.

19. *The O.C.* isn't exactly a gay show. As Generation Y's *Beverly Hills 90210*, it's more of an homage to the tortured lives of rich southern California kids. So you can imagine our surprise when the show featured a fairly accurate representation of a bisexual teen relationship between Mischa Barton's character, Marissa, and a smart bi gal played by Olivia Wilde in a 2005 story line. Too bad it predictably ended in stereotypical lesbian psychodrama, with Alex pulling a 180 and stalking Marissa. Ugh, when will these writers ever learn?

20   *All My Children* has been a groundbreaking soap opera since it debuted in 1970. Daytime TV's first lesbian kiss was between characters Riegel and Sosnovska, who had an insatiable sexual appetite and whose motto was: "Men for business, women for pleasure."

WORST BIPHOBIC SLUR ON A TELEVISION SHOW

Aside from the fact that all of the bisexuals on the show either turn gay or cheat on their lesbian lovers, *The L Word* reached new heights of biphobia during the 2006 episode in which the character Dana died. In poor taste, the creators of the show decided to lighten the scene by having the bisexual character Alice joke to her dying friend in the hospital bed about how bisexuals are gross. True, the joke was made to condemn the character Tina for leaving her lesbian partner for a man, but seriously, Ilene Chaiken—wake up! Just because you have the bisexual character say a bisexual slur in jest doesn't mean you're not offending half of your audience. Not funny.

WORST DEPICTION OF BISEXUALITY ON TV

Sex and the City unfortunately wins this award for its episode "Boy, Girl, Boy, Girl" in which Carrie dates a bi guy and is plagued with insecurity about whom he's looking at in a crowded bar. When

Carrie meets with Miranda, Charlotte, and Samantha over lunch they discuss the nonexistence of bisexuality and how all bi men and women they knew in college ended up with men. By the end of the episode, Carrie locks lips with a bi character played by Alanis Morissette during a game of spin-the-bottle and decides she's too grown up to entertain bisexuality as anything more than an immature phase that her bi boyfriend has not grown out of.

BI CARTOON CHARACTERS

We don't need religious leaders defining the sexuality of our cartoons. Yes, you have to look closely, but there are a few characters in kids' cartoons and comics that seem to be colored purple. Of the more obvious cartoons, there's an Internet comic strip called *Jake the Rake* about polyamorous bisexuals, and there's a German one called *Biester*. A famous Marvel bi hero is named Paradox, while Vertigo has Lord Jesus de Sade and DC has Frostbite. The beautiful boys and sexy girls in schoolgirl outfits from Japanese anime are mostly bi. Peter Cheung, the Korean artist who created *Aeon Flux*, says that his sexy killing machine is not only bisexual but "metal-sexual, she has sex with robots." But consider these too . . .

BUGS BUNNY. Overly dramatic, cool, and very clever, this carrot-chomping cartoon character is perhaps the best bi role model. He's kissing guys and gals with reckless abandon, doesn't care what anyone else thinks, and is pretty open about his fetish of dressing up in women's clothing. There's no question about "What's up" with this Looney Tune.

STARMAN. This DC comics hero has blue skin and is from another planet, but he's quite bi, bouncing from a dark brown–skinned male to a snow white–skinned female. The strip's writer, James Robinson, says the alien doesn't think of gender as humans do. Good thing!

PEPPERMINT PATTY. The butch gal in the Charles Schulz *Peanuts* strip likes Charlie Brown, but geeky Marcie has a crush on her.

JOHNNY QUEST. Handsome, blond Race Bannon of this classic cartoon is the companion and bodyguard of Johnny Quest's father. Race sometimes sleeps in the same room as Professor Quest, and he does sneak off to a lady spy that he seems to have some history with, but his loyalty is to this new family, raising Johnny, Hadji, and the little dog Bandit.

KYLE from *South Park*. Trey Parker has told us himself, "If any of the guys was going to come out as bisexual, it most likely would be Kyle." He's the one with the Jewish mom who throws up every time he kisses Wendy Testaburger. Butter's father is technically bi, and the mayor of South Park was also declared a "bisexual slut" in one episode.

ICE MAIDEN. From the Justice League of America, she flirted with Fire, another female character in the 1996 edition, after heating up the hearts of men.

ANIMA. Part of the New Titans series, she's a trendy character who's open about playing around with anyone, thus her name. Fortunately, despite a liaison with a character who had AIDS, she was safe and didn't get killed off.

TWEETY BIRD. Of undetermined sex, this little yellow critter seems to be attracted to all sorts. His fetish is being caged. Director Garry Marshall outed this Warner Brothers character at a GLAAD awards show one year, declaring, "We should all support animation; after all, Tweety bird is the most bisexual cartoon character ever."

ROCKY THE SQUIRREL. It's quite unclear if the flying squirrel of Rocky and Bullwinkle fame is a boy or a girl, but his character seems to be attracted to bad guys Boris and Natasha at times, as well as characters of all species. The bigger, brawnier, and dumber Bullwinkle is undoubtedly the bottom in this relationship.

THE THUNDERBIRDS. These British marionettes of the '70s starred five handsome brothers—although they didn't quite look like brothers—who never seemed to leave their luxurious island where they hid their cool rockets. The only woman ever making an appearance was wealthy and campy Miss Penelope, who seemed willing to offer her services to any of the hunks as they needed.

MULAN. This cross-dressing gal in the Disney feature sings, "I can't hide who I am inside though I tried, I would break my family's heart." The girls in fields think this "boy" is handsome.

THE GREEN LANTERN. This shady, disguised hero is penned by openly bi cartoonist Bob Schreck, who's on the record as wanting to create a comic book character who reflects his own sexuality and is introducing that into the story line. But wearing a green suit all the time? Gosh, even a bisexual would shirk at that.

TINTIN. Three guys were arrested in Belgium for showing this boy from this European cartoon having a fun time in gay bars in an unauthorized book, *Tintin in Thailand*. Although the character has been attracted to women in previous story lines, and has had close male companions, the B-word has never been put into that bubble.

SPONGEBOB. No one who dresses in those square pants could be just gay. His strong friendship with Sandy, the underwater squirrel, and Patrick, the starfish, reveals that this sponge soaks it up any way he can get it.

STORMBOY. He started off in Holland in 2002 with *Steal Your Heart Away*, but this bi horny superhero hasn't stopped winning both masculine and feminine hearts (as well as other organs).

THE SCARECROW in the *Wizard of Oz*. A bit of a goof, but even at his introduction to Dorothy, he very clearly says, "People do go both ways."

POPEYE THE SAILOR MAN. Never truly interested in Olive Oyl, even after being at sea with other sailors for so long, Popeye seems much more interested in roughhousing it with Bluto and hanging out with his friend Wimpy. Besides, he's always insisting, "I'yam what I'yam!"

COLEY COCHRAN. Perhaps the sexiest bi comic superhero ever created, the blond stud created by John Blackburn has his way with women and men rather equally, and discards them just as equally. A porn star, artist, and voodoo love god, he goes on incredible adventures, mostly in the nude. So when is that movie coming out?

You have now completed Chapter 5. Your brief moment of escapism has concluded. Before you make a b-line to your nearest video store, keep in mind that you've got to conquer the complexities of dating both genders in about, oh, a page. Don't worry, though. We'll hold your hand . . . that is, as long as it has been washed.

CHAPTER 6

DOUBLING YOUR CHANCES

Bisexuality immediately doubles your chances for a date on Saturday night.

—WOODY ALLEN

IT SOUNDS LIKE A simple thing—going out for dinner, having a few drinks, and getting to know someone, be they female or male. But in actuality, dating sometimes feels more like a chore, a tedious exercise to filter out the bores, the losers, the overeager, the unintelligent, the unattractive, the sleazy, or the humorless. Though we might get twice as many dates on a Saturday night, it's often twice as depressing when we go home at the end of the night wondering why we can't meet Mr. or Ms. Right. But don't worry . . . as usual, we've got your back.

This chapter will help you better hone your bidar to detect nonheterosexuals so you can meet them and mate with them (if they're lucky). We cover the clues and the warning signs associated with nearly every type of orientation you might date. (We left out most of the heterosexual dating stuff, because let's face it—millions of books exist to give you tips about how to attract members of the opposite sex.) We've organized this section to specifically address bi gals and bi guys separately, with Nicole writing for the ladies and Mike writing for the gents (notice: his tips are shorter because guys don't really overthink this stuff). We also spoke with dozens of our bi, straight, gay, and lesbian friends to develop these tips, so we're not completely talking out of our asses.

Let's start with those ambiguous, label-free folks who are all the rage lately.

GETTING SOME PLAY: THE POWER OF INDIFFERENCE (BY NICOLE)

AT AN OFFICE LUNCHEON, a coworker of mine surprised the whole table by admitting she had gone to a lesbian night at a bar and made a complete fool of herself when she approached a woman and said hello. Someone at the table asked her, "So are you a lesbian?" My coworker shook her head and said, "Oh, I date everyone." Everyone at the table nodded, instantly understanding she was bi, but not needing to clarify it by actually saying the word.

My coworker's unspoken bisexuality didn't factor in at all to her failures to mack on the girl at the club. Instead, it can purely be attributed to her inability to remember the first disgusting rule of dating—indifference is sexier than eagerness.

It's fucked up, we know, but somehow that's a universal rule of dating in het, homo, or ambiguously bi situations. Be yourself—just don't care too much. Sound impossible? Consider this . . . because you're fluid, you probably have flowed more to the straight side out of convenience for most of your dating life. This means that when you finally spot a same-sex dating opportunity, you salivate so readily at the prospect that you totally blow your wad. Your hunger for the same sex and your desperation—while attractive to some lesbians and gay men eager to de-virginize straight people—lead you to place too much importance on whether that one person at the club or bookstore, wherever, rejects you. There's only one solution: exposure training.

When people suffer from anxiety disorders, obsessive-compulsive disorder, and a panoply of other mental illnesses not caused by their deviant sexuality (sorry, we had to put that one in for the Bush administration), they learn exposure training to cope. That, my friend, is exactly what you need to soothe your raging hormones and calm your nerves. There's an old saying, "Out of the closet, back into adolescence," which pretty much means if you have little experience with the same sex, you're starting in that twelve-year-old place whether you like it or not (only this time it will, we hope, be without the zits or the braces). But just because you're in that mental and emotional headspace doesn't mean you have to act like it. Be yourself, be honest, but be optimistic that you will meet a lot of nonheterosexuals in your future, so you need not place your entire hopes for your romantic future on one encounter with someone you saw at a bar and thought was hot. The only way you're going to overcome this concern is through exposure to nonhets and lots of it.

Go to every gay bar you can find. Every guy night. Every girl night. Get used to being around homos, queers, dykes, queens, and fence-sitters. Though you might still get a few extra butterflies in your basket, you'll eventually, little by little, feel less intimidated by the scene and realize that once you start approaching people, not everyone will reject you. Sure, some might, but it's their loss. The others, well, they were just perceptive enough to sense your confidence and sincere laid-backness. Sound impossible? Just chill out. First you have to find some gay people. Read on, you label-free whore!

BUTCH OR FEMME?

Many of you know whether you're butch or femme or any of the lovely gray areas in between. Whether you hate dresses or love them. Whether you like short haircuts or loathe them. Whether you do or don't care if you look gay. The real question is what draws you in. Do tomboys get your motor running or effeminate men? Do girly girls annoy you or attract you? Does a macho man in uniform ready to take charge force you to take notice, or does he make you want to send him to sensitivity classes? You know the answers to all of these questions, and knowing what types of men and women get you hot is the first clue to what type of bisexual you are and what you're truly looking for in another person.

Bi women who consider themselves more on the straight side sometimes go for more butch women. Masculinity in all forms is their predominant turn-on, so naturally it still appeals to them when it's on another woman's body. Likewise, women just coming to terms with their adoration for the female figure sometimes turn to femmes because of the comfort factor. Others go for butches because they want someone "who really knows what they're doing" and like not having to make the first move. Ultimately, once a true female bisexual grows more comfortable with her chameleon-like status, she learns whether her dislike of butch women really stems from a physical aversion or just a discomfort toward dating or sleeping with someone who looks really gay—whether her love of high heels stems from watching one too many *Sex and the City* reruns or because they secretly envy the women who work at the makeup counter at Nordstrom's. Or whether they chase after tomboys because they themselves played cops-and-robbers with the neighborhood boys after school.

Bi guys who are more on the straight side might lean more toward femmes, especially if they're bi, too, with the hope of re-creating a potential three-way that's good enough for taping. Bi guys on the more gay side won't be so threatened, and perhaps will be even more turned on, by a more masculine woman. Veteran bi guys might go for men who are more sensitive, but ironically, it's rather common to see fully gay macho guys team up with bi men who are far more femme than they are.

You don't have to figure it out this moment; just be mindful of your preferences. Knowing who you are and what you dig are the first steps toward exuding the confidence you will need in order to have fulfilling flings, dates, relationships, sex parties, whatever.

FOR BI GALS . . .

WHERE CAN I MEET WOMEN? (BY NICOLE)

AN EXCELLENT RULE TO follow is that if you don't hang out with any bi/gay people, you won't meet many to date (oh, and that one gay person at work doesn't count). So the first step is to develop a strong stable of bad-ass bi/gay friends. Some bisexuals prefer the company of monosexuals (a.k.a. people who only like/date/screw one gender) because they find the ambiguity of a bi crowd unsettling. One bi woman told me she prefers not to hang with fence-sitters because she never knows who's hitting on her and who wants to be her friend. Other bisexuals prefer bi company because their level of self-censorship is lower. For example, you can say, "Oh my god, your friend Tara is hot." Then two seconds later gawk, "Who is that cute guy who just walked in?" and feel understood.

So get your friend situation stabilized and satisfactory before worrying about dating. Clearly, this won't be an issue if you're having a straight day, or a straight week, month, year, whatever. If that's the situation, you might feel content with your straight friends and have little trouble meeting straight guys because, let's face it, you can't throw a stone in this world without hitting one. Then again, if you're bi and have no bi or gay friends, you're probably going to feel like something's missing or, worse, feel like an outsider in your own life. Not good. Get some friends. How do you do this? Everyone knows a gay man. Every gay man knows a gay woman. Ta-da! (But if that doesn't work, just keep trying to hang out in gay neighborhoods, coffeehouses, or clubs as much as possible. Or better yet, join a bisexual Listserv online. Regardless of which strategy you employ, you'll be surprised at how many out bisexual and lesbian women are just as desperate as you to make queer friends.)

Once you have your rock-solid core group of bi/lesbian women, you're ready to hit the town. A lesbian friend of mine once told me that every lesbian is a bridge to another lesbian, so she views every gay or bi friendship as an opportunity to possibly meet her dream girl. But we're not going to blow smoke up your ass. It's a nightmare out there. The club scene is shallow and sucks for anyone who isn't fresh out of college, but at least at gay clubs you know most people are gay. Same goes for gay/lesbian parties.

Getting over the intimidation of attending an all-lesbian or gay party can be a bit daunting if you're new to the scene, but bring a herd of friends so you look popular as you mingle among the gay people as if you're one of them. No need to tell the gay people you're bi. Like the wild buffalo, you will frighten them. Maybe you'll get lucky and find the one nonbiphobic person there. Also try to find the other token bi person at the party by hinting at your own sexuality to determine whether they are bifriendly and date-worthy. If not, at the very least you'll have one more bi friend. But if so, see where things go; just try not to get too invested in an outcome, and if things don't work out make sure they don't end badly. The dating pool in gay circles is small, so you don't want to get a love-'em-and-leave-'em reputation or—worse—that of a stalker.

FOR BI GUYS . . .

WHERE CAN I MEET MEN? (BY MIKE)

FINDING A FELLOW BI guy isn't easy. As we've suggested, the openly bi political and social scene isn't always filled with lookers, and the Internet guy who says he's bi is usually a big flaming liar. The club scene does have some bi-oriented themes sometimes, but often those go to the extremes—like extreme drag (and often ugly drag) or extreme leather (where whips are mandatory in the dress code)—and they're not hard to find because they have names like Club Fuck or Crossover. Those clubs are usually transient, they're usually freak shows, and they're usually filled with people you don't want to see in the daytime.

My favorite bi club in the L.A. scene was the Vampire Club in the 1990s. It was sometimes held in dark warehouses downtown, sometimes in mall parking lots, sometimes in cool club spaces, and at a club owned by Prince. Because vampires, as we all know, are bi by nature—just pick up any Anne Rice book—this club prided itself on nonjudgmental sexuality. The dance floor often had threesomes gyrating in various combinations. The problem was that you really did feel like you were in a meat market, and not just for sex—a few of these people really did look like they wanted you for dinner.

The clubbers dressed in capes (often with nothing underneath), many wore fangs, and all looked rather pale. The parties started at midnight with all the members howling, and they often lasted until just before sunrise—and were always on a Thursday. Scream queen Brinke Stevens, Mistress of Darkness Elvira, Alexis Arquette, and other bi-list stars popped in. I met a young married couple who would put food coloring in their eyes to cry green and red tears before they swooped down and tried to bring someone home for a three-way. He had bright-red hair, and she was ravenesque, and I ended up not taking them up on their offer.

Anyway, the club scene isn't always the best place to go, but it doesn't mean you can't find a guy who might swing both ways. At a sporting event, if a dude is checking you out at the trough urinals or seems to be overly friendly, you may want to mention that you know it's Freddie Mercury's birthday, or hum an Ani DiFranco song. Such sensitivity may show this sports jock that you're multidimensional.

Going to a movie is always a way to hook up too. Obscure art films like *Dying Gaul* or *Adam & Steve* could open a discussion about what you are, or what you'd do, while standing in the popcorn line. Wearing your pink, purple, and blue rings around your neck or a Pansy Division T-shirt can't hurt, either.

A lot of bi guys seem to congregate at mostly gay parenting groups. Maybe Baby, Gay Dads, and other groups have men who've had their "one mistake" tagging along with them, or share custody of their kids, or are looking for others to share child-rearing responsibilities with them. If you're child inclined, it's a nice spot to find handsome, shy, caring guys who may want a relationship too.

The best thing I can suggest is find a club that holds your interest, whether it's straight or gay or a twelve-step program, and eventually show them how flexible you are. But if you're really into vampires, just be careful what you get sucked into!

CAN I MEET BI'S ON THE INTERNET?

SINCE EVERYONE AND THEIR mother joined MySpace, it seems Internet dating has steadily shed its überfreak image and became a somewhat common practice. Really, we mean it. What do you mean you haven't noticed? It's amazing. Even straight people are doing it. Mac, a San Diego bi activist, has collected an e-mail list of 140,000 bisexuals and says, "It's incredible how many married guys are sneaking out on the Internet looking for connections with other guys." Just like nightclubs and bars, each Internet Web site has its own vibe and unspoken rules.

Some sites exist purely for bi dating. The only thing is that they cost money, and a subscription of ten to thirty dollars per month to a bi dating site is something that a lot of twenty-somethings can't afford. This means these sites might be populated by more thirty-somethings or baby boomers and that you're not going to meet a lot of poor bums on these sites who can't afford to buy you dinner. So there are positives and negatives to paying the fee. The good news is that many sites offer trial memberships.

BICAFE.COM is populated by a lot of bi activists and down-to-earth types. Some just want to network with other bi's for friendship or more. It really runs the gamut. Since 1997, BiCafe has helped bi people who want to socialize with fellow bi's. The site's intention: to be the best online resource for bisexuals who get a charge out of sitting around a table and chatting with like-minded fence-sitters. Features include a search list that shows those who have logged on recently. Michael Page, the site's creator, says, "We do not collect e-mail addresses for bragging rights. Our goal is simple: to provide the best possible means to unite bi's."

BICUPID.COM is predominantly a bi dating site for singles and couples around the world. You can join for free, but you're forced to abide by the site's specific search criteria—if you want anything more, you have to pay. A lot of twenty-somethings populate this site, some of whom are "just looking for good times," others who seem to want friendship or something more substantial—so there's a good mix. Then again, about half of the gals who contacted me already had boyfriends, many of whom liked to watch. So it's a tough call. If you want to know what the person is seeking (man or woman), you have to pay. (Clearly, we didn't, so our impression of the site is limited.) BiCupid offers a six-degrees-of-separation feature like Friendster, with the added bonus of daily bisexual news, yet again, only if you're willing to shell out the bucks. Their main goal as stated on the site is to make bisexuals feel at home, and given that most of the people on the site look cool as opposed to downright scary, perhaps they've succeeded.

If you're looking for lesbians and bi women, take a peek at **Q-GIRL CONNECTIONS,** "a lesbian-owned and operated site for women only." Plenty of butches and femmes to choose from, but a lot of the user profiles don't have photos. A lot of lesbians, but quite a few bi gals, and for a fee you can boost your membership and your options.

BISEXUALPASSIONS.COM is part of the larger Passion Network, devoted to bringing together people with overlapping interests. For example, if you join the yoga-passion site and the bisexual-passion site, you'll meet bi folk who like yoga. Get it? Really, not that tricky. But hey, it's free! So you can join as many passion groups as you like after you join the bi site.

The Dating Network offers a bunch of bi dating sites such as **DATINGBISEXUALSINGLES.COM** and **BIFINDER.COM.** The membership is free, and the folks on the site seem fairly interested in making genuine connections with people. Though the profile info isn't very specific, a lot of people on this site seem relationship friendly—you know, not the type of people who want to talk about anal fisting.

BISEXUAL.ORG, a general resource bi site, features personals mostly from middle-aged folks. If you're looking for a baby boomer, you might want to check this site out. A lot of bi guys on this site, and given that many of them like to talk about their penises, they don't seem too shy.

FRIENDSTER is populated by alternative mid- to late-twenty-somethings, some of whom are bisexual, yet it's been somewhat of a dead zone for dating for a while.

Sure, for a few years everyone was hitting on everyone else, but Friendster messages from strangers just don't happen much anymore. Just like a popular nightclub, Friendster's moment as the hot spot has passed. Bi's, gays, and straights are switching to more predatory sites like the one listed below.

MYSPACE.COM is like Friendster for sluts, which naturally means a lot of bisexuals populate the site. The problem is that they're slutty bisexuals, many of whom are barely legal. If you write in your profile that you want to genuinely connect with people and not just fool around, you'll get messages from trashy college kids that read something like, "Yer cute! My boyfriend and I like your hot body, blah blah blah, please have sex with us." Actually, there usually isn't a "please." (Which brings us to a quick point before we proceed: women shouldn't hit on each other as poorly as men hit on women. Sure, there's something to be said for straightforward honesty, but what makes anyone think a simple "You're hot" will excite a woman? That strategy certainly doesn't work for men. Hello, it's trickier than that! Try harder next time you send an e-mail message. Compliment something in the person's profile.)

CRAIG'S LIST, though not specifically gay or bi, provides free personals—and everyone and their mother populate this site. It's not just for apartment hunting. You can find quite a few queers lingering on there, seeking either casual encounters or something more substantial.

FOR BI GALS . . .

WHO APPROACHES WHOM? (BY NICOLE)

Whether you're new to the gay dating scene or not, one frustrating aspect of meeting women will instantly become apparent to you: most women have no idea how to approach other women they find attractive. The reason is obvious: women are far too accustomed to being approached by men, or they've been conditioned to think they should be pursued. But once you enter the precarious world of same-sex dating, gender roles become obsolete. Shy newcomers and old veterans of the gay scene often struggle to answer this simple question: who approaches whom?

Lesbians are a little better at making the first move than bi women, who are often fresh from the straight dating world, where men do all the work. This passive attitude works great if you're a femme looking for a butch. A butch usually has no problem approaching you. But if you're a femme looking for a femme, you're going to have to suck it up and make a move or two. Two femmes will almost always have a rough time negotiating who will make first contact and often will never meet because these divas wait forever for the other to make the first move. Even two nonstraight femmes who are friends will often waste months waiting for the other gal to reveal some attraction. Perhaps femmes fear rejection more than butches, and for that reason they play coy, but more likely, femmes play coy because it's in their nature. And how can one thwart one's nature?

Here's a tip: don't go to gay places with just one female friend. When you travel with just one same-sex friend, you look like you're with that person. Though you may avoid touching one another, it's still more confusing for outsiders to determine whether you two are a couple. Also, if want to approach someone and you're with just one friend, what are you going to do—just leave your friend alone in the club, bookstore, whatever, while you go mack on someone? See our point? It's much more difficult to approach people when you're with just one other person. So bring a lot of backup and travel in herds. Then you can approach someone as friends and introduce them to all of your nice friends. It's seemingly innocent and enables you to meet the girl and metaphorically feel out her degree of interest without placing yourself on the chopping block.

You can assemble your herd by collecting those gay/bi women you met either through your gay male friends or online. I once created a short-lived herd with a lesbian friend that I met through a gay male buddy. We had a similar goal: to assemble a group of bi/gay girls to hit the town with. For a few months, before I dated her roommate and it ended badly, the group fulfilled my unique bi social need and also helped me meet women.

Remember: you can't thwart who you are or deny your comfort level, but you can stretch it a little. If a cute girl smiles at you, be it in a club or a movie theater, smile back, and maybe even bite the bullet and say hello. Use the quintessential pickup line of all time: "Hi, I'm _____" (Usually this proves to be an excellent cue for the girl to tell you her name.) Crack a joke if you have a sense of humor. If you don't, too bad. A good joke early on will help break the tension. Also lament how difficult it is to meet cool girls, but not in a hopeless, depressing way, more in a "I think you're cool" way. This one works a lot because almost every nonstraight woman can relate to the difficulty of meeting women, and everyone is a sucker for casual flattery.

Most important, if you approach a woman and she refuses to make eye contact or respond to your penetrating charm, walk away and don't blame yourself for the woman's obvious shortcoming: her inability to notice your undeniable desirability.

FOR BI GUYS . . .

WHO APPROACHES WHOM? (BY MIKE)

It's an odd world in the single dating scene for the bi guy. He's cast with suspicion, intrigue, doubt, and scorn by many of the communities that he'd be seeking a mate from, and so he has to tread carefully.

The general feeling among the guys is that bi men have to be more aggressive and overt when it comes to approaching guys, but have to be more sensitive and shy when it comes to approaching women. It makes sense, when you think about it. Women are so overzealously hit on by creepy guys with silly lines that it's a rare event to find a guy who's a bit subtle, wary, and even hard to get.

Being a product of the touchy-feely, Alan Alda generation, I was always taught not to be too aggressive, but polite, fair, and equal toward women. Now that didn't make me bisexual, but it makes me a bit of a wimp when it comes to scoring with the ladies. That is, until they find out that I'm bi, and then they are supercurious.

At first, the girl may want to be a friend, but then get surprised when friendships become more than that. So when a bi guy's interested in a woman who knows he's bi, he should wait for her to bring up her insecurities about the potential relationship. But when she finds out how you now think a woman can fully satisfy you, and how you were always safe with men, and how you're itching to have a meaningful liaison, she'll swoon. You can even compare notes about how all men are pigs.

And, to get to that side of things, when a bi guy approaches a guy, he's got to compete with all the expert gay guys out there, and so he's now got to be a bit more aggressive than his nature may allow. Gay guys will sometimes flee when they hear you're bi, or they may see you as someone who's in denial. And so you're going to have to be more direct, more macho, more adamant, and more sensual than you ever would for a female counterpart. And with a guy, you can complain about how crazy and unpredictable women are.

TO SHAVE OR NOT TO SHAVE?

SO THE DATE'S BEEN set. The plans have been made. Someone saw you somewhere, you had a decent conversation, and now you're going to meet over drinks or dinner to decide whether you should mate. But don't break your arm patting yourself on the back just yet. You have some serious decisions to make. For example, what to wear? Rule: never spend more than an hour selecting what to wear, or you will lose your mind and grow far too nervous for your date. A good dress tip is to wear something casual that's only slightly nicer than what you would normally wear. You want this person to accept you the way you are and not feel tricked or unpleasantly surprised when she/he realizes you don't wear Armani and makeup every day. Bottom line: the person is far too concerned with what she/he is wearing to worry about your outfit, so chill out.

Once you place your perfect outfit on the bed and head for the shower, the real question hits you: to shave or not to shave? Now, boys have it easier when it comes to this question. You can make a snap decision based on the gender of your date. For instance, if it's a woman, she'll probably be cool with your hair down there as long as she doesn't get a big handful when she grabs your dick. Hairy balls can also be a turnoff for some women, but bottom line, if a woman likes you, she won't care as much about the amount of hair as long as it's not excessive. But gay men . . . look out! They want you shorn down there, especially around a certain nether region. And boys, when you're going out on a date with another man, you need to be groomed and prepared to get down quickly because that's what a lot of men do. Women, on the other hand, have much more to consider in this department.

Before shaving it all off, consider the place you live and the gender of your date. If you live in Eugene, Oregon, no one is going to give a crap whether you've gotten a bikini or Brazilian wax (psst: Brazilian means bald). They're not cosmopolitans up there, so they pretty much don't expect much more than a courtesy trim, if that. But if you live in New York or Los Angeles, you need to give the hair down there a little more thought. Some guys in Los Angeles are so shallow that they'll dump you over having anything more than a porn-star-size bush. Those guys should be shoved in a cannon and shot to Planet Shallow, but because Planet Shallow doesn't exist (yet), you'll just have to tell all of your friends that they were just bad in bed.

Most men are just happy that you're naked, so trim within

your comfort level. Some guys are really uncomfortable and have their friends wax their backs, or they shave their chests before going to the beach or the White Party. Some guys go overboard with their pube trimming, so remember that although guys could look bigger down there if there's some judicious shaving, most people don't want you to look prepubescent—and you shouldn't want to go out with people who want you to look that way.

Most women, who aren't shallow, will be cool with a courtesy trim as well, but not all women. If you're dating a gal who makes a big deal about how she loathes the pubes and gets Brazilianed all the time, you know she expects you to be smooth as a whistle down there as well. If you're not comfortable with shaving or waxing it all off for her, don't do it. If she dumps you over that, she's as shallow as those wretched men mentioned earlier, and you can tell all your friends that she was really straight.

Overall, the basic rule: shave within your comfort level and according to your partner's preference, if the partner's worth it. Remember: whatever you choose will set a precedent and an expectation for your partner. To some, it's the difference between sandpaper and silk, so choose wisely. Some people like silky hair. Some people like sandpaper (let's face it, hair grows back real quick!). Figure out which one you are, take a shower, and head to your date with confidence. Even if you don't plan on giving more than a good-night hug, it's good to be prepared.

HOW TO SEDUCE
A STRAIGHT GIRL (BY NICOLE)

SO IF YOU'RE A curious straight girl reading this, you probably want to stop reading now if you plan on keeping that denial thing going, because let's face it: you people have tendencies. Come on, admit it. Fine, put the book down. This section isn't for you anyway. It's for all the beautiful queer women goddesses who know how utterly ambiguous situations can get with their straight, yet not-so-straight, female friends.

We've all been there with that one "straight" girlfriend who touches us emphatically a few times too many during a not-so-noteworthy conversation. She's the same girl who gives us multiple good-bye hugs at the end of the night and squeezes a little too tightly. Sometimes when nestled safely in a group setting, that same woman flashes us a serious "look," the same look that disappears after her friends disappear. So what gives? Do these women want us, or are we just hypersensitive to any and all signs of queerness?

First, pat yourself on the back, because your odds of helping your friend explore this, ahem, virgin territory are better than your lesbian counterparts. Because you're bi, you're safer to experiment with. Odds are, you're more femme, and thus "less gay" (a.k.a. dangerous). The woman in question can probably look at you and say, "She's just like me." Through your bi-ness, your mere presence forces her to question her own identity because you contradict many of the damning "gay cues" that scare these experimental girls away. Plus, when she looks at you, she thinks "threesome," which means her creepy boyfriend probably won't object (though you might). No matter, let her think that or whatever might be floating around in her head. You're about to create the safest environment for her to explore.

To truly determine whether your straight friend is willing to get down, you must ascertain her level of attraction without ruining your friendship. This can be rather tricky, so use caution. Given that you're bisexual, you're undoubtedly a master flirt (if not, practice!). The good news: women flirt with each other all the time. The bad news: they're usually kidding. But in order to amply test the waters, you must slip in a comment here or there to test your friend's reaction. An instant sour face usually means game over, but a coy laugh accompanied by a slight blush could work in your favor. True, this reaction could just mean she's being polite . . . but it also could indicate that she realizes you're onto her and is acknowledging the chemistry between you.

The next step involves a bit of sass, followed by a strong regiment of teasing. Dare to disagree with her, but be cute and funny about it. If she fights back with a lot of spunk, you've succeeded. Competitiveness walks a fine line with some bizarre form of sexual energy, perhaps because it involves game playing—something you are both pros at, given your gender. When you add alcohol to this spirit of competition, you've created yet another safe space to pick your friend's brain about otherwise verboten topics and to push the already tenuous boundaries of your friendship. Next time she playfully touches you, create an excuse to playfully touch her back.

By now, of course, you've already scoured her video collection for any gay titles and her bookshelf for any steamy lesbian literature. If you didn't find any, don't despair. Your friend may be at the very beginning of her exploration, which means if she has any of these items, they aren't out in the open.

A word of caution about these ambiguous straight girls: as they struggle with their attraction to you, their desire will ebb and flow, giving you hopeful hints one moment and devastating "What was I thinking?" reminders the next. Don't let these discourage you. Studies have proven that women often show desire for men through intermittent reinforcement—staring them down one minute and ignoring them the next. Female desire is not as consistent as male desire, so signals are always harder to read.

One thing's for certain: determining whether your straight friend can truly blossom into a bi identity is going to take a lot of work, usually spanning many visits and possibly many months. You must question whether this project you've undertaken is worth that much of an investment and remind yourself that you may never see any returns . . . but that doesn't mean you can't have fun in the meantime. If all odds fall in your favor (as they have for me on multiple occasions), you'll move from playful conversational touching to harmless massages to meaningful cuddling to . . . well, you get the picture.

HOW TO SEDUCE
A STRAIGHT GUY (BY MIKE)

SEDUCING A STRAIGHT GUY is rather easy. In fact, talk to a straight woman about it, and you'll find that often a bi guy has more luck seducing straight guys than a woman has trying to do the same. She becomes a slut, or too clingy, or not the kind of girl he'd bring home to Mom if she's too aggressively seductive. You just become interesting.

To a straight guy, a bi guy isn't carrying the baggage that a woman may seem to be carrying. There's no talk of a marriage, or another date, or even who's paying for dinner. And if you have a girlfriend, you have a connection. You can talk about her body parts and how great sex is with her, and it's less threatening to him.

If a straight guy is so inclined, he wants to get it over with quickly, and he knows you don't expect a long-lasting relationship. So whether it's a quickie after a hot workout at the gym, a fast Internet hookup while the wife and kids are away, or a curious moment before marrying his fiancée, the straight guy sees a jaunt with another guy merely as an emotionally meaningless diversion for quick sexual satisfaction.

And, for the most part, if you're bi, the straight guy isn't going to worry too much about being seen in public with someone who may appear "too gay," so you can outwardly be "hang-out" buddies without anyone being the wiser.

The biggest problem with trying to land a straight guy is that you may be putting yourself into a dangerous situation. Don't set yourself up in a Matthew Shepard scenario where the guys are luring you out with their bi-curious questions and then ending up beating the crap out of you. Too many friends of mine who are straight-chasers end up going home with straight guys who freak out as their zippers get pulled down, and turn into self-hating, psycho bashers.

One good way to test the dude: before agreeing to go anywhere private, try kissing him long and hard on the lips in public, and even finagle a tongue between those lips. If he resists, if he panics, if he calls you a faggot, then don't pursue this one. There are plenty of straight men curious enough for the picking out there. Or, if you're really horny for this particular one, just meet him at a bathhouse, and if he tries anything rough there, he's going to have a bunch of naked homos beating the crap out of him.

My best straight-guy conquest was a professional baseball player. Macho, rugged, and with a girlfriend, he seemed overly friendly with the guys, always slapping everyone on the butt, and adjusting his crotch cup. A female friend of mine got us in the dugout during a game, and he came over to talk to us. There were plenty of double entendres, talking about how big he likes his bat and why baseball players scratch themselves so much, and we were amused and charmed. He seemed to flirt with her, but when he slapped me on the backside, he grabbed one of my butt cheeks and gave it a firm squeeze. It was breathtaking, but I wasn't sure what it meant.

After the game, he invited me into the locker room, saying girls weren't allowed—but they were, because female journalists were doing interviews all around—but I followed him like a puppy dog. When he undressed and sported a bobbing bit of wood, I looked away, lowered my voice, and tried to say something macho, but he simply said, "Playing really gets me worked up; you'll notice it in all the guys."

After three double dates with the player and his girlfriend, our talks became more personal, and he complained about the blow jobs he was getting from his girl. Now this is always an easy "in" with straight guys: all you have to insist is that you know that guys must know how to please guys more than girls do. If he questions it, then simply add, "Well, do you think you know how to go down on a girl very well? Don't you think another girl is going to figure out how to do things better than you?"

If he's honest, he'll agree. Then, it's only a matter of time before he can feign being a bit sloshed and ask to stay the night. In our case, the baseball player arranged it so that we dropped off our dates first, and then he suddenly felt too drunk to drive. He came in with me and seemed to sober up pretty quickly, opened up a beer, and stripped to his underwear as he looked on my shelves for porn.

This is also another way to gauge a straight guy's interest. If he's willing to watch porn with you, he's unafraid to get hard in front of you. If he gets hard watching guys go at it, then it completely fucks with his head.

The baseball player knew by then I had a history with guys, but he never even copped to being "bi curious." He said he didn't want to see any videos with the "gay shit" but was willing to watch a bisexual tape—always have a good one on hand, and have it cued up to the two-guys-and-a-girl scene. And as soon as he watched two guys going at it with a girl in *Valley of the Bi Dolls*, he was massaging himself through his undies on my couch, and like a bad porno, it was my cue to dive in.

He claimed it was his first time with a guy, but I never believed it, and we "saw each other" for about eight months until he was traded to another team and later got married. He said it was easier to be with me because I had a girlfriend and I wasn't interested in anything more than our casual encounters.

It was more than casual for me, though, and I had to keep it a secret, although my gay friends always asked about how close we were, and his fiancée seemed to get a bit jealous of our suddenly intense friendship.

I've had the chance to seduce a few straight guys—the scout at camp, the tennis jock in school, the politician, the rock singer, the soap opera star—but they all allowed themselves to be in positions of opportunity, and so it's up to the bi guy to recognize those opportunities and make the move.

By the way, my story about the baseball dude is true. It was loosely made into a porn movie by Studio 2000 called *Playing to Win*, and so the bad porno that I felt I was in at the time became a reality after all.

HOW TO SEDUCE A LABEL-FREE BISEXUAL

WHETHER THEY'RE VETERANS TO the scene who would just never use the B-word or a newbies who doesn't like labels, bisexuals who don't call themselves bisexuals are, well, still bisexuals. They hunger for both sexes just like the rest of us. They just don't like to talk about it. So if you want to seduce them, don't make them admit it. But once they drop that signature noncommittal, ambiguous comment about how they swing both ways, go in for the kill . . . that is, if you find them attractive. Don't say, "I'm bi too!" Just roll with it and casually say, "Yeah, I go out with men and women too." Your nonchalance will win you major points and will signal to your label-free friend that you might be interested. From there, just look for the basic reciprocal signs— compliments about your body and your being, subtle touches, constant stares, legs crossed in your direction, nervousness only when they're talking to you, and so on—then make your move, that is, if she or he doesn't make it first.

FOR BI GALS . . . (BY NICOLE)

ADVANTAGES OF DATING A STRAIGHT GIRL

First of all, one doesn't date a straight girl. If a straight girl goes for you, neither one of you will call it "dating." Dating happens intentionally, and straight women don't intentionally date nonstraight women. It just happens, often without longevity, usually when one of your straight friends decides to experiment. If you're into high femmes and being a woman's "first," then straight women might be for you. Closeted bi women often have a proclivity for straight women because they will both be interested in keeping their involvement/fling a secret.

DISADVANTAGES OF DATING A STRAIGHT GIRL

If you're not into secrets or inexperienced, femme-y women, then straight gals aren't for you. Straight girls often go bi just for the sex and are incapable of giving you their hearts. Others fall in love with you, but just can't get turned on by you because you are a woman—and repeated make-out sessions won't cure this setback either. Ultimately, you deserve someone who will be hot for you and in love with you, at least if you're looking for that special someone. A lot of bi gals really crave a relationship with a woman but settle for straight girls who aren't hot for them or really smitten because they just can't meet a nice bi or gay girl. For this reason, many finally take the plunge and date a lesbian.

ADVANTAGES OF DATING A LESBIAN

The first obvious advantage of dating a lesbian is that she's certain she likes girls. Instead of the usual bi-curious, closet cases, an out lesbian will usually exhibit a fairly consistent attraction to you. She knows you get her hot, and she doesn't hide it or feel ashamed about it. In fact, at times, she can be rather straightforward about wanting to sleep with you. Many bi gals will find this refreshing after dealing with frequently ambivalent bi gals. On occasion, you can find a lesbian who has an actual preference for bi gals, which is supercool. Many lesbians dig monogamy, so if you want a real relationship with a woman that will last, lesbians are your best bet—that is, if they don't mind the bi thing.

DISADVANTAGES OF DATING A LESBIAN

A lot of them do mind the bi thing, and sometimes their own insecurities about it can ruin the relationship. They might view you as experimental or simply as a straight person pretending just for a roll in the hay with a gal. If you're dating a lesbian who has this attitude, there's not much you can do. Verbal assurances will do little to quell her fears that you will leave her for a man. If that happens, dump her. You don't need to be dating someone that insecure anyway.

ADVANTAGES OF DATING A STRAIGHT MAN

By default, straight guys are what and whom most bi gals end up doing. Simply put: straight guys are the pinnacle of convenience. They approach you. They pay for stuff. They open doors, if you're into that kind of thing. Gentlemen offer chivalry—something that's lacking in more unconventional relationships. Assholes offer you misery. You've got to figure out which type of straight man you're dating. Hope that it will be the former. Straight men don't hide their affections, and most don't play games. All will appreciate a straightforward bi gal because many straight girls are passive and leave them guessing. Guys identify with your masculine side and feel they've got the best of both worlds—a gal who doesn't mind a wandering eye, whom they can check out chicks with, who is straight-up about what she wants. They can be ideal life partners for bi women who want a storybook ending with kids, so long as they don't get bored with their hubbies.

DISADVANTAGES OF DATING A STRAIGHT MAN

A lot of them are boring. Sorry, guys, it's true. It's not like encyclopedia boring, but more like "your lips aren't soft, and you don't have tits" kind of boring. Most bi gals have had their fill of the male body. We can enjoy nicely toned abs or a waxed chest just like straight girls, but sometimes we want something just a little bit softer. Sometimes we want the climax of a sexual experience not to be ejaculation. Sometimes we want hours upon hours of sex play and intimacy without the expectation of intercourse. Though some straight men might claim to want that as well, they're few and far between and sometimes liars.

ADVANTAGES OF DATING A GAY MAN

Whoa there, you mean bi gals date gay men? Well, not date exactly. More like screw occasionally when really drunk and often hard up. Usually, closet-case gay (or even bi) men go for bi women because they'll feel safe exploring their sexuality with someone who's already queer. Hey, see above: half of them have slept with women. Sure, you probably won't enjoy yourself, but the conversation in between will be fabulous.

DISADVANTAGES OF DATING A GAY MAN
He's gay.

ADVANTAGES OF DATING A BI MAN
Many bi gals would love to date a male bisexual. The male bisexual offers every bisexual's ideal: dating someone who understands dual attraction. Bi men embrace the gray areas of attraction and will never fault you for craving a same-sex partner. Bottom line: they get it in a way that a straight or a gay person never could and offer endless possibilities in bed. Things will never get boring.

DISADVANTAGES OF DATING A BI MAN
They're hard to find. Uncovering one to date in the first place is incredibly tricky. So if you do happen upon one, whether he has someone or not, you want to hold onto that guy. Sometimes, though, these "bi" guys aren't as bi as they claim. Some would never go further than kissing a man, whereas others never date women—only men. Others might have a much stronger proclivity to wander and leave you wondering why you're spending another Friday night alone or listening to him bitch about the girl or guy who just dumped him. If you're looking for simple or for a white-picket-fence fantasy, a bi guy might not be your best bet. If you're looking to find the first member of a triad, a bi guy is a great place to start.

ADVANTAGES OF DATING A BI WOMAN
She's just like you. She must be. After all, you're both bisexual. You're both women. Therefore, together, you can, in all probability, take over (or at least deconstruct) this cruel world. You can commiserate over the foibles of dating men and lament

your inability to relate to lesbians and straight people. You can maintain endless conversations about *The L Word*, lust after Johnny Depp, and hypothesize about whether that mystery girl at your office is really straight. You can shop at Whole Foods and cruise men and women as you toss vegan TV dinners into your cart. You can attend nightclubs with your gay friends, brunch with your lesbian gal pals, and go to baseball games with your straight buddies. Even better, you can make out and make out and make out and share your most out-there fantasies with someone who won't judge you and might not expect you to maintain a "traditional" monogamous relationship, which is a good thing if you're dodging those lesbian moving vans.

DISADVANTAGES OF DATING A BI WOMAN

Not to reinforce stereotypes here, but some bi gals are flighty. Many have a much more difficult time committing to women than to men (perhaps scared to tackle a same-sex relationship), so if you're looking for something serious, be up front from the get-go on your expectations. By dating a bi gal, we hate to say it, you're also risking getting a closet case or a bi-curious straight girl, so be sure your lady feels confident in her identity. Plus, finding bi gals who aren't already in relationships with men can be a challenge, especially if you're looking for something serious. (Don't believe us? Check online. They all want sex.) Also, the femme factor with bi gals might require some high-maintenance grooming that might not be worth your time, but then again, there are plenty of bi gals who don't even shave their legs and want a commitment—and the two don't always have to go hand in hand.

FOR BI GUYS . . . (BY MIKE)

ADVANTAGES OF DATING A STRAIGHT MAN

It's easier, quicker, and could be relatively anonymous. Want to feel used, want to feel like a piece of meat? Then, this is the relationship for you. Of course, if you're both in the closet about your relationships, this is a good way to cover by double-dating with your girlfriends or wives and fooling around on the side with your good buddy. Trouble is, *Brokeback Mountain* ruined it for all this closet playing around.

DISADVANTAGES OF DATING A STRAIGHT MAN

He is the most likely to go psycho on you, or pretend like nothing ever happened. Think about it: if he's still insisting he's straight after giving you a great blow job and he's kissed you on the lips more than once, his dabbling is more than an anomaly, and there's something seriously wrong with his reality. However, due to the "down-low" awareness these days, his girlfriend or wife is going to be very suspicious, and you can bet she'll be checking his fishing-tackle box.

ADVANTAGES OF DATING A GAY MAN

You don't even have to watch *Queer Eye for the Straight Guy* anymore. He's going to keep you up on all the latest trends on Broadway and in fashion, the best clubs, and who's in the closet in Hollywood. There's nothing beating the latest dish in the gay gossip crowd, and there's always someone who knows someone who cuts so-and-so's hair that makes it all sound so legit, too.

DISADVANTAGES OF DATING A GAY MAN

Inevitably, when he finds out you've been with a woman, he's going to want all the dirty details about what it's like to explore a vagina. He's going to squeal, retch, and gag along the way, no matter how tasteful you are. Remember, he'll have a vested interest in turning you off to the female anatomy. Don't let him think that dressing in drag is going to make him more attractive to you. And you'll quickly get tired of the "Ditch the bitch and make the switch" chant.

ADVANTAGES OF DATING A STRAIGHT GIRL

She's not stupid, but she generally won't notice if you take an extra look at a cute waiter's butt or are noticing the guy's bulges while at the ballet. They will tend to be more clingy but blissfully naive about your homo past. A straight woman may be more family oriented, and it's more likely she's going to want to keep you on a tight leash. Find one who likes sports, and then pretend like you know something about the game while watching it with her.

DISADVANTAGES OF DATING A STRAIGHT GIRL

Whether she tells you or not, she'll always be threatened about not having a penis. She'll always wonder if you're missing out what you had before with a guy and wonder what she can offer that she thinks she's lacking. It's a good way to turn this into a sex-ed class and have her demonstrate the best ways to please her and vice versa. Another way to turn the tables on her is to ask if there's anything she misses that you're not providing. Then maybe she'll see how silly she's being.

ADVANTAGES OF DATING A LESBIAN

Occasionally, a lesbian wants to dabble with a man, and finding a more sensitive and willing bi man is a better option for her. She'll know how to tie a tie, and she's good at shining boots. She'll also have cable because she watches *The L Word*. But be warned—you're going to totally screw up all your social circles because no one is ever going to figure you out. A big plus: she can fix your car.

DISADVANTAGES OF DATING A LESBIAN

Look out! A lesbian is going to bring all kinds of whirring, spinning, gigantic sex toys to bed with you, wanting to try them all on, and without lube. She's going to want to use a strap-on too, and she's going to insist on being a top. This has happened to more guys than you'd believe, me included. Negotiate how many tools from her toolbox she's going to bring to bed before things get too far.

ADVANTAGES OF DATING A BI MAN

Like attracts like, so what could be more perfect than a relationship with another bi man? Well, you know what he's like for one, but that includes you knowing what a wayward horndog he is too. He'll be cute, and hung, and he'll think he knows you. It's fine to discuss women with a bi guy, but as soon as you discuss guys, jealousy rears its ugly head. Just make sure he doesn't live the stereotype.

DISADVANTAGES OF DATING A BI MAN

He could be rather voracious, and you could feel like you don't live up to his past relationship with a woman. He will have had his heart broken, many times. He will ask you to change for him. But before you think about cutting anything off, realize that at least half the time he's hot for you and what you've got.

ADVANTAGES OF DATING A BI WOMAN

No matter who walks by, no matter who you're looking at, you can judge, compare, discuss, and analyze without fear of shock or judgment. She'll certainly be very open and carefree. She may be more open to bringing in someone else to the relationship, so be prepared, and don't get jealous.

DISADVANTAGES OF DATING A BI WOMAN

She may be so hip, so cool, so carefree that she'll figure you're not good enough!

DOES BIDAR EXIST?

bidar (BI+dar) n. An intuitive sense that enables someone to identify whether another person is bisexual.

AT THE TURN OF the twentieth century, gay men wore bright-red ties to indicate their sexuality and availability to each other. If only it were that easy today. No, no, no! Though most would argue that one too many trips to the gym and stylish haircuts have replaced red ties in the gay community, even gay folks can't always peg a fellow queer with their gaydar (especially since the rise of the sensitive male and the metrosexual revolution). That doesn't mean that sensationalistic news shows haven't tried to prove its existence.

On October 29, 2004, Dateline aired a segment that examined the existence of gaydar through an experiment. A panel of straight and gay men sat before straight and gay audience members who voted on which individuals appeared to be homosexual. (Bisexuals were naturally excluded.) Sixty percent of participants accurately guessed who was queer. We wager that if the panel had mixed bisexuals with straight people, that percentage of accurate guesses would have been much lower because sensing someone's bisexuality purely through their physical appearance can be nearly impossible.

Unlike most gay men, bisexuals do not, as a collective group, fit certain molds, at least not in our physical appearance. Bi guys don't necessarily go to the gym, style their hair, and flip their wrists like stereotypical gay men. In fact, neither do a lot of gay men. Likewise, not all bisexual women sport short haircuts and wear masculine clothes like stereotypical lesbians. Though the gay community laments all of these lame stereotypes, at least it has visual indicators that enable gay men and women to identify one another in public places. Bisexuals don't have that. Even sports fans are luckier than us.

Take asshole jocks, for example. Collectively, they look alike because they share the common interest of sports and thus express their common interest through the group norm of wearing jerseys, caps, and the occasional foam finger. Gay people subconsciously do the same thing: they follow the norms of their group—be they ribbed T-shirts or gender-bending haircuts—to attract like-minded people. But when you're bisexual and have no community, there are no specific modes of fashion or behavior to imitate. If a bright, obnoxious orange T-shirt indicated bisexuality, you can be damn sure that despite how stupid we'd look, bisexuals everywhere would be wearing bright-orange T-shirts. The only problem is that because we have little to no community, unlike our gay counterparts, we probably wouldn't even hear that wearing an orange T-shirt means someone is bisexual.

For this reason, the bisexual appearance quite collectively seems schizophrenic. Bisexuals could look like hippies, goths, preppies, nerds, sorority girls, frat boys, musicians, actors, surfers, lawyers, or really anyone from any scene. For this reason, unless bisexuals go out of their way to look gay, they often are mistaken for straight people. Aside from maybe a straight-looking couple in a gay bar clearly looking for a threesome, it's hard to peg bisexuals in gay places. Maybe that's because most bi's identify with the straight community by default and thus look more straight; or maybe that's because many bi's identify with the gay community, and thus appear more gay.

So how in the hell can you spot a bisexual in public? The answer: through the process of elimination. Take a gay bar, for example. Scan the crowd. Determine who seems the gayest, and discard them visually. Then, rescan the crowd and attempt to pick out all the straight people. Don't discard them. They very well might be bi. Now, attempt to establish eye contact with one of them. Go ahead. Blatantly check out a cute prospect until he or she notices. If you get a smile, keep staring, but not in a lecherous way. If the person looks at you again and smiles, you know he or she may be gay or bi.

Using this strategy in a straight bar is easier sometimes. Instead of looking for straight-seeming people, look for that one tomboy gal or slightly feminized guy—you know, gender-bending or gay characteristics—or just notice that one member of the same sex who keeps checking you out. Bi people hang in straight places a lot, and given that you are also bi, they will probably stand out to you in an indescribable, nonverbal way. And that, my friend, is bidar.

Sure, it's not completely accurate. Neither is gaydar. But by not being straight, you are born with a natural ability to detect other not-straight people. You don't agree? Spend more time in gay bars, hone your instrument, and watch it improve its accuracy. And if that doesn't work, you can always ask or, better yet, drop a line about how you date boys and girls, oops, men and women (don't want anyone to get the wrong idea) and see what happens. If you get an "I think everyone's bisexual," then you're in.

If you're around someone a lot, like at work or in social situations, you can better assess their bi-ness through the person's androgynous manner and style of dress, though that's not always a sure bet. Moreover, look at what the person says, his or her attitude, and so forth, but don't reveal yourself if the situation could later bite you in the ass and prove unprofessional or inappropriate. But hey, sometimes being open is the best policy. You decide. But remember, in general, bidar is accurate only about 40 percent of the time (OK, we made this number up, but that's our estimation). But seriously, even veteran bisexuals can't always reliably detect the presence of other bi's. Verbal confirmation is the only surefire method to determine whether someone goes both ways . . . and even that's not 100 percent reliable.

WHEN A STRAIGHT WOMAN LOVES
A BI MAN (BY MIKE)

AS AN OUT BI man, my longest relationship with a straight woman was for three years, but she always introduced me as her "gay boyfriend." I was monogamous with her, and I didn't want to go out with anyone else. Interestingly enough, I was almost living more of a "gay lifestyle" with her than I ever was before, because she kept insisting on having me keep my aura of queerness.

She wanted us to go dancing at the gay clubs ("Better music," she'd say, as she was the lone blonde-haired beauty gyrating under the disco ball surrounded by sweaty guys, and me).

She insisted on attending all the Gay Pride events ("It's so much fun," she'd gush, as she slapped rainbow stickers on our bumpers.) She'd go out to rent gay porno ("to learn from them"), we'd go to art-house theaters to see gay mainstream movies ("Gregg Araki is so edgy"), and we'd listen a lot to Elton John and Boy George ("Their songs are for us all, not just for you people.")

She'd buy my clothes so they were tighter, more flowery, and more frilly than I'd ever bought them before ("You want to fit in, don't you?" she'd say). And she'd often ask me the words to show tunes if she couldn't remember ("Don't get so offended, I just figured you would know").

It occurred to me that she loved the gay side of me more than she did the hetero side. Parading me around as the "guy she turned around" was a badge of honor among her friends, but she couldn't do that if I were bi.

She knew what bisexuality meant, but as a het woman, she had a hard time dealing with the fact that I could turn my attraction on and off like a spigot. I tried to entice her bi side, but she said she was attracted to only one other woman in the world, and that was Roseanne Barr. "I just find her so sexy," my girlfriend said.

We had fantastic sex—never with Roseanne, or any other person, and always with a condom. She would come with me for regular "checkups" for AIDS tests, but the beginning of the end of our relationship was when I asked her to get tested too.

She suddenly backed out of going on *The Phil Donahue Show* to talk about bisexuality with me because there were a few issues that we hadn't yet resolved privately. And it wasn't until Phil asked me on national television about her that I realized and said, "You know, my girlfriend is actually more dangerous to me than I am to her! She has me go get tested all the time, but she's never been tested, and she's slept with more guys than I have."

It got a big laugh, but I was faced with a big scowl when she picked me up after the show. She had watched it live with her family.

Straight women may find that bi men are more sensitive, less abusive, and even better lovers. Maybe they feel more equal, less fearful, and more comfortable. But, ultimately, there's sometimes a sense of inadequacy that a woman may feel she can't match.

The first time my girlfriend sneaked a dildo into bed, I jumped and said, "What's that for?" She tried to explain, "It's to make up for something you may have missed."

No, I had mine, and didn't miss it at all. As far as anyone else's, it wasn't an issue, nor was it anything I missed.

It's possible to have a very good relationship with a straight woman—I know many bi men who have been married for decades and more—but be careful. Don't let a straight woman turn you gay!

JUST ONE BEER AWAY

Everyone's bisexual when they're drunk.

—CONFUCIUS, 500 BC

OK, SO MAYBE THAT'S not an old Chinese proverb, but let's face it—we've all heard it if not experienced it. But are the rumors true? Will straight people fall into bed with members of the same sex after one too many vodka Red Bulls? Will gay folks become breeders because of booze?

We all know that alcohol allows our inner id to run free. What most monosexuals don't know is that our inner id is bisexual. Once the liquor sets it loose, it likes to run around nightclubs and house parties with carefree abandon. The mere suggestion of fooling around with a gender the id usually ignores sends it into spasms of reckless delight. But whether you believe this depends on your philosophical interpretation of alcohol.

People view alcohol in either of two ways: that the booze sets your inhibitions free and makes you who you really are or that it makes you become someone else entirely. Usually, the people who believe the latter have made one too many bisexual mistakes while blotto and have tired of justifying their bisexual hangovers in the morning. But if college teaches us anything, it's that a hundred drunk coeds can't be wrong for accidentally participating in unplanned orgies. So embrace your inner bisexual wino. He or she may just be more fun than you'd like to admit.

RULES OF DATING A BISEXUAL

NOT MANY FOLKS LEAVE their houses on a Friday night thinking, "I hope I meet a nice bisexual tonight." Very few people, with the exception of frat boys, plan to date one of our kind unless, of course, they themselves go both ways. Most often, our preference is sprung on them during a first date or a few months into a relationship, a marriage, whatever, when they least expect it (though any time would be "when they least expect it," because the possibility of not being straight or gay doesn't even occur to most people).

Instead, everyone inaccurately assumes that their dates or partners share their identical sexuality and, thus, make an ass out of you and me. For example, straight men assume their female partners are straight, while straight women assume their boyfriends are hetero. Gay people assume their dates are homos. This sort of self-centered thinking leads only to massive shock on the straight or gay partner's end, especially because many of us don't look queer. Likewise, butch bi women and femme bi men are often assumed to be lesbians or homos by their gay dates. Aside from perhaps accidentally dating a closet case, dealing with this circumstance—that is, the one where you have to come out to your date or partner—is almost exclusively an awkward by-product of being bi.

So we've created this section for you to hand to your straight or gay partners to help them better understand how to date you. We know it sounds silly, but seriously, hand it over. You'll thank us later.

RULE #1: DON'T BLOW IT OFF. We've come out to dates or people we've been seeing and had them simply brush our sexuality under the rug, claiming to be cool with it. If that's the case, why the sudden need to ignore it? Though we'd like to assume you are as progressive as you claim, we need a little proof. Humor us. Tell us about some bi girl or boy you knew in college or how you "think everybody is." Anything—just don't drop the subject like a hot plate.

RULE #2: DON'T JOKE ABOUT IT. We know you think calling us your "damn fence-sitter" is hilarious, but unless you want to earn the new nickname of "breeder booty call" or "fag'a'muffin," you better zip yo' lip. Poking fun at our "confusion" is about as funny as that humiliating moment you barely survived in middle school (you know the one). If you're kinda dense and just now realizing what an ass you've been, you had better start buying us stuff. Lots of stuff. Now. That is, unless you've already been dumped.

RULE #3: DON'T SIGH, ROLL YOUR EYES, OR TELL US WE'LL GROW OUT OF IT. Nuh uh. No. The only thing that's going to be grown out of is your outdated ignorance. Repeat after us: "I believe in bisexuality. I believe in bisexuality . . ." Click your heels and repent. Only then will we consider future dates.

RULE #4: DON'T ASSUME YOU WON'T GET YOUR WHITE PICKET FENCE. A lot of us, especially the women (well, some), want to settle down and have kids with a nice, open-minded straight man who's willing to let his wife sleep with the occasional woman—or not. Each couple reconciles each partner's bisexuality differently, but that said, there are some traditional bisexuals out there.

RULE #5: DON'T ASSUME YOU WILL GET YOUR WHITE PICKET FENCE. A lot of us think that monogamy doesn't make a whole heckuva lot of sense. Those of us who flip-flop a lot or just don't feel balanced with just one gender probably won't want to get married. This kind of bi might suggest a more unconventional route. Be prepared for anything, but, most important, determine what kind of bisexual you're dating: traditional or nontraditional or someone who (we know) runs down the middle.

RULE #6: DON'T ASSUME YOU'RE NOT PLEASING US SEXUALLY. Many straights and gays fall into the trap of assuming we fall in love with genitals, not people. Stupid, we know, because quite frankly, you can't even hold a decent conversation with a vagina (well, more so than with a penis, but we digress). For some, it might be just about the sex and only the sex. There's a name for those people (and it's not bisexual): shallow. Sure, some of us are, but you know how someone who's not that attractive can get hotter the more you get to know them? Same goes for bisexuals: the more we like you, the less focused we are on your genitals. Seriously, when you've got that wicked sparkle in your eye, we've almost forgotten entirely whether

THE BISEXUAL'S GUIDE TO THE UNIVERSE

you have boobs or a schlong, and how greatly that will impact our lives or at least the rest of the night.

RULE #7: DON'T ASSUME YOU ARE PLEASING US SEXUALLY—NOT BECAUSE WE'RE BISEXUAL, BUT BECAUSE MOST IDIOTS DON'T ASK. Seriously, would it kill you once in a while to check in? Sure, we might be moaning, but some honest communication in the bedroom never killed anybody. Yeah, there might be an issue at some point when we're craving someone of the same or opposite sex, but we promise that if you are considerate enough to ask us whether you're hitting the right spot in bed that we'll tell you when or if we want to bring other people into the bedroom.

RULE #8: DON'T ASK TO BRING OTHER PEOPLE INTO THE BEDROOM. It's tacky. We know as an American you're probably an opportunist, but you don't want us to think that's the only reason you're dating us. The best way to get a threesome is to not ask for one. Then, if you're lucky, we'll grow tired of you after a while and suggest one ourselves.

WHEN TO TELL YOUR DATE

IN AN IDEAL WORLD, you wouldn't have to tell anyone about your sexual flexibility. Instead, being bi would be as obvious as being gay. But until an ample bi stereotype is invented that enables monosexuals to develop bidar, which, let's face it, most bisexuals have barely honed, we're gonna have to tell our dates that we're bi, fluid, pansexual, hetero-flexible, or, our personal fave, "a people person."

There are a number of choices as to when or if you tell your date about your sexuality. Keep in mind that there's no right answer to this. Coming out is a comfort-level thing, and bottom line—it's never comfortable. Unless you're Miss Cleo or psychic John Edward, you will not be able to predict with 100 percent

---

TIPS FOR STRAIGHT GALS ON SEDUCING BI WOMEN

Straight women often grapple with the best strategies for seducing one of their bisexual female friends. The only advice we can give them is to be straightforward about your availability and desire. This means if you're hot for a bi gal, don't just sit awkwardly on the couch giving her mixed messages about your interest, especially if you have a boyfriend. A lot of bi women have felt misled by their straight friends' body language in the past, so crossing your legs toward her in interest and smiling a lot may not be enough. Though verbal confessions can kill the mood and the mystery, bi women won't usually be too offended if you make things easier for them. But do be straightforward about what you desire. If you have a boyfriend, explain whether you would want a relationship with a woman or just some sex with a friend. Be clear on whether you would ever want a primary relationship with a woman. A lot of bi gals won't care if you have a boyfriend. Some will. Just don't be afraid to be honest and flirt, but don't expect them to jump you as a guy would on the slightest hint of interest. In fact, bi gals will find it insanely hot if you make the first move.

---

accuracy your date's response. Depending on how well you know this person, he or she could respond in a variety of ways. Here's how to tackle the timing . . .

OPTION #1: Never. This option involves, yep, you guessed it, never telling your date or partner about your sexuality. This highly unevolved approach, though we're not being judgmental, will lead to only more self-loathing and hatred in the end. You might argue that going both ways is just too difficult to explain, so why bother? You might argue that telling your date/partner has led only to abandonment in the past. Or you might just be a complete chickenshit. Whatever your rationale may be, keep in mind that real intimacy involves sometimes telling people what they don't want to hear or things that make you feel vulnerable. If you're not shooting for intimacy, hey, good for you! You're fulfilling your goal.

OPTION #2: Sometimes. This option has been adopted by most of us because we can apply it on a case-by-case basis depending on our partners. Bisexuals who employ option two know that it's not always necessary to tell a meaningless date about their sexuality, especially if the relationship is going nowhere or is just about sex. These bi's wait to reveal their sexuality until they are certain that the person is worth it. Part of this strategy involves a sort of bait and switch, where the bisexual gets their significant other hooked on their winning personality before tossing out what might be perceived as a complication. True, it's not like telling someone you have a sexually transmitted disease, but it's similar in that your sexuality could, sadly, be a turnoff. But everybody's got that one thing, that one hang-up, that one turnoff that they put off revealing. Nobody knows how their date/partner will take it. The sometimes-ers don't want to come off like their sexuality is a large part of their personality but acknowledge it is a part of who they are, and for that they must be respected.

OPTION #3: Usually. You've got to love the "usually tell their partners" bisexuals. They promote visibility by being up front about their sexuality but, most important, demonstrate a lot of self-respect because they don't want to bother getting involved with somebody who wouldn't accept them. These bi's tell their dates straight up—if their date is worth telling. Often, newbie activists or strippers (kidding) have lifestyles that enable them to be quite out, if not all the way out. They usually have a grandparent or a cousin who doesn't know or a job working with children or in some capacity where they can't be out. Aside from these contingencies, the usuallys usually find a way to 'fess up to their sexuality and weed out the losers who won't get it.

OPTION #4: Always. Much like the "nevers," the always-tell bisexuals belong in an extremist category, but a more respectable one. Often, professional bisexuals or queer activists have built their lives around their sexuality and promoting social change. Most people heading out on a date with these bisexuals know they're dating a bisexual. In fact, they probably met them in a bisexual context or at a gay event. No surprises with this bunch. Their policy is simple: date me, and you're dating my politics. You've got to hand it to the members of the gay community who can withstand this amount of pressure and say, "Cool. Sign me up!"

TIPS FOR BI'S ON DATING OTHER BI'S

A LOT OF US prefer to date fence-sitters rather than people of other persuasions because "one of the nice things about being with a bisexual is that you don't have to talk about being bisexual. It takes a lot of things off the table," said one friend of ours. Then again, just because you like both genders doesn't mean you know how to date a bisexual. After all, we are chameleons, masters of many different styles and scenes. To aid you in your quest, we've compiled a brief guide to dating our elusive breed (a.k.a. other confused fence-sitters like you).

DATING THE "I DON'T LIKE LABELS" BISEXUAL

What might appeal to you while dating the "I don't like to label myself" bisexual is his or her comfort with ambiguity. In a world forcing us to choose Pepsi or Coke, they say, "Whatever— they're both soft drinks." This style of free thinking and open-mindedness is what drew you to them in the first place. It plays like nonchalant confidence and forces you to go, "Yeah, labels are a pile anyway." Sure, it's annoying when you're hanging with your queer buddies, and they ask, "What is so and so?" and you reply, "I don't know. S/he's not into labels." But their unwillingness to bite the bullet and define their sexuality is what makes them flighty and at times dangerous to date if you've got a big heart or feel strongly about someone actually using the B-word. But if you're the type of person who hates all of the pressure to be outspoken about something as private and fluid as your sexuality or would rather use no label than the wrong label, then you've just met your ideal match.

FOR BI GALS . . .

Dating the Bi-Curious Straight Girl

Most lesbians will caution against dating the "experimental" bisexual, a.k.a. the bi-curious straight girl. But many of us will give the experimental bisexual a chance because either we started out as open-minded straight girls or because most lesbians won't give us a chance. Let's face it: a lot of us have to take what we can get because most gay girls wouldn't dream of involving themselves with complicated fence-sitters. But unfortunately, the caution that your lesbian friends advise is unfortunately usually warranted. Here's how it often plays out . . .

The experimental bisexual will usually be introduced into your life through a mutual friend. You'll probably mistake her for being straight, despite the gay company she keeps. After hitting it off with her at a few clubs while in the safe company of your mutual friend, you swap numbers. You start as friends.

Then she puts it out there: a "You look hot" comment here or there followed by a blatant romantic gesture. The sexual tension will escalate to an unbearable degree before you realize that this chick has no intention of making the first move. It's all you, baby! She's scared shitless, and that is why, ultimately, dating the "experimental" bisexual will not work out.

Her ability to dance around you, fearful of the inevitable intimacy, can be rather daunting. The space between you can sometimes feel like two magnets trying to connect at opposite poles. For this reason, copious amounts of alcohol are usually needed in order to initiate any physical contact. In some cases, even verbally acknowledging an attraction isn't enough to initiate contact because of her fear factor—she's afraid of disappointing you.

One night you finally find the right moment and boldly kiss her. Her hesitation seeps through her kiss as you realize you're the only one touching her face, hair, and so on. This is more than a subtle hint. Cut to four hours later when she's in your bed, frozen, a mere recipient of your touch as opposed to an active participant. But you're an optimist, so you tell yourself her comfort will come later ... which it doesn't.

The next morning, you both discuss how wonderful it was and how you plan to see one another as soon as possible. But don't be surprised when she calls later in the day about picking up the belongings she left at your place and returns to you the lesbian sex book you so slyly loaned her a few weeks ago. And though you may cringe when you try to make plans for the next weekend and discover she has friends sleeping over each night—who live in town—don't worry, she's not cheating on you ... just avoiding you and proving all of your lesbian friends right.

You might mistakenly think a sweeping romantic gesture will solve the growing awkwardness and the distance that have developed during your phone calls, but you're wrong. That action will be perceived as yet another attempt for intimacy, an attempt to be alone with her, and, well, this lady wants the white picket fence and a lot of babies, and not through insemination. To her, you were just another dish on the buffet while she's moving to the big dessert: a big white wedding cake and a hetero happy ending. Don't expect an invitation.

FOR BI GUYS . . .

Dating the Bi-Curious Straight Guy

The bi-curious straight guy should be thought of as one thing, and one thing only—an experiment. Though you may have a history when people considered you the "experimental straight guy," don't expect too much from him (not even a one-night stand). But the main thing you shouldn't expect is any sort of verbal confirmation of an attraction. Men in general are of few words, and this breed is made of even fewer. The only confirmation you'll receive will be physical. Like that night he was supposed to be crashing on your couch after a long night of drinking and just happened to slide into your bed without a word. Don't expect a confession in the morning.

If he does dare confess an attraction, he'll probably be open to attending all the twenty-four-hour orgies that you know about, where the drugs are free and the girls and guys are plucked from fashion magazines and going at it like bunnies all the time. In other words: he wants you to support his gay fantasy without telling anybody. If you get this far, he might ask about your past history or sexual escapades, not that it'll matter. He won't remember because you'll rarely find this guy sober in your presence. He will always drink too much intentionally so that you can take advantage of him, and so he'll have an excuse the next morning.

This dating experience can result only in disappointment—his. One night he'll stop crawling into your bed and return to the couch, and then without a word go back to his wife.

Dating the Closeted Bi Gal

Dating the closeted bi gal is a bit safer than dating the "experimental" bisexual—but not much. Because of her Bible-thumping roots and complete ineptitude about gay culture, your out lifestyle will shake her to her self-loathing, anxiety-ridden core. The good news is that she's probably been with women before, and her hunger to once again indulge her naughty desires makes her a total firecracker in the sack. Enjoy it, because the guilt will set in sooner than you think, and before you know it the sex and her brief foray into the sinful gay world will probably be over.

In my experience, you will encounter the closeted bisexual in a gay bar. Though seemingly contradictory, this breed does venture out once in a blue moon when the longing and the depression drive them to once again attempt self-acceptance. Case in point, I met my closeted bi gal at a lesbian club. The first words out of her mouth: "This is my first time at a gay club ever." And though that's the absolute truth for many closet cases, that won't stop them from making eyes at you all night and stalking you around the bar. Keep in mind, she's usually not there alone. Mine was accompanied by a "straight" woman with whom she'd had a sexual relationship for three years and was the only person she knew who (a) knew she liked the ladies and (b) was willing to go to a (gasp!) gay place. But don't worry. A situation like that won't prove to be much of an obstacle.

After boldly making the first move, her gratitude will be extensive. She will express all of her longing—to have gay/bi friends, to meet more women, and more. Her almost tangible excitement will remind you of a child during their first trip to Disneyland, eager to learn about this strange new world. The closeted bi woman makes things very personal very fast because, after all, who else does she have to talk to about this stuff? So expect a barrage of questions about your gay and personal life in her attempt to establish an immediate connection.

In my situation, she told me at the club she'd call the next day . . . and actually did. After a series of phone conversations, I discovered we really didn't have much in common. This left her relatively unfazed, and we met for our first date that Friday evening. The conversation consisted mostly of stuff like, "So when did you know you were bi?" "My parents are so unaccepting," "Why do you think people are gay?" Sure enough, she told a predictable tale about a fundamentalist Christian upbringing in the South and spoke sadly about how her family hates gay people. I felt sympathy for her, though I couldn't relate, being spawned from liberal parents in Marin County.

She drove me back to my car and as we arrived at our destination invited me back to her apartment to watch a Sade DVD (code word: sex). I followed her back, where we sat on opposite ends of the couch for a good hour before I decided to announce my departure because it seemed neither one of us had the courage to make the first move. I was wrong. She pounced and literally bowled me over on the couch, and before we knew it we were in her bedroom and she was asking me whether I liked to be tied up. Suddenly, this innocent southern girl had transformed into a fearless force. We separated for only a brief moment for the rest of the night . . . when she went to go looking for the handcuffs. (She couldn't find them.) We did what girls do—we made out all night long without even getting too naughty. After all, we had to leave something for the second date.

By date two, her discomfort set in. She mixed comments like "I love being inside of you" with questions like "You won't get attached, will you?" because the closeted bi girl can't commit to really being . . . gay. To continue this liaison would require her to admit her gay side more than once every six months, and that simply would send her entire world into upheaval. In the end, I told her if she ever needed a bi friend that I'd be there for her.

She responded a few weeks later with thanks, apologizing for not contacting me: "I'm just not comfortable with it."

The good news is that someday closeted bisexuals might change their label and actually hunker down with a hot bi woman like yourself . . . just know that that probably won't happen on your shift.

FOR BI GUYS . . .

Dating the Closeted Bi Guy

He may have some educating needed, but for god's sake don't try to recruit him into carrying the bi banner, as obscure as that may be. He's going to be concerned about being seen at some place that's "too gay" or doing something that isn't hetero enough.

The dangerous thing about this dating experience is that it can turn into a teacher-student relationship, but if you're into that kind of lover-beloved role-playing you might want to get him into one of those schoolboy uniforms before the date.

FOR BI GALS . . .

Dating the Hippie Bi Womyn

I must admit that the hippie bi womyn is my favorite breed. True, they usually don't shave their legs, but they sure as hell know how to kick back on the couch, smoke a bowl, and cuddle. Not ones to balk at a neglected bikini line, these womyn (don't call them girls; they will correct you) will argue with the butcher about the upbringing of their free-range poultry. And just when you think you can no longer bear their politically correct antics, you'll find yourself on a hiking outing, staring at the purple flowers braided into her beautiful hair, and realize you could hang out a bit longer . . . even if you are smoking a little too much pot.

Maybe I'm just a low-maintenance gal, but you won't have to watch them fuss over manicures or makeup, which is a major plus. Hippie bi gals also aren't stingy with the affection. If they like you, you'll fucking know it, though don't be mistaken: the bullshit mind reading will still exist because, hey, they are still women. The cool thing is that they're usually educated in most elements of bi-ness or are at least willing to learn more. One hippie bi girl, I mean womyn, I met in a women's studies class had actually read *Bi Any Other Name*. I interviewed her for a bi article I was writing (an excellent excuse to get to know her), and things progressed into a brief involvement from there.

The main disadvantages of dating the hippie bi womyn will surface if you're expecting any sort of committed relationship. These ladies are all about free love and probably will have a boy on the side, whether they tell you about it or not. But that doesn't mean that in their minds you're not special to them. You're the apple of their eye, especially when they're shrooming. (Note: hippie lesbians are a different story. After dating one of them for two weeks, I noticed on Friendster she had changed her profile to "in a relationship" over a gal she had also known for two weeks.) Don't expect the hippie bi womyn to move fast. Start with friendship, and let her open-minded, liberal nature take it from there.

FOR BI GUYS . . .

Dating the Hippie Bi Dude

If you like long hair and the smell of incense, the hippie bi dude is worth a try. It's funny being seen holding hands with him because people don't give you attitude until they realize that the beautiful long hair and the nice ass that you're connected to is that of another guy. It freaks out both men and women, and sometimes your bi hippie is so androgynous that you can't tell for yourself at first.

The trouble with a guy like this is that he's going to always be a bit lackadaisical and want you to take charge, whether it's deciding what film you want to go to or what to do sexually. Sometimes hearing "Sure, whatever, man" in response to everything you say can get irritating. Before it's all over he's going to want you to try some sort of tantric position, or attend some spiritual seminar, and you're no doubt going to hear Hendrix or Joplin playing in the background no matter what you do. But, hey, at least you know that this guy is always going to have a fine stash of weed in his nightstand.

FOR BI GALS . . .

Dating the Corporate Bi Gal

The corporate bi girl is almost as difficult to spot as the bi-curious straight girl. Their chameleon-like tendencies force them to blend imperceptibly into their corporate surroundings. This species usually remains closeted at work and dresses very straight. Because they feel empowered by the mainstream, convincing them to tread into the unfamiliar gay world can be a bit of a challenge. When you're ready to dive in, she's just placing her toe in the water. Usually untrusting and tentative, the only way to snare the yuppie bi gal is through an initial friendship. Keep in mind that the yuppie bi gal differs from her brethren, the power lesbian. Power lesbians set their target and go in for the kill. They're direct, confident, and together. Yuppie bi gals usually are less likely to readily embrace their queer identity, and probably will need a little persuading.

The pluses of dating a yuppie bi gal include intelligence, wit, a high pop culture 'Q, and excessive grooming. With razor-sharp eyebrows and a wicked manicure, these ladies could fit in better at a reading by Hillary Clinton than an Ani DiFranco concert, though they might attend both. The main problem with dating them is that they play their cards close to their chest, like the good businesswomen that they are. You'll probably have a hard time trusting them or their affections for you because they feel so comfortable in mainstream society, and let's face it—taking your girlfriend to the company picnic and explaining to your coworkers how you're not a lesbian is just logistically a complete bitch. For most yuppie bi gals, fitting a gay relationship into the corporate world is just too tricky when they could opt for the straight norm. But sometimes their hearts make decisions that their perfectionism cannot ensnare, and at that point they, well, "move in with a friend."

FOR BI GUYS . . .

Dating the Corporate Bi Guy

Don't go out with this kind of guy unless you have the wardrobe to live up to his Abercrombie & Fitch attitude. Once considered the "yuppie bi guy," this attitude-laden date is even worse than the yup because intelligence doesn't necessarily accompany the 'tude. So consider having an intellectual conversation about anything other than fashion and Broadway musicals an added bonus.

This guy will always criticize what you're wearing or driving or have in your stock portfolio or on your coffee table. (And no, leaving catalogs out is not cool to this kind of guy. It's about as tacky as having a porn video on display.) Just don't get offended easily. He's going to greet you at the door saying, "You're going out with me like this?" Then he'll go through your closet and redress you as best he can like Carson on *Queer Eye for the Straight Guy.* These types are eye candy, and they're out there. They like sports, money, and sex with women, but, most important, they like wearing nice clothes and like being looked at. If they deem you worthy for a date, all you have to do is pour on the flattery and not expect much substance.

FOR BI GALS . . .

Dating the Female Bi Head Case

First of all, nobody intends to date a head case unless he or she is a head case. Now you might be wondering what makes a bisexual head case different from other head cases. In our experience, the bisexual head case flips out not just about minidramas all day but over her confusing sexuality as well. Because head cases don't know themselves very well, and if they do, they don't accept themselves, their bisexuality proves to be yet another maddening component of their already cluttered existence. Rankled with instability, the head case uses her confusion and insecurities as a scapegoat for unacceptable behavior. Example: "I wish I wasn't so fucked up right now, or I'd come over and sleep with you." Or, "I was crying the other night just thinking about what a great love we could have if I wasn't so crazy."

Get it? She flakes because she just "couldn't handle things," and you tell her you understand. And you do . . . until the fourth or fifth time her emotional problems take precedent over one of your dates. Like a great illusionist, what you see is never what you get with this bi girl. You might take her to a party only to watch her take refuge in your car because she saw someone who reminded her of someone she kinda didn't like somewhere. You see, her unpredictable nature makes her one of the most unfulfilling partners you'll ever have.

She'll tell you she's in love with you, then make out with some other girl at the bar because she didn't want to hurt your feelings. Er, what? See, it all makes sense in her head, but give up now because that's all the clarity you're gonna get from this sometimes-lovable nut case. Be careful, though, 'cause her words rarely match her actions, and they will keep writing checks that her heart can't cash. For this reason, she won't treat you half as well as you deserve to be treated.

The danger of dating the bi head case exists mainly when you desperately desire a healthy, functional relationship. Granted, functional relationships aren't for everyone. You still shouldn't question whether the bi head case will ever truly be yours. She can't be because she doesn't even belong to herself.

Dating the Male Bi Head Case

It's amazing how many bi guys wear their borderline personalities as accessories these days. Characteristics include insisting on seeing a health certificate before even shaking your hand, impotence, and complete control freakdom. This type will be controlling about where you're seen in public together, holding hands, and going dutch (anything else requires too much commitment and an expectation of maintaining an erection.)

Go ahead and try some new lines and new moves on these crazy blokes, but don't push for the long-term relationship because he's going to turn psycho after the third month. It's been proven scientifically.

Dating the Bi Goth Girl

Don't let this raven beauty fool you. Beneath the pale makeup and the jet-black (or bleached-blonde) hair, you'll find a fairly normal gal. Sure, she might listen to Bauhaus and sport multiple tattoos, but that doesn't mean you have to feel intimidated. Odds are, she just appreciates the beauty of being sad a little more than others.

The good news is that you won't have to stomach the shallowness that accompanies dating the bi corporate or the shame of the closet case. This gal's probably got depth to spare. That she's willing to wear those frightening clothes means she's probably fairly comfortable with who she is and will be willing to let the world—or maybe just her boyfriend—know she adores you. Relating to her won't be difficult. Just quote some poetry about death, and you're in.

Also, stereotypically goth bi gals don't shy away from fun, experimental sex, so decide beforehand whether you want to wield the whip.

Dating the Goth Bi Guy

Just don't be scared if this guy tries to give you a piercing or tattoo while you're sleeping. He's not going to want to go out in the daylight very much, and if you suggest going to the beach when the sun is still out, you're not quite getting him.

Don't think of his Eeyore-like depressive state as a personal affront—that's the charm of this dude—and don't be put off by his insistence on replaying the Tones on Tail bootleg he owns over and over again; just tune it out.

This could be a very cool dating experience; just don't ask him to remove the Prince Albert, and be careful about cutting yourself when kissing around that nose ring. There are major benefits if you date him long enough: you'll find out the reason for that tongue stud and some of the amazing feats that can be done with it.

Dating the Bi Punk Girl

This gal could quite literally rock your world, if you could just stop staring at that lip piercing. If you can find a punk who has got the personal-hygiene thing down, you're in for an exciting encounter. Sure, she might act like kind of a brat, but that's just part of her charm. And hey, she certainly looks hot in combat boots and a wife beater (as un-P.C. as that may sound). Boyfriend or not, this chick is all about riot grrrl power and reaffirming her societal rebellion with alternative relationships and sexual encounters—not to mention many different hair colors. If she does go for a dude, he'll be a gentle feminist capable of balancing her out (think Courtney Love and Kurt Cobain). Just monitor her white-drug intake. This girl likes to take things pretty far. But if the music's already giving you a headache, you might want to rethink this relationship.

Dating the Bi Punk Guy

He may come across as being a bit too CBGB's for his own good, like he never left a certain period of the '70s and '80s that really shouldn't be revisited. He's not going to show much tenderness as a general rule, and if he bashed into you in bed, or uses a four-letter-word pet name for you, or puts on a fake brogue when he's horny, then don't be surprised. It's part of his nature.

These guys aren't going to shave, so you're going to get some whisker burns on your face and maybe other parts of your body. He's going to take you to alternative clubs you never knew existed, and a pair of secretive earplugs may be something you want to bring as an accessory on your date (not to mention a stick of deodorant if you feel like pushing the issue). Punk may be dead, but the guys who created it—rough, rugged, bald, and bisexual   still linger and are ripe for the picking.

Dating the Female BUCK (Bisexual Urban Cool Kid)

The most pretentious of the bunch, the bi cool kid can ironically be more fashion conscious than any of these bi women. If you don't have the uniform down, this exclusive chick won't even give you the time of day. And the look goes something like this— Betty Page haircuts with cute barrettes, vintage skirts with colored tights or kneesocks with garish high heels or combat boots, T-shirts from Goodwill with ironic slogans or art, and a ratty hoodie, used sweater, or jacket. The bi cool kid usually hangs with the lesbian cool kids. Penetrating this scene can be impossible if you don't look the part or have strong liberal politics or are not prone to exhibitionism.

Yup, these gals throw and attend a lot of really obnoxious

costume parties, so if you don't have the energy or the time to say, "Hey, look at me!" you probably will go unnoticed. Her appearance might change drastically from date to date, so be prepared to see her as a soft butch one day and in full face paint the next. Bottom line: this gal is high-maintenance in a highly unpredictable way, so you might not have the stamina for her.

Trying to be cool all the time can be exhausting and suffocating. When the hell do you get to just be yourself? The good news: if you get accepted by her and her cronies, you'll have a panoply of bi/gay girls reassuring you of your overwhelming superiority to, well, the rest of the girl nation and possibly the world.

FOR BI GUYS . . .

Dating the Male BUCK (Bisexual Urban Cool Kid)

The bi urban cool kid at one time was called a "slacker." But now he's more ambitious, a better dresser, and more open about doing anything with anyone when it feels good. This is the surfer guy with the winning smile who thinks nothing of inviting you over for a homemade seaweed shake after you've been watching him in the water for hours. He's the guy in the park with a backward cap, baggy clothes, and a big book who isn't threatened by your casual conversation and may ask you to go for a drink.

He is secretly high maintenance because behind that "whatever" attitude he has toward the world, he is rather insistent about maintaining a "cool" image and staying on the cutting edge. You'll be around only as long as having a bi partner is deemed "chic."

FOR BI GALS . . .

Dating the Butch Bi Dyke

She'll open doors for you in more ways than one. Unlike her über-bi-femme counterparts, she's not afraid to look gay. This means dating the butch bi dyke means dating one confident, strong gal. She'll challenge you to be proud of who you are as well and to possibly experiment with some gender bending.

She might wear too many button-up shirts and prefer calling herself "queer" instead of "bi," but you gotta respect a bi gal that wears a dykey haircut and then still shoots the boys come-hither stares. Butch bi dykes are one misunderstood bunch, but they're not apologizing to anyone for their tough exterior, especially not one of their hot bi conquests who is supposed to understand. Their dominant nature means you won't have to rack your brain about what to do on a Saturday night. She already knows: you.

FOR BI GUYS . . .

Dating the Macho Bi Guy

Don't let him intimidate you—there's a softy somewhere inside that well-toned muscled exterior. Whether you're a gal or a guy going after the macho bi guy, you better know how to throw a football, catch a baseball, and help hold onto the rigging of a sailboat. In other words, you're going to have to catch and receive.

Because he has the outward appearance of a straight guy, and because he knows he exudes testosterone with every step, he's going to be aware of the looks he receives—whether he's jogging, washing the car, or nude parasailing. He'll entice you into his workout schedule, put you on his macrobiotic nutrition plan, and feel comfortable you won't tell anyone about that time he cried in your arms. Yes, he cries, but not as much as he sweats, so bring a towel.

BI ASTROLOGY

SO WHICH IS THE most bisexual sign in the Zodiac? Is it the twins, Gemini? Or the balanced scales of Libra? Read below to find out.

ARIES You're assertive, passionate, and quick to pick a fight with male and female lovers (that is, if you don't get bored and lose interest first).

TAURUS You're bullheaded and stubborn like a man and overwhelmingly intelligent like a woman.

GEMINI Your sign means the twins, which means there are two people inside of you (a male and a female). They're both bisexual, and they both cheat on everybody.

CANCER You're very sensitive and sympathetic, and these traits make you a knockout in the sack and a complete pain in the ass to both your male and female lovers. (Better cancel that three-way!)

LEO You think both men and women are in love with you.

VIRGO You're equally uptight and anal whether you're dating a man or a woman, but the ideal social coordinator for bi orgy. (P.S. Throw that virginal stereotype out the window. We know what you've been up to.)

LIBRA You're extremely beautiful, and you know it, so you have lots of sex . . . with both men and women. Plus, you keep the scales balanced between men and women.

SCORPIO You're all about the sex. If you don't think you're bi, you just don't know it yet. You're way too sexual to limit yourself to just one gender.

SAGITTARIUS You loathe boundaries, thrive on freedom, and are extremely friendly—so friendly that you will practically do it in the gutter with both men and women.

CAPRICORN You're conservative in the bedroom, strong willed, but in love a complete pushover for both men and women.

AQUARIUS You're a "people person," extremely open-minded, and one of the most experimental signs in the Zodiac. Slow down and you just might connect with the guys and gals you're doing.

PISCES You're sensitive, receptive, infinitely complex, and so emotionally intricate that both men and women call you a lesbian—even if you're a guy.

BI NUMEROLOGY

BASED ON THE "VIBRATION" of numbers, numerology translates dates of birth, names, and even addresses into a basic number that reveals the secrets of your personality. So what in the hell is bisexual about that? you might ask. (By now, you should know, we can make anything queer.) For starters, take the number 2—quite bisexual. Look at its sensuous curves, it's flagrant . . . duality. Or, say, the number 3—the triad. By combining the potent 2 with the forceful 1, you get a powerful dynamic. Er, something like that. Three sides hold up a triangle or a pyramid, so that must mean something, right? Absolutely. The number 3 stands for socialization and "the joy of living," according to numerologists. Mmm, they got that right.

The sexually explosive number 5 represents intense pleasure seeking, though number 8 gets the most action (that's just what we've heard). When there's a pair of deuces together, such as in the number 22, a powerful bi force is created . . . just ask your neighborhood psychic.

But we know what naughty number you have in mind, and to answer your inquiry, 69 brings together traits of both the 6 and the 9, numbers that symbolize "community," "giving," and "creative expression." It's enough to almost make you want to crack open a math book . . . Nah!

BI TAROT

ON THE TAROT DECK, the "Fortune" or "Lucky Wheel" card can represent bisexuality because we're fortunate to have the most evolved sexual orientation on the planet. Latent or repressed bi feelings are represented by "The Hanged Man" (not hung), whereas the sexually experimental is represented by the powerful XXII card, "The Fool." "The Seven of Wands" and the "Three of

Cups" may also represent bisexuality, according to some tarot readers, whereas "The Magician" is an omnisexual or transgender character, sometimes depicted as a naked woman.

You have now completed Chapter 6. Now go out there and hone your bidar, herd together your queer friends, and boldly ask out that man or woman who has caught your eye. Remember: the power of seduction is just a skill you must sharpen. But most important, it can lead to finding Mr. or Ms. Right—or in your case both.

ADVANCED

CHAPTER 7

WHY YOU'RE NOT GETTING LAID

BY NOW IT'S PROBABLY no secret to you that the world at large (gay or straight) has a major stick up its ass when it comes to sexual ambiguity. We get blamed for spreading AIDS to the heterosexual community and for leaving gay relationships for "a normal life." You name it, we've been blamed for it. Here are a few reasons this societal glitch might translate into you not getting any.

WHY STRAIGHT PEOPLE HATE US

ASIDE FROM BIBLE-THUMPING rednecks, most normal, well-adjusted straight people hate us for (a) making their boyfriend think it's cool to pressure them into a pornlike threesome, (b) being more interesting than they are, and (c) comparing them to the gay lovers we've had who allegedly knew how to give better head.

That's right, straight people aren't that different from gay people. They don't like us 'cause we make them feel nervous and inadequate. Although some evolved straight people in the art world might feel intrigued by bisexual chic, many will freak when they realize you've had other peas in your pod.

Straight women will think about the yuckiness of anal sex and worry about whether their boyfriend has contracted any diseases. The image of their boyfriend pounding the puddin' with a man just kills their Harrison Ford fantasy. And then there's the issue of where that tongue has been.

The bi guy who tells his girl about his past is doomed. Despite the fact that you're probably more sensitive than her last asshole trucker boyfriend, your effeminate or inexplicably masculine manner suddenly becomes a massive turnoff. Next time you're in public, she'll worry about whom you're checking out and who's looking at you.

Straight men are another story altogether. They love bi women . . . or so they say, and will hold it as a matter of pride. In fact, when out in public, don't be surprised if he wants you to wear your blue, pink, and purple bracelet or something else that will spotlight that you're a hip bi chick. And even if you ask him not to tell his friends, forget about it, he's already planted threesome fantasies in all his buddies' heads that he'll someday get you with another girl.

Straight men are completely freaked by bi guys, but straight women are often curiously intrigued by bi women.

WHY GAY PEOPLE HATE US

THE FIRST THING A gay man will say after you reveal you're bisexual will be something like, "Sure you are, honey. So was I." You see, gay men don't believe in bisexuality because so many of them once called themselves bisexual—because in the past they were either cowards or just more open-minded. But that open-mindedness had long since disappeared, and now you have to bear the brunt of their irritating, catty comments about how little you know about yourself. Being bisexual, you're a big fat affront to their static sexual identity and just need to get over your "breeder" ways.

To most gay men, you're now a potential conquest. It's going to be just a quickie so they can tell the boys at the bar about having to move the baby seat so you could fool around in the backseat and add another notch to their "straight-recruiting" tally.

Telling a lesbian that you're bi is like spraying a mosquito with repellent. Their lips will curl, their eyebrows will rise, and you will get the distinct impression that you are being judged. As you watch their eyes wander to other parts of the room, you can be confident they are remembering the last bi girl they dated who inevitably cheated on them with a man. Terrified you'll never see their fingers or tongues as a proper substitute for a penis, most of them refuse to even give you a chance.

The ones who do will keep an eagle eye on you during the duration of your time together and tell you every so often that you don't understand when queer issues arise because part of you (the part that's straight) just doesn't get being gay. You can chameleon out and play straight, unlike them. This aside from the fact that all the faggot-hating lowlifes lump bisexuals into the gay, not straight, category. If you try to explain your preference lies with women (if that is your preference), they will probably tell you that you're gay and just need to open your eyes and stop wasting your time with men.

So what's the big deal? Why are we such a threat? Is it our shocking good looks? Unfortunately, no. Most gay people and the rest of the world see bi people as having a choice in their sexual preference on any given day and, thus, a huge problem for them politically. If we can "choose" to marry and lead "normal lives," why can't the rest of the queers? You see, that's the crap-ass part of being bi—everyone thinks it's so convenient, that we choose what gender turns us on on that particular day and then flippantly change our minds. The fluidity of sexuality cannot be addressed because that might denote some evolved level of thinking that most of the morons—straight and gay—in our country just can't wrap their pea-size brains around.

It sucks being the sharpest tack in the box, doesn't it? So don't take that bullshit biphobia lying down. Tell your close-minded gay friends to grow the hell up and get over their ridiculous insecurities because if they don't, they'll never know what they're missing.

WHY STRAIGHT MEN LOVE BI WOMEN (BY NICOLE)

WHEN WE BI WOMEN tell a man we're dating about our sexuality, immediately his eyes begin to sparkle. A smile creeps upon his lips because we've just transformed from the woman he probably wasn't going to marry anyway into the stuff of late-night porno fantasies. Congratulations! Don't you feel special? As the silence dangles in the air, you can practically read his thoughts as he scans through all of your hot friends he'd like to lure into your bedroom. After all, because you're bi, you must want to sleep with all of your female friends. And really, nothing would please you more than satisfying his lifetime desire of spending night after sordid night with two women in bed, fawning all over his rod.

Now listen to me carefully: at this point it's important to raise your hand before his eyes, bring your thumb to your middle finger, and SNAP! Tell him a woman gave you the best oral sex you've ever had and that he needs practice. So what if it isn't true? Make him feel threatened and remind him you're a regular girl, not a prostitute. And even if you want a threesome with him, don't tell him that. You just started dating the guy, and you don't want him to think this whole threesome thing is about him. No, no, no, it's about two people completely focused on you, if at all. It's about him getting off and then leaving the room, so you and your girl can get down to business. And at about that point in the conversation, his face will start to drop.

Don't be alarmed. It's just the onset of insecurity, the fear of inadequacy, the sound of his little male ego breaking. You see, you're no longer the girl next door. You're naughty, and probably comparing him to every woman you've ever slept with. This once-exciting prospect now turns his blood to ice. You're suddenly the bearer of expectations, expectations he can't possibly meet. What most straight guys don't realize is that it takes a lot of confidence to date a bi girl. The question is: do they have it?

WHY STRAIGHT WOMEN HATE BI MEN (BY MIKE)

TO SAY THEY'RE "THREATENED" would be an understatement. Most straight women, (with few exceptions) won't ever consider dating a guy who's crossed over even once. The yuck factor often proves to be much too high for them. They picture what may have once been in his mouth or other orifices and cannot deal with the potential diseases those orifices may carry. Though I'd like to see straight women reject the yuck factor and realize that they're falling for the stereotypes, some events have forced me to lose faith.

When New Jersey governor Jim McGreevey said he was a "gay American," he acknowledged that he had been married not once, but twice! His poor wife, Dina, stood next to him, head bowed, as he mentioned his first wife, Kari—and his kids! All the commentators shed tears for the poor "widows" because those ladies couldn't compete with a man. Um, hello? If a gay man is stupid enough to get married twice, he should at least have the common decency to call himself bisexual. Instead, books are being written and support groups are sprouting up for women to deal with their "gay" husbands. At least when Arianna Huffington's ex-hubby, Congressman Michael Huffington, came out, he used the B-word and didn't negate their past sexual relationship when they were married.

The truth is that the guys aren't turning gay because their wives have done something wrong or they're bored with them. It's because their wives have unwittingly married a promiscuous bisexual. Sometimes the wife has the unfortunate experience of watching her husband expand his sexuality during their marriage, and it unfortunately leads to straight women feeling inadequate and making gay assumptions about their hubbies. With stats showing that 68 percent of married men cheat anyway, wouldn't it be nice to know that at least if your husband cheats, he won't do it with another woman?

Not that bi men are incapable of monogamy. Many have a preference for women and would just like to have a partner who understands his attraction to the male physique. But because straight women see the McGreeveys of the world publicly announce their homosexuality, they have little faith in the possibility of a safe, fulfilling relationship with a bisexual man. These straight women are missing out on a bi man's stereotypical sensitivity, openness, and cooking skills.

Of course, there's always the realistic fear that bi men spread communicable diseases—so do straight men, and gay men, and straight women, and lesbians—but that's where straight women need to remember safe sex wasn't designed just for bisexuals.

CONVOLUTED SLURS

BI'S ARE SO INVISIBLE that we don't even have a nasty, mean-spirited, derogatory word like *fag* or *dyke*. Here's a list of derogatory euphemisms we've heard. (We've excluded "in denial" because then you're in a river in Egypt.) Anyway, here's what they're calling us, but what are they really saying?

→ AC/DC
→ Afraid to Choose
→ Always Available
→ Ambisextrous
→ Chameleon
→ Coitally Confused
→ Comme ci, comme ça
→ Fence-sitter
→ Fifth Base

→ Flip-flopper
→ Going through a Phase
→ Looks for the Easiest Hole
→ Neither Fish nor Foul
→ Nonpreferential
→ Organ Attraction Denial
→ Pandrogynically Inclined
→ Perpetually Horny
→ Plays for Any Team
→ Screws Anything That Moves
→ Sexual Dyslexic
→ Sexual Misidentity
→ Sidesaddle Queen
→ Slumming for a Quickie, Then It's Home to Mama
→ Stage 1 to Coming Out Completely
→ Sushi/Hot Dog Dilemma
→ Switch Hitter
→ Tits-or-peno-pic-aphobia
→ Totally Yin-Yang
→ Whatever (yeah, like this ever caught on, whatever)

NOW YOU'RE BEING BI-PHOBIC

IF YOU'VE THOUGHT THIS, YOU'VE BEEN IT . . .

→ Everyone is either heterosexual or homosexual.
→ People use the bi label just to be chic and trendy.
→ Dating a bi woman guarantees a three-way.
→ Dating a bi man means STDs galore.
→ Bisexuals are never monogamous.
→ Bisexuals have had LOTS of sex.
→ Gee, a bi person will want to explore all of my kinky fantasies.
→ You're young; you'll grow out of it.

➤ Why wear that "bi" label when your rights are included in gay and lesbian rights?

➤ Oh, god, does dating him/her come with bi buttons, T-shirts, and explaining to all our friends he/she's no longer gay?

➤ Gosh, if I introduce my friend as bi, everyone will think I'm bisexual too.

➤ Bi people will leave me for the "normal" lifestyle.

➤ They just want to have their cake and eat it too.

➤ I'll start dating that person when he/she makes up his/her mind.

➤ I could never be enough for a bi gal/guy. They need both to be satisfied.

➤ A bi date will be willing to pass for whatever I want him or her to be.

➤ It doesn't matter if they're attached. I can make a play 'cause they're bi.

➤ I couldn't go down on a bi girl. With all the women she's been with, I'd never be good enough.

➤ I couldn't go down on a bi guy. With all the guys he's been with, I'd never be good enough.

➤ Bi women only want straight girls or lipstick lesbians.

➤ Bi guys only want straight guys or straight-acting gays.

➤ I can't really trust my bi friends: they're not really gay, lesbian, or hetero and don't really understand.

➤ That bi friend of yours will always want to talk about sex.

➤ You can get great sex advice from a bi person.

➤ If they just found the right lover, then they'd settle down and be just one way or the other.

➤ Two women holding hands are lesbians, two guys holding hands are gay, and a man and woman nuzzling are heteros. (Think again!)

ARE YOU A MODEL BISEXUAL? QUIZ

LET'S FACE IT: OUR role models in the mainstream media just plain suck. Despite popular conceptions, many of us are not exhibitionists who do blow while searching for spaceships in the desert . . . except for that one time. Are you the one to break the mold and make Jerry Falwell eat his tongue? Take the quiz below to find out.

1. You've never collected dragons, unicorns, wizards, or fairies. T/F
2. You have a piercing that's never seen the light of day. T/F
3. You're into designer drugs. T/F
4. You have implants of any kind (breast, pecs, calves, penis, and so on). T/F
5. You have a tattoo or envy people who do. T/F
6. You vehemently defend Scientology. T/F
7. You have been or want to be on a reality show. T/F
8. You call yourself straight. T/F
9. You take members of only the opposite sex to your friends' dinner parties. T/F
10. You have a history of cutting yourself or others. T/F
11. You have never voted in your life. T/F
12. You're a Republican. T/F
13. You're a member of the National Rifle Association. T/F
14. Instead of breaking up with people, you just never call them back. T/F
15. You've never been in a monogamous relationship. T/F

Now tally the number of "False" answers . . .

13-15 FALSE: Congrats! You're a model bisexual! You're stable, together, and capable of representing bisexuals everywhere.

10-13 FALSE: You're not ideal, but we'll take you. Sure, your politics or body décor might not epitomize the ideal bisexual, but, hey, people change.

10 OR FEWER FALSE: Don't speak at any Pride parades or appear on the *Barbara Walters Special* yet. You'll just reinforce the stereotype.

You have now completed Chapter 7. Now you know what we're you're up against. We're sorry we couldn't soften the truth. Next time you feel like you're getting dumped or ditched for the wrong reasons or hear one of your alleged gay friends tell you that you don't exist, speak up. If you don't feel up to fighting the good fight, just walk away knowing you're light-years wiser than them—and better in bed.

CHAPTER 8

BETWEEN THE SHEETS

Going down on a woman gives me a stiff neck, going down on a man gives me lockjaw and conventional sex gives me claustrophobia.

—TALLULAH BANKHEAD, in Lee Israel's biography, *Miss Tallulah Bankhead* (1972)

SEX REALLY SHOULDN'T BE that much more complicated for us. After all, bi sex should in theory encompass all of the nuances of straight and gay sex, should it not? Then again, we do have some unique issues to contend with. For starters, we have not one but two virginities to lose, orgies to attend, and polyamorous possibilities to ponder. Here are some tips on navigating those inevitably cloudy gray areas.

TWO VIRGINITIES: AH, TO BE A VIRGIN AGAIN

ONCE YOU COME TO terms with your bisexuality, be it at sixteen or sixty, you'll have to confront a rather disturbing fact: you now have two virginities—like one wasn't humiliating enough. But seriously, we all have two virginities, though some stupid heteros might claim that "intercourse" can only occur between a man and a woman and that deflowering involves a penis thrusting into a vagina. Little do they know, sex can be defined as simply as a man's lips sliding down your cock or a woman's tongue swirling around your clit. Some lesbians consider fingering each other to orgasm as great sex. Some gay men consider a hand job . . . anyway, you get the picture.

You get to define what sex is (just like former presidents), and whether it's intimate or casual, meaningful or drunken, special or regretful, you get to be a virgin again. As long as you know sex involves more than talking, you're in good shape. Sometimes you lose one virginity and don't lose the other for years. Some bi women start with women and then once they're past the typical "virgin" age screw a guy. Or maybe they start with guys and don't dive into bed with a woman until they're past thirty and have had kids.

Same goes for guys. When Mike was a facilitator at the first-ever coed bi rap group in L.A., he heard plenty of guys saying they've fooled around only with other guys and now are attracted to women but never did the deed. He heard married women say they are now tired of their hubbies and are looking for women to fulfill their desires. You can know what and whom you want to do but just haven't had the chance to do the deed.

Sometimes you have stronger emotional ties to one sex and wait until they develop for the other before losing your second virginity. Sometimes you're just a horn dog and lose them both in a hot threesome . . . not that all bisexuals must have threesomes (though most of the bisexuals we know really, really want to if they haven't already).

Own your virginity. It's always sweet to hear, "Gosh, I've never done that before" or "Heck, I've never had that in there" or "Gee, I've never thrown my back out in that position before" or something like that. But don't ever fake it! Do what makes you feel comfortable. Most important, take responsibility for your own orgasms and your partner's orgasms; otherwise, you're going to be frustrated, and really, there are enough straight people having frustrating, unfulfilling sex for the rest of us already.

I don't think there's any difference between what I find sexy in men or women. I think it's definitely an attitude and it's definitely something that's about a certain kind of confidence and self-awareness that makes somebody attractive and strong. I don't think it's something all that tangible. It's certainly not a look in somebody's eye. It's something that transcends hair color.

—SANDRA BERNHARD,
Lesbian News, February 1998

TURN-ONS

MASSAGE

You can't fail by offering a sensual, thoughtful, and thorough massage. Massage is a great way to feel out whether someone is bisexual, especially if you're a woman making the moves on another woman. (Sure, it seems a little queeny for a guy to offer another man a massage, but if he says yes, odds are he's not straight.) Just let your fingers wander and linger a little bit over . . . well, you know the places. If your guy or gal moans, odds are they've got those tendencies you predicted.

HANDS

Have you ever noticed how attractive another woman's or man's hands can be? With subtle gestures and light touches, hands often prove to be one of the most underrated, sensual parts of a woman's body, and they don't go unnoticed by bi women and lesbians. In fact, it's not uncommon for bi and gay gals to compliment another woman's hands. Such a compliment can sometimes be employed as a subtle come-on, a way to say she sees their potential. Men who take care of their powerful hands with nicely trimmed or manicured nails can also prove to be a major turn-on.

FINGERS

Though fingers are technically part of a person's hands, we felt inclined to expand upon their blessed beauty by glorifying them in their own section. Men's and women's fingers offer completely different sensations, whether they're fingering women or squeezing a man's cock. Besides, there's something just so intimate about someone touching you down there, be they man or woman, and taking the time to do it right. Men have larger and often longer fingers, which provides for a different sensation than women, who often have smaller and softer hands and provide a uniquely sensual approach. Bi women and men can appreciate the differences in both male and female touch and crave them both, desiring either. The gender doesn't matter as much as the person's ability to satisfy us and take responsibility for our pleasure.

TONGUES

Tongues are softer than any other body part. If you need an explanation for why that makes it so erotic, you might need to take a breather before reading the rest of this section. If your mind instantly jumped to visualizing its soft, gushy loveliness in naughty places, then thank god, your mind is as dirty as ours. Tongues can lightly trace the outsides of ears, swirl around nipples, and lick us in the holiest of holies, and bi gals and guys appreciate it when the fellas and the ladies do all of the above. True, some people have gotten us licked better than others, but we know it's all in the individual. Some men are great at oral sex, some women suck at it, and vice versa. The only truism that holds for both sexes is that whether a person likes using their tongue (for oral sex in particular) can determine how good they are at pleasuring someone with it— and that goes for you folks with the tongue bars as well.

BREASTS

We like the way they look. We like the way they feel. We like them in all sizes. Though many women get caught up in societal bullshit that makes their breasts more of a source of insecurity than pleasure, bi women and men never fail to appreciate them fully. We like the way they feel when they press up against us during hugs or brush against us accidentally. We notice them under tight T-shirts and tank tops. We dig nipples. Most important, we know how to treat them. We like licking them, sucking them, and biting them until we hear a satisfied groan. Any questions?

BUTTS

Both guys and girls have them, so what's the big deal? Well, for starters, a cute butt in tight jeans just has this undeniable effect on us. A medical article once said human beings stare at behinds because the walking motion reminds them of thrusting, which in turn reminds them of mating. We think it's simpler than that. A hot ass in whatever shape or size you prefer can quite simply give you a goal—grabbing it. True, you kind of have to be intimate with the person before that can be deemed appropriate behavior (be wary—grabbing or spanking men's or women's asses inappropriately can be deemed offensive), but for the most part we just like them. Though some of us are more into other body parts, we all notice them. In fact, the butt can often be a deciding factor in how attracted we feel toward a certain individual. Women's butts are more about the hips and curves. Guys' asses are more about definition and muscle. Either way, some of us are butt girls or guys . . . just maybe not up-the-butt girls or guys (but really, who knows?).

MUSCULAR ARMS

Though some women find them to be a bit too butch, many bi women and men find it extraordinarily hot when another woman or man has clearly defined arms and shoulders. Though toned arms in women didn't seem to come into style until Madonna sported them after her yoga phase, tons of women now sport muscular biceps and forearms, much to our delight. Same goes for the guys who draw their inspiration from, well, other guys. Toned arms scream strength, and there's nothing sexier than a strong woman or man.

LEGS

Bi women who are into women's legs usually are into femmes, which conversely means they are into shaved legs. Silky and revealing, athletic or slender, they catch our attention, especially in skirts or dresses. Guys with toned or muscular calves always stand out as well. Usually legs aren't our main concern, but a nice pair never offends us.

STRAPPING IT ON AND DOING HER

Freud thinks it's penis envy. Rednecks think it's the only way two women can have sex. We call it fun. Sure, it might make women feel kind of like they're violating the feminist code of ethics to fuck a woman like a guy with a fake dick—and of course women can have perfectly satisfying sex with each other without ever using a dildo—but hey, doesn't the thought of fucking your girlfriend sound kinda cool? It'll take some practice. Most important, it will take a lot of lube and a visit to the sex store. Let your girlfriend select the dildo she likes, or you can surprise her. Whatever you choose, read the instructions on cleaning the dildo carefully.

STRAPPING IT ON AND DOING HIM

The only thing hotter than watching a guy submitting to another man is watching a guy submit to a woman. Come on, ladies, we know you've thought about it—bending over your boyfriend and letting him take it for once. One bisexual couple we know admitted that they have sex mostly in this manner because the woman prefers to penetrate than be penetrated and the man prefers to, well, bend over. True, they sometimes have sex in the traditional way, but gender bending in this role-reversing way proves to be a bigger turn on for them. But that's a couple where both partners are bisexual and, thus, more open-minded to experimentation. What if your boyfriend's straight? How in the hell are you going to talk him into this?

First of all, if you and your partner are remotely intimate, you'll know whether or not he's "a butt guy"—if he likes a finger up there or has hinted at anal play in the past. If he hasn't and you're looking to persuade him, you might want to go buy the video *Bend over, Boyfriend: A Couple's Guide to Male Anal Pleasure* to make a strong case for your fantasy. Aside from being one of the few educational videos in which you can witness women doing their boyfriends with strap-ons, *Bend over, Boyfriend* is pretty damn informative. Before it gets into downright penetration, the video makes a very strong argument for anal play, debunks stereotypes, and offers crucial safety tips.

I find it hornier looking at women than men. Sorry, I love experimenting with my sexuality. If that means with girls, so be it.

—CHRISTINA AGUILERA,
Zoo magazine, January 2004

WATCHING TWO GIRLS TOGETHER

OK, so this section seems like a no-brainer, but the bi gals and guys we know say watching girls go at it really makes them hot. Who knew? Some high femmes said they enjoy watching any type of lesbian porn, even with the Pamela Anderson types. Other bi gals said the typical L.A.-looking, long-nailed, plastic-looking women turn them off and prefer more organic porn videos from more women-friendly sources like Fatale Media, which shoots videos in San Francisco that feature normal women with real breasts. Guys pretty much don't care—if it's two women making out, fingering each other, or doing each other with dildos, they're pretty much psyched.

Bi gals prefer authenticity. Be it a regular indie flick, trashy L.A. porn, or Fatale-style lesbian porn for lesbians, bi gals can tell when two women are faking it and not really that hot for each other. (So, guys, take that into consideration if you're out video shopping for a special treat.) We bi gals get hot not just from the physical but also from the emotional elements of sex. Watching two women together who have a genuine attraction or emotional connection is always hotter than watching women fucking each other like men for men.

Like most Americans, we like to watch. The experience of watching the tenderness and sensuality of two women together always beats the pants off watching boring straight couples or really anything else . . . aside from maybe watching two guys together.

WATCHING TWO GUYS TOGETHER

What is it about two boys, all over each other, that just makes us go gaga? For starters, you won't see it anywhere outside your local gay bar—well, that is, except on Pay Per View. Because so many straight men (and straight women even) find the image of two men together entirely repulsive, we have been entirely deprived of this titillating stimulus by the mainstream media and our general surroundings. Yet watching two bi or gay men confident and overt in their sheer sweaty lust for one another can be an enormous turn-on because of its honest carnality.

The first obvious reason guy-on-guy action gets our engines running is basic: we like men. Even more so, we like men with hot bodies, and usually those bi or gay boys sucking face on the dance floor have washboard abs (did we mention they usually aren't wearing shirts?), ripped biceps, and smooth skin. But the fascination doesn't end there. When two men kiss and touch one another, they often do so without a hint of tenderness and instead, well, manhandle each other. They move fast, like the hunters that they are, and then move in for the kill. No hesitation. No insecurity. They both want it, and they both know it. And there's nothing emasculating about that. It's a battle for domination, and, eventually, one must submit. And that's the best part.

The sexiest aspect of watching two hot guys together is the moment of submission. We women have seen literally hundreds of films in which women submit to men, ready and willing to be taken. In fact, most of us know that exact feeling as much as the average guy knows the feeling of dominance. But seeing a man taken by another man and willingly submitting to another guy is simply exciting and unique. To see a man forced to take it lying down and close his eyes, bite his lip, and ride it out is just fucking hot. The look of near pain on his face as the sweat pours down his brow . . . need we say more?

POWER DYNAMICS: TOP, BOTTOM, OR BOTH?

BY NOW, MOST OF you have probably heard the terms *top* and *bottom*, especially if you've been hanging out in the gay community. Tops and bottoms exist in the hetero and gay worlds as well. A top simply refers to someone who prefers to be dominant in bed, whereas a bottom prefers to be more on the receiving end of things. You could argue that by nature in heterosexual sex, women are natural bottoms and men natural tops, but just because you're being penetrated doesn't mean you're passive, and just because you're penetrating doesn't mean you like to dominate. Quite simply, a top likes to be in control, whereas a bottom likes to be taken. This means different things depending on which gender you're with, and bisexuals aren't always tops with both genders or bottoms with both genders. It all depends on the circumstances. Likewise, straight and gay people who are tops sometimes want to try being bottoms and vice versa, sometimes discovering their true calling. You don't have to be a top or a bottom all of the time.

For example, some bi guys are bottoms with men and tops with women. Others are always bottoms or always tops. Some bi women are tops with men and bottoms with women or vice versa. It all depends on your comfort level. Some women have to be in charge with men, while others have to be in charge with women, or both. Get the picture? It's really not as confusing as it sounds. Oh, and one more thing: just because someone is dominant in their professional life, like CEO of a major company, doesn't mean they aren't big fat bottoms in their sex life. Likewise, someone who's a wallflower and generally shy can often take charge in the bedroom. Bottom line: you don't know what you're getting—top or bottom—when you go out with someone. We just hope next time someone jokingly asks you whether you could try out for *America's Next Top Bottom*, you know they're not referring to a reality show.

SEX GUIDES FOR BISEXUALS

WANT TO BECOME A better lover or at least grow more comfortable with your sexuality? These books will effectively pave the road to sexual self-confidence for any bisexual:

THE STRAIGHT GIRL'S GUIDE TO SLEEPING WITH CHICKS by Jen Sincero guides curious straight gals down the tumultuous path of fooling around with the ladies. With a lot of humor sprinkled throughout, Jen encourages women to masturbate to fantasies with women and to trim their nails and teaches them how to pick up women in bars.

LESBIAN SEX SECRETS FOR MEN: WHAT EVERY MAN WANTS TO KNOW ABOUT MAKING LOVE TO A WOMAN AND NEVER ASKS by Jamie Goddard and Kurt Brungardt. Ideal for women and men eager to learn how to push that special lady's buttons! From kissing to massage, hand jobs, and going down, this book will effectively teach you how to make her moan.

SEX TIPS FOR STRAIGHT WOMEN FROM A GAY MAN by Dan Anderson and Maggie Berman. Ideal for women and men eager to learn how to satisfy their man! From hand jobs and blow jobs to turnoffs, this book will give you confidence in bed whether you're a man or a woman.

THE ETHICAL SLUT: A GUIDE TO INFINITE SEXUAL POSSIBILITIES by Dossie Easton and Catherine A. Liszt. With sections explicitly titled "How to F**k Up" and "The Ten Commandments of Sluthood," this manual describes in step-by-step detail how to embrace your inner slut without hurting anybody in the process. A must-read for any bisexual who wants to maintain a primary relationship but still continue to play around.

BOX LUNCH: THE LAYPERSON'S GUIDE TO CUNNILINGUS by Diana Cage is written for both amateurs and pros. Bi men and women have a responsibility to be good at this for the sake of their partners. For god's sake, buy a book like this!

GOING DOWN: THE INSTINCT GUIDE TO ORAL SEX by Ben R. Rogers and Joel Perry is written for men and women interested in giving guys the one thing on the menu they always desire and sometimes rarely get (well, at least from some women). People usually hate giving blow jobs because they literally suck at it. Buying a book like this can make the entire act more palatable and (gasp!) even fun.

EXHIBITIONISM FOR THE SHY: SHOW OFF, DRESS UP, AND TALK HOT by Carol Queen. If you're a shy guy or gal allowing your fear to prevent you from fully embracing and enjoying your sexuality, this book might help. Written by a recovering shy person turned famous sex educator, this manual provides exercises to help readers build sexual self-confidence.

THE TOPPING BOOK and **THE BOTTOMING BOOK** again by Dossie Easton and Catherine A. Liszt playfully tackle the psychology behind, you guessed it, tops and bottoms.

These books reveals what inspires tops and bottoms, including turn-ons and frustrations. Not sure whether you're a top or bottom? You might be after reading these books.

FUNNIEST BI PORN (BY MIKE)

They're not necessarily the best adult films, although some of them will get your juices flowing no matter what your persuasion. The names alone should drag a grin across your lips.

ATTACK OF THE 50-FOOT TRANNY. While leaving a party, Christy is spirited away by a spaceship and undergoes a sexual transformation of massive proportions. Now she can exact a nasty revenge on her cheating husband and her best girlfriend who've both betrayed her.

BI CLAUDIUS. Seize her, seize him! Let my people come! Romans are impaling Romans; guys are going Greek. Hail viewers: see the costumes, hear the oratories, swallow big swords, witness lots of debauchery. The rest, after all, is history. Long-schlonged Vince Harrington lets us see what the gods have under their robes.

BI DREAM OF GENIE. Randi Hart plays a ditzy, meddling genie who with the blink of an eye can get the gardener to go down on her hunky boyfriend and service her as well.

BI LOVE LUCY. Latino stud Dicky is cast in a porn video, but his wife—that wacky redhead Lucy—decides she's going to give adult videos a try for herself. This is as grotesque as it seems, and it's been banned by the Ball estate, so if you find it, you're lucky.

THE BI-SEX PROJECT. Three couples disappear into the world of bisexuality, seeking the biggest cocks ever. Two months later, their footage is found. See, there's a reason for shaky, poorly shot scenes in adult videos after all.

BI-TANIC–THE SHIP WHERE EVERYONE GOES DOWN. Talk about iceberg-interruptus! Filmed surreptitiously on the *Queen Mary* in period costume, this vid is equipped with mini ship effects and over-the-top dialogue. Follow Rosebud as she's torn between an entire shipload of lovers.

THE BI VALLEY. Drag diva Lana Luster plays the Barbara Stanwyck role as the Widow Tartley who rustles up studs to satisfy her three rather horny children.

GILLIGAN'S BI-LAND. In this one, see what really went on among the castaways, and Ginger, played by bi director Karen Dior, has a big surprise between her legs for the little buddy!

GOOSED–A BISEXUAL FAIRY TALE. These fractured fairy tales take a look at Jack Sprat, Bo Peep, and three men rub-a-dub-dubbing in a tub. Boy Blue isn't so little anymore. Peter Peter eats more than pumpkins, and see how nimble that Jack can really be. There are two sequels.

THE HILLS HAVE BI'S. Trash meets class when Chi Chi LaRue and her lesbie lover, Moist Towelette, drive into Beverly Hills—with the boys in the trunk —to meet their new in-laws. Sharon Kane and Chi Chi LaRue go at it (not sexually, but in a great catfight), and their caviar spitting is sidesplitting.

NIGHT OF THE LIVING BI-DOLLS. Steve Rambo and Sam Crockett battle the undead along with Sharon Kane who plays three roles in this film, including a vain dead actress whose face keeps peeling off. At the tail end, the zombie who devours Sharon's left breast is this book's coauthor Mike.

VALLEY OF THE BI DOLLS. Sharon Kane plays the drugged-out Ceily Fontana in this brilliant musical spoof that also stars porn legend Gloria Leonard. There's an even better sequel, *Revenge of the Bi Dolls*. Both have become bi porn classics.

BEST BI PORN STARS

THEY'RE LISTED IN ORDER of the amount of titles they're in, including fetish, gay, bi, lesbian, hetero, tickling, S&M, and more (bet you didn't know there were so many genres!)

SHARON KANE is the longest-working bi porn starlet with more than one thousand titles to her name and a great songstress and musician too. She also appears in a "freak" video where she has two working penises!

DREW ANDREWS, married with children, has more than five hundred titles to his credit.

GEOFFREY KAREN DIOR was the first HIV-positive transgendered adult film star to come out about his status and performed as Rick Van as a man.

JEFF STRYKER calls himself "just sexual," doesn't like labels, but has a type of guy he likes.

JOHN HOLMES couldn't keep his long appendage to just the girls and loved whipping it out.

SHARON MITCHELL, a nurse by trade, has done it every

possible way over three decades.

RYAN IDOL, a Tom Cruise lookalike in younger days, grew into being bi through porn.

NINA HARTLEY, a blonde swinger in real life, debuted in *Educating Nina* at nineteen in 1984 and now directs. She's the grand dame of porn who made it fashionable to be bi.

KEN RYKER. Kids used to call him "firehose" at gym in school; now he's figured out what to do with it.

TINA TYLER is an enchanting brunette who's good at switching from coy librarian to whipping dominatrix in an instant.

VINCE ROCKLAND brought his two brothers into porn for a while, but then he found God.

JEANNA FINE is a fiery temptress who always seemed to like it more with girls, but she's a good mom.

GINO COLBERT made the switch from star to director and always shows he loves the ladies as well as the gents.

JOHAN PAULIK and **LUKAS RIDGESTON** are the beautiful eastern European studs who have wowed audiences of all persuasions, and both of them are bi and personally attached to women now.

69 BI TITLES

THESE TITLES ARE JUST too funny to pass up.

MOVIE SPOOFS

As Time Goes Bi
Bi Bi Birdie
Bi Chill
Bi-Dazzled
Bi-Laddin
Bi on the Fourth of July
Bi the Rear Window

Bi Voyager
Every Which Way You Can
Genderella
Good Bi Girl
Lust Horizons
Where the Bi's Are

TV-SHOW SPOOFS

Bi-Bi American Style
Bi-Nanza
Bi-Witched
Entertainment Bi Night
A Family Affair

BUSINESS SPOOFS

Bi American
Bi Now, Pay Later
Bi 'N Sell
Corporate Bi Out
For Sale Bi Owner
Jizz Bizz
Toys Bi Us

SPORTS SPOOFS

Bi-Athelon
Bi Cycling
Super Bi Bowl
Switchhitter Series

STAR SPOOFS

Bi George
ElBira
Good Bi Norma Jeannie
Kourtney Luvs

PUNNY TITLES

AC/DC Series
Bend over, Boyfriend
Bi Agra
Bi Bitches in Heat
Bi-Butt Invaders
Bi-Ceps
Bi-Coastal
Bi-Dacious
Bi Friends
Bi Golly
Bi Linguist
Bi-Ologist
Bi Spy
Blow Bi Blow
Crossing Over
Days Gone Bi
Drag King
Drive Bi
Fence Jumpers
Fly Bi Night
Get Bi Tonight
Goldie Locks and the Three Bi Bears
Inch Bi Inch
Karen's Bi-Line
Mass Appeal
Miss Kitty's Litter
Read Bi All
A Real Man Wouldn't
Remembering Times Gone Bi
Score
Semper Bi
Slide Bi Me
Split Personality

Threesomes
VamBires
Why Not Cum Bi?

YOUR FIRST THREESOME

FAMILIARIZE YOURSELF WITH THE following terms because you will be expected to be a master of all three of them: *threesome or three-way*, *orgy*, and *group sex*. In fact, when most straight or gay people hear the word *threesome*, they immediately think, "Oh, isn't that the way bisexuals have sex?" And they're right. It's the only way for bisexuals to have completely satisfying sex, given that we must be with a man and a woman at the same time in order to receive any sexual satisfaction whatsoever. In fact, we are only capable of jumping into bed with two other people at a time. That one-on-one, making-love thing just never happens. So read up!

Threesomes differ from group sex in two ways: they involve only three people (duh!), and the participants usually already know one another. Most threesomes start with a couple that invites a third person, "the guest star," into their relationship for a night of fun.

Some folks prefer to be "the guest star" because there's no commitment involved, no jealousy to be experienced or relationship to be screwed up, and as the newcomer they often garner the majority of the attention. True, they don't have the home-bed advantage, but, hey, if the couple starts fighting, they're out of there.

TIPS FOR THE GUEST STAR

IF A COUPLE TELLS you that you're the "secondary" partner to their relationship, believe them. Respect that you will never become a third "primary" partner, and by all means do not go into the relationship hoping to become one. Don't expect to be treated as an equal.

Be secure in yourself and keep dating other people. Don't let the couple become the focus of your life unless you are the focus of theirs.

If you don't feel like both partners are equally into you, let it go. Don't raise hell and try to fight your way into the relationship. Accept your position. If for any reason you feel uncomfortable with the situation, get out of it.

Don't be more high maintenance in your friendship with the couple than they are with each other, or you'll get the boot.

Don't have the threesome/orgy/relationship at your house. It's easier to walk away if things get uncomfortable

Some people prefer to be the couple because they don't have to worry about getting attached or feeling used or ignored after the fun is over. They get to spice up their love life from a position of security. If things go wrong, hey, it was just one night (or a few weeks), and they can give the guest star the boot.

Threesomes don't always involve couples and a guest star. Sometimes bi singles seek out a three-way. Though we strongly recommend bi singles prioritize seeking out threesomes with friends over strangers, sometimes a fantasy encounter with two hot strangers sounds enticing. Here are three strategies for single bi gals, (besides begging their friends) to find two hot strangers for a threesome:

1. Have a guy find a girl for you. Most girls don't consider this tactic, but some women we know have found it quite effective. Simply go to a club with an attractive fellow and send him on a mission to find you a cute girl. The guy will jump at the chance because what hot-blooded male wouldn't want to have a threesome? (Little does he know, he might be going home alone!) This strategy alleviates the awkwardness of approaching the woman yourself or facing rejection. Instead, your guy friend can simply approach other women, ask them whether they're into

girls, and then point you out to them. If one girl finds you attractive and you find her attractive as well, then you're set.

2. Find a hot couple and hit on both of them. A lot of bi women find this strategy advantageous because not only do you flatter a sexually adventuresome couple, but once you hit the sheets you also get the bulk of the attention. If you like being the center of attention, this strategy might work best for you. Then again, it can backfire sometimes. One twenty-something friend of ours notes, "I had a threesome one time where the guy was, he was kind of dating the girl. I think he was more into her than he was into me, and I was really into her, too, and she was more into him. It was more like they were having this straight thing and I just happened to be there. That sucked. I didn't like that at all. After we all had our sex and everything, they were just like together, and I was like, 'Fuck this, I'm leaving!'"

3. Be approached for a threesome. This option is highly unlikely, though it has happened to some gals we know. Sometimes a couple will spot you in a club or ask you as a friend to have a threesome with them. Other times, a man will ask you to have sex with his girlfriend, and he'll not be involved sexually at all.

Guys can use the same three strategies, but they must use more caution. Option one works if they can find a female friend willing to find them another guy at a gay club or somewhere not straight. But this can prove more challenging for guys because of the straight-girl gross-out factor, so try to find a fag hag who fantasizes about being with two guys at once. The only problem she might have will occur when she realizes her fantasy didn't necessarily involve the two guys diddling each other. (Find a really open-minded fag hag.)

Number two will be more difficult because finding a straight couple at a gay club where the guy is bi instead of the girl is nearly impossible. If you go and hit on them, you could find yourself in a very awkward moment. Hey, if it's any consolation, option three works for almost everyone.

FINDING THE PERFECT GUEST STAR: A TEN-POINT CHECKLIST

If you and your partner are interested in having a threesome, you must chat and discuss your criteria for this third person. Here are some required attributes in our opinion:

→ good hygiene
→ attractive
→ emotionally mature
→ a good communicator
→ honest
→ respectful of boundaries
→ secure in him/herself
→ generous in bed
→ comfortable with being the guest star
→ does not expect a relationship

A lot of people say, "Oh you're a bisexual, you guys just get together and have orgies." Of course, what do you expect us to do? You get a group of 10 people in a room and you realize that everyone in here is attracted to each other. Checkers anyone?"

—DAN ROTHENBERG, comedian

A RECIPE FOR AN ORGY (HOW TO PLAN ONE WITH YOUR FRIENDS) (BY NICOLE)

THOUGH *PLAN* AND *ORGY* seem antithetical, the two terms can go together if one lays enough groundwork to make it happen. One can inadvertently create the proper scenario by placing certain elements together.

If you're in college, you'll have an easier time creating the circumstances needed because every weekend usually involves experimenting with many things, including copious amounts of liquor. If you're not in college, bring the topic up to friends at a dinner party and feel things out. Get someone else to admit they'd be interested in having a threesome someday. Then get more people to admit that same fantasy. Then get all of those people together in one room.

Your next step, once you've managed to gather these orgy-friendly people together, is to create an innocent-seeming event that could precipitate your fantasy. If you have a friend with a hot tub, tell everyone to bring their suits. After a few cocktails, they might want to jump in, if you catch our drift. Or throw on some music and see where the dancing leads. Or be totally obvious and offer someone a massage and hope everyone else doesn't think you're a complete weirdo. Remember, these are friends, so relationships with them will change postorgy, so choose wisely! If you don't want the baggage and you're really brave, check out a sex party.

SEX PARTY ETIQUETTE (BY MIKE)

SEX PARTIES ARE FOR people who are cool with having sex with strangers, albeit very, very safe sex. A lot of bi singles prefer to take this route rather than trying to construct a threesome or orgy out of thin air.

If you've ever been to an orgy (for you neophytes, that's three or more people where clothes are off and people are touching more than themselves), you know it's tricky enough to keep track of all the wandering hands and flailing body parts. Throw in the bi element, and things get even more confusing.

Here are a few rules for navigating a bi orgy or sex party (sometimes referred to as a Jack-and-Jill-Off Party in more enlightened communities):

STAY SAFE. It is the highest priority, so you should assume that everyone in the room is HIV positive for your own protection. But that doesn't mean you can't have a rip-roaring good time despite that terrifying assumption.

NEVER ASSUME. Yeah, that old saying about it makes an "ASS out of U and ME" takes on bigger dimensions when you're in a situation where you don't know if the guy or gal is into you or what you want to do with them. Never assume he/she/they want you. Asking first is always polite to see if that "ASS" is welcome for both U and ME.

DON'T JUDGE. That means, never judge a limp wiener for its full potential. Never think that those erect nipples under a gal's tight white blouse are the real thing (unless you live outside of Los Angeles). That little dangling turkey neck that you see when he first slips off those boxers may turn out to be a fine supersausage, and those perky breasts may in fact be fake. Just be happy with what you've got when you've got it and shut up.

AVOID THE "EWW!" Sure, there may be some unpleasant types around, and there may be some people doing some pretty nasty things in some fascinating positions you've never dreamed of, but don't say, "Eww!" Being grossed out can be par for the course, so don't be obvious about it.

TOPSY-TURVY. It sounds weird, but don't think that just because one person is a top with one gender that they're a top all the time. The guy who's great at topping a woman may be a superpower bottom with the boys, and the gal who likes being dildoed by a lady may prefer strap-ons with guys.

HOT-TUB FLOPS. Don't expect the gang to get all steamed up by stripping naked in the hot tub. Not only is there the often unpleasant blast of cool air during your rush to the tub, but once inside, if it's too hot, it's impossible to get any blood rushing to the right spots. For older folks, it's just too much on the heart. For young drunk folks, the hot tub poses the risk of fainting. No, the hot tub is ideally a good foreplay spot where y'all can get warmed up and cleaned up, but after you size up your connection, take your fun indoors.

FIND A FRIEND. If there's a familiar face in the crowd, don't go up to the person and talk about their spouse or most recent girlfriend or boyfriend. Bad form! And, if the person doesn't know you're going to pop into that party, don't surprise them. (I remember the one time I surprised an old friend by massaging his back when he was going at it with a gal, and he turned around and shrieked, "Omigod, it's like finding out that my grandmother was watching." Needless to say, it temporarily killed the mood.)

PLAY THE STRAIGHT CARD. Guys, if you're going to freak out when there's a dick in your face, or gals, if you're going to be squeamish about touching a pair of breasts, then get out of there and rent a few more of the *Switchhitter* porn series before trying this again. Sometimes a hand is going to grab you and you don't know to what gender it's attached, so don't freak. If you say, "I don't do that because I'm straight," that's as bad as someone letting their cell phone ring during a movie. You shouldn't be high-strung about whatever balls you think you have.

BEWARE OF SHARP OBJECTS. Clip your fingernails, and toenails, and be aware of any studs, piercings, or other sharp items you may have on your personage. And if you do have them and insist on wearing them, use them well.

RECRUIT. Don't think of this as a job, and don't go around seeking out the straight person who's doing this for the first time so that you can be the willing teacher to lend a hand. Sure, there will be a few virgins in the group, but let them join in on the grope in their own time, or else you'll frighten them away.

GENTLE WITH THE GENITALIA. Hey, if you're in unfamiliar territory, take cues from the people around you. If you're not sure how to handle those testicles, don't just reach out and squeeze. If you're not sure where that man in the boat is, don't go digging too deep into her like you're on a fishing expedition. Frankly, getting 86ed from an orgy is really the most embarrassing thing that can ever happen to you . . . that is, aside from being caught masturbating by your mother.

NEVER COMPARE. Don't you dare talk about what it's like being with girls when you're with a guy or how great it is with guys when you're with a girl. Certainly, you're not going to score points with this sort of chitchat, so nix it if you don't want to find yourself relegated to a corner.

OFFER A HAND. The best way to join in on a really hot interaction is to caress a body part that isn't interrupting the couple's interaction. If they want you to continue, you'll hear the appropriate grunt or groan. If they don't, you'll hear the appropriate grunt or groan. It's not so bad to just stand back and watch.

LADY LUSTING. Don't be creepy, and certainly don't leer at the women whom you want to be with. It's unflattering, and it's scary to watch guys (or even gals, for that matter) leer at the gal who just has arrived and is considering stripping off her clothes and looking for someone to play with. If she doesn't give you any signals, go for someone else and leave her alone until she acclimates to the situation. Also, don't think that you're such a stud that

you can handle two or more gals at the same time, you
arrogant prick.

FAKE WHEN NECESSARY. It's OK to fake it—yeah, even
guys can do it—and the best way to do that is to stop
something that isn't getting your rocks off or just to
get away from some vampiristic creature who has been
stalking you all night. Rather than getting your clothes
on and hightailing it out of there, you might as well fake
a quickie. Then you can get rid of your stalker for at least
twenty minutes.

BE REALISTIC. It's time to get a reality check. You're already
in your fantasy situation with naked men and women
around you, so don't go overboard. Gals, it's not likely
you'll do well shoving two dicks in your mouth at the
same time, and guys, double-penetrating a woman is
tricky (that's having two guys enter a woman, one from
the front, and one from the back door). Start off slowly,
and have one of you start at one end and then work your
way down. And remember that although orgasms are
infinite, they may be finite for the night.

NAVIGATING THE MIDDLE. It's a big bi fantasy, I know,
to be in the middle, but the reality is pretty difficult.
Whether you're a guy who wants to get penetrated by a
guy and be inside a gal or a gal who wants to languish in
the middle, the logistics are something akin to trying out
for a Russian gymnastics team. Don't let those porn vids
fool you—some pieces just don't fit together, and getting
three people to fit just right while keeping up a rhythm is
about as hard as winning the lottery. But keep trying!

KINKINESS 101

IF YOU'RE GOING TO introduce advanced sexual activities or
even role-playing in the bedroom, for the love of god, know what
you're doing! Here are some tips for the kinky queer in you.

ANAL PLAY

Whether you're a bi gal doing your boyfriend or a bi guy doing another guy, you should mess with the nether region only if you know what you're doing. This is definitely something that can turn a bi guy straight if it's handled incorrectly, or rushed too much. Some gals freak out a bit, some guys get squeamish, but once you pass those portals, you'll always return again. Here are a few hard-core tips:

→ Good communication is a must, and we're not just talking out of our asses.
→ Safe sex is a must. Sheath anything that squirts.
→ He's in charge 'cause he's being penetrated. If he says stop, then listen.
→ Don't let him eat spicy food, seeds, or sharp, crunchy things.
→ For first timers, lay off the coffee or alcohol beforehand.
→ Clean up down there very thoroughly. Don't douche. It can cause irritation.
→ Use a bath, deep breathing, vibrating toys, massage, or regular sex to relax your guy.
→ Anal rimming (a.k.a. oral sex on his hole) can be done without having to lick his hole. Slap a sheet of plastic wrap over his crack and go to town without a mess.
→ Finger play with latex gloves can be more fun than it sounds.
→ Use plenty of lube, and don't use a numbing agent on his bum.
→ Don't dive too far unless he begs for it.

Reasons to Try It Even If You're Scared

→ Anal play/sex can make your man feel softer and more, ahem, receptive. It can open him up . . . emotionally.

→ Your man can be actively receptive while you're doing him. He can be on top. It's doesn't have to be a passive act, as you may know from experience.

→ The prostate is the male g-spot.

→ Regular prostrate stimulation can decrease the risk of health problems in that area later in life.

→ Anal play doesn't make guys "all loose up there." It can actually improve their sphincter control because they are having more muscle activity and more blood pumping through that area.

→ Extra bloodflow caused by anal play can actually make hemorrhoids disappear.

→ Men can have orgasms through anal stimulation without any contact with their rod. Who'd have ever thought that?

UNISEX TOYS

IF YOU'RE LOOKING FOR sex toys to use on your male or female partners, here are our suggestions. The double-sided dildo provides limitless possibilities. Women can use it on each other, and so can men. Other items such as the Bunny Rabbit Clit Flicker, the Slim Probe Teasing Tongue, or the Vibrating Sausage (for the meat lover in you) also offer unisex functions but, most important, supply plenty of giggles in the bedroom. Open your mind! Start looking at your silver-bullet vibrator as girl-friendly and boy-friendly. Just slap on some "Happy Penis Wild Cherry Lube" on your rod or a purple-shaped plastic butterfly toy, and you're good to go. Whatever goofy toy you've got stashed in your bedside table, remember as a bisexual you're practically required to try some nontraditional gender bending. Don't worry—the people at work will never find out.

ROLE-PLAYING

UNLIKE MONOSEXUALS, WE BISEXUALS can play with people's assumptions about our relationships and sexuality like nobody's business. Girls can take their girlfriends to straight bars and pretend to be mere friends while their hands wander beneath the table. Bi guys can do the same with their male buddies. If you're with a member of the opposite sex, one of you can play gay in public and then sneak away to a parking lot for a secret make-out session. You can pretend to meet like strangers in a restaurant or a bar for the first time. (Be sure to find a public bar that's quiet enough to have the regular pre–happy hour patrons listen in as you woo each other, pretend to fight, and eventually go home together.) If you're particularly adventurous, you may try to hit up on someone else at the bar for a three-way (whether you have any intention of going through with it or not), or for true sport, try posing as the opposite sex and finding each other in a public place.

STRIPTEASE

YOUR PARTNER/S, MALE OR FEMALE, will always delight in an impromptu striptease or lap dance. The bi secret is in what s/he strips down to. With those kooky bisexuals you never know if a gal will be wearing boxers or a guy will be wearing a thong. Will s/he strip down to silk panties, a g-string, or a tight Speedo that will make you giggle? Not to mention the stripping opportunities outside of the bedroom. There's nothing more unconventional than taking a willing date or partner to a strip club.

Taking your bi gal to a female strip show can turn bi guys on for a panoply of reasons: she'll be the center of attention, and you can watch her while she receives a lap dance. Bi guys can take fellow bi guys to a strip joint 'cause there's nothing more fun than two bi guys playing macho men in public and buying each other lap dances, stealing the occasional kiss as women writhe on their laps.

Likewise, bi gals can take their women to strip shows (with male or female dancers) and do the exact same thing with or without the "macho" part.

> We don't choose our sexuality. It chooses us. My honest belief is that we're hard-wired the way that we are. I say celebrate it. I say come on, have fun with it. You've been given something that gives you intense pleasure. Let's get out of the shame about it.
>
> —fetishist filmmaker on HBO's *Real Sex*

BI FETISHES

BECAUSE YOU'RE BISEXUAL, YOU'RE expected to be a walking encyclopedia of fetishist culture. And really, what separates a bisexual from a foot fetishist? Aren't we one and the same? Given your proclivity for kinky sex, you're undoubtedly already practicing all the fetishes listed below. But just in case . . .

- **FEET:** A highly mocked fetish that can be interpreted as bisexual. Take your pick—with polish or without.
- **UNIFORMS:** Whether it's a leather daddy or your het boyfriend in a cop uniform, a sexy drag queen in a nurse's uniform or a soft butch in a fitted suit . . . you get the picture. Uniforms are hot
- **LEATHER:** This fetish has a strong affiliation to the BDS&M scene, but it can be hot even when it's not strung tightly over a whip or body part. Women in black leather jackets can play butch or femme, while guys can ham it up as leather daddies or GQ models. With its

rough or smooth textures, you never know what you're in for when it comes to this material.

LATEX: Most commonly used for safe sex, this material has a silky, seductive quality most people fail to consider— that is, most people except for kinky bisexuals. You can buy spray-on latex and seductively peel it from your lover's nipples or climb into a full bodysuit and prove to your lover that you're willing to sweat for them!

LINGERIE: Yes, it's true. Both men and women wear lingerie, especially bi people 'cause we have lots of sex (if only). Some men slap on garters. Some women climb into silk boxers. Though a lot of guys admit they don't give a crap about lingerie (what matters is what happens when the lingerie comes off!), a lot of women find it oh-so-sexy on other women. Others think it's a big ol' waste of money. (In truth, you could be spending that money on sex toys!)

CORSETS: A favorite of drag queens and hot mamas, you've got to have the boobs (or an ample way to fake having boobs) to fill these hot items. Corsets can be used in role-playing or cross-dressing or just to accentuate that hot moment when your lover unfastens the ties in the back. Either way, they'll steal your breath away.

CROSS-DRESSING (A.K.A. "GENDERFUCK"): This means something different for both men and women. Some bi men do it because they like the soft textures of women's clothes, while some bi women wear suits to express their dominant side and attract femmes. Men and women cross-dress "to pass" as the other gender because the excitement of going undetected turns them on. Others just dress up in the bedroom to fantasize with their lovers.

SHAVING: Taking a razor below the equator on your girl or boyfriend can be either really dangerous (if you don't know what you're doing) or really hot. The key to this fetish is vulnerability. Shaving makes your lover vulnerable. If it's a man, it's possible he's never been shaved in his life and will find the whole thing really arousing and, if you're lucky, kind of humiliating in a superbly erotic way. If it's a woman, she probably considers shaving an intimate experience and will find it extremely intense to have someone else doing it. And really, what better way to say "I trust you" than by letting your guy or gal act out their shaving fetish? Bottom line: shaving fetishists get really aroused by silky smooth skin. (P.S. If you try this, go with the grain, not against it!)

BI SADOMASOCHISM

SO WHAT EXACTLY ABOUT bisexuality screams bondage—we mean, aside from our predictably naughty nature? Naturally, since we're capable of doing it with both sexes (as some most tastefully put it), the slippery slope to dressing like that gimpy guy in *Pulp Fiction* and consequent bestiality is somewhat inevitable. In order to help accelerate that process, we feel it's our responsibility to teach you how to wield a whip, so you don't disappoint the religious Right. (We must also note that, ironically, the practitioners of S&M have more of a community than we do.)

WHY DO BISEXUALS, OR ANYONE FOR THAT MATTER, LIKE S&M?

Many people wonder what in the heck is so fun about getting hit during sex. What on god's green earth could make pain pleasurable? Most fetishists argue that while sexually aroused, people chemically have a higher pain threshold and can now enjoy pleasure on a different level. Plus, the human body creates endorphins to counter pain, so many S&M practitioners do it for the endorphin rush, much like a jogger who digs the "runner's high." Others just do it for the intense physical and emotional experience and to build trust with their partners in a safe, consensual manner. Pain is a continuum, much like sexuality. From playful pinches and bites to smacks and spanks, everyone has their place on it.

Some bisexuals participate in S&M, much like certain sects of the straight and gay communities, because when they come out as an alternate sexuality, they have a little bit more freedom and courage to come out or indulge in other appetites. Whether that's S&M or drag or foot fetishism, that's for you to say. Coming out lessens the barriers to meeting people involved in subcultures such as S&M. We do want to assert, however, that being bi does not make you any more inclined to loving sadomasochism or any other type of fetish.

HOW DO I KNOW WHETHER I'M AN S&M BISEXUAL?

Only you can answer this question. Many bi's get into kinkiness out of curiosity. Some love it. Some hate it. There's only one way to find out. But before you give it a shot, learn the lingo and the rules, so no one gets hurt or freaked out. If you have no interest in trying it, don't, and never get talked into doing something you don't want to do, even if your partner is pressuring you. Also, if you have really low self-esteem, S&M is probably not a good idea because playing the submissive could possibly further reinforce your feelings of worthlessness. Allegedly, good S&M is supposed to be "self-actualizing" and help teach people things about themselves and their partners.

THE LINGO

Because you're bi, you're obviously into the kinkiest sex practices known to man. As a pervert, you probably already know the following kinky S&M slang and have in all likelihood shared it with as many small children as possible. But just in case, we've included a list to keep it all fresh in your mind. You wouldn't want to disappoint anyone, now would you?

S&M: sadism and masochism

B&D: bondage and dominance

D&S: dominance and submission

SCENE: a sexual situation that involves two willing participants role-playing as the dominant and the submissive

NEGOTIATION: before the scene begins, each partner negotiates his/her limits and comfort level, so no one gets hurt or too freaked out

SQUICK: something that pushes beyond the bottom's limits (a.k.a. an unwanted ouch)

SAFE WORD: a word the dominant and submissive decide will be used if the play becomes uncomfortable or too intense. If either says the word, all sex play stops immediately. If the submissive has a gag in his/her mouth and can't speak the safe word, a nonverbal signal is usually agreed upon. Sometimes an object is placed in the submissive's hand, and if the submissive drops the object, it functions as a safe word.

PUSHY BOTTOM: a submissive who doesn't know how to just shut up and be a submissive; a bossy submissive

WHAT SHOULD I USE TO TIE UP MY LOVER

Apparently, some objects are better than others. Who knew? Here's what the experts say . . .

SILK SCARVES/BANDANNAS: Often get too tight when under tension and have to be cut off!

METAL HANDCUFFS: Cheap ones from sporting goods stores often break and have to be filed off. If you decide to go this route, splurge on some brand-name ones—such as Peerless for around thirty dollars—because they won't get tighter under pressure like the cheap ones, but beware: metal can pinch nerves.

ROPE: Difficult to master the tightness level and to learn how to tie good knots. If used improperly, rope causes discomfort. Apparently, nothing distracts you from pleasurable torment like a foot that's fallen asleep or lost all circulation.

ANKLE/WRIST CUFFS: Made of leather or Velcro, these are your best bet because they won't cut off circulation. Sure, you have to buy them at an adult store, but the humiliation far outweighs the risks of getting a blue hand or foot or worrying about finding a lost key.

S&M PARTY ETIQUETTE

BE POLITE. THIS MEANS observe quietly. Loudly yelling, "Whip that ass good!" is not observing quietly. Also a furtive glance in your direction is not an invitation to join in. Also, it is possible to watch the wrong way. In the S&M community, these people are called "energy vampires." Energy vampires destroy the intimacy of a scene by gawking like teenagers at a substitute teacher's breasts. These observers lack "empathy," which is a key trait for an S&M party observer. Watch people at these parties like a porno with a sick grin on your face, and you won't get invited back.

If you want to get in on the action, don't ask to join in during the middle of a scene. Instead, mingle politely and build a connection with someone outside of the action. There are rooms for talking and dungeons for whipping—don't try to mix activities in the inappropriate areas. Also, be prepared to take rejection easily because not everyone's gonna want to get their butt whipped by the likes of you. As for your attire, don't expect to get any in jeans and white sneakers. The dress code is leather, leather, and more leather. The sexier you are, the more likely you'll get to suck on someone's stiletto.

You have now completed Chapter 8. Remember that as a bisexual you're obligated to go out and buy some chaps and/or dominatrix gear and use it in your next threesome. But keep in mind that whether you're kinky or conservative, bi or boring, we all have one shared responsibility—having superbly safe sex. So buy some latex and use it!

CHAPTER 9

PLAYING BI HEART

I think it's much more the person that you fall in love with—and why would you close yourself off to fifty percent of the people?

—Natalie Portman, *Rolling Stone*, June 2002

DESPITE POPULAR OPINION, BISEXUALS actually do have relationships. Some even involve only one other person. But settling down with just one sex always leads to people assuming we're gay or straight, while jumping into a relationship with more than one person can lead to other complications. Here's the lowdown on making it work.

BATTLING ASSUMPTIONS

BISEXUALS IN RELATIONSHIPS CONFRONT a unique problem that heteros and homos never face: we have to deal with our sexual identity being incorrectly perceived based on the sex of our partner. For example, a bisexual in a relationship with a member of the opposite sex will be perceived by the rest of the world as straight. A bisexual in a relationship with a member of the same sex will be considered gay. So basically, unless you're walking down the street arm in arm with a man and a woman in a triad, your relationship won't look bisexual, which is one of the many irritating realities we must tolerate. To deal with the assumptions of the rest of the world, and hey, on occasion we are guilty of them too, you have a few options.

The first option is to tell these assuming bastards that you go both ways. Correct them every chance you get. If they call you gay, tell them, "No, actually, I'm bi. And so's my partner," or whatever. Maybe your partner's straight or gay. No matter, just tell the truth. This will stupefy many who either can't wrap their pea-sized brains around the concept or just don't believe it exists. Plus, correcting people forces them to realize we aren't willing to chameleon-out and hide in either the straight or gay community just because it's easier. You'll feel better about yourself and be fighting the invisibility of our people at the same time.

On the other hand, correcting everybody can be freakin' exhausting. One bi activist friend of ours said that in his twenties he corrected everybody, from his coworkers to his neighbors. Now he's older and just doesn't give a crap what they think. He accepts their assumptions because he's sick of explaining himself to the rest of the world.

BI WITH A BOYFRIEND

"BI WITH A BOYFRIEND" gals usually veer more toward the straight side. Their sexual preference might be equal for men and women, but their emotional commitment usually tends toward the fellas. Many of them cannot envision themselves in a long-term relationship with a woman and feel fulfilled just dating or sleeping with women on the side (with their boyfriends' permission, of course). Some of them feel that if they settled down with a woman, it just wouldn't be enough for them. Something would be missing.

Not to say that many of them don't stray from their boyfriends once they begin to date women on the side. Remember: preferences are preferences, but women still fall in love with "the person."

"Bi with a boyfriend" guys sometimes veer more toward the gay side or are at least perceived that way. Many have had long-term relationships with women, but happen to find themselves settling down with a guy. They sometimes bring women or additional men into their relationships, and they usually don't have a problem avoiding falling in love with them. Other bi guys with boyfriends whose preference lies with men settle comfortably into a monogamous relationship without feeling like much is missing. It just depends on the person.

BI WITH A GIRLFRIEND

"BI WITH A GIRLFRIEND" gals often identify more with the queer community and don't mind being mistaken for lesbians. In fact, many of their girlfriends are gay. Though their preference might lie more with women (or maybe they just flip-flop a lot), these gals still aren't afraid to admit their bi-dom if they find themselves in the middle of a bi-phobic lesbian crowd. The only complication that may arise in these otherwise blissful unions emerges if the bi gal starts to crave a fella. If her female partner's bi, an arrangement might be possible, but for the most part women tend to get more jealous if their girlfriends stray. So if you find yourself bi with a girlfriend, craving the penis, be honest. Don't be another bisexual cliché and just take off!

"Bi with a girlfriend" guys may have strong sexual appetites for both but just happen to end up in a seemingly het relationship because of convenience. Some fulfill the bisexual cliché by cheating on their girlfriends with men. Others tell their women up front that they need to be allowed to enjoy sex with men on occasion, while some have a preference for women and have no problem being monogamous with them. "Bi with a girlfriend" guys who lean more toward the straight side very well might just want to make out with the occasional dude but don't necessarily want anything to do with his cock. As usual, it depends on the person.

BI SINGLE

BI SINGLES OR SERIAL daters often go out with men and women, but rarely end up in relationships with them. Some of them just can't find the right person. Others can't reconcile their desire for both, while a few have plain old intimacy issues. Bi singles sometimes find themselves frustrated with hanging at gay bars trying to meet the right man or woman or are tired of going on blind-date setups created by their helpful straight friends. Consequently, they may just prefer not to be tied down. Maybe they don't have time for a relationship because of their job or hobbies, or maybe they never feel like they have enough time for themselves. Either way, bi singles usually acquire plenty of dating and sexual experience over the years and have been with their fair share of straight, gay, and bi folks.

OPEN RELATIONSHIPS

A LOT OF MONOSEXUALS assume that bisexuals are capable of having only open relationships. This is untrue. Many of us happily maintain monogamous relationships. Others have open relationships because they define themselves as polyamorous, or lovers of many. As with everything, each bisexual must be taken on a case-by-case basis. No rash assumptions or generalizations can be made about bisexuals' ability to be monogamous or polyamorous. But as a bisexual, you might want to figure out which one you are and whether you will be content in an open or closed relationship.

WHAT IS POLYAMORY, AND WHY IS IT BI?

POLY IS THE OPPOSITE of *mono,* as in *monogamy.* It means many loves, or loving more than one in an emotional or sexual way. It doesn't always have to do with sex.

But often polyamory is what happens after you and your partner have a threesome or attend a sex party and like it a lot, enough to invite extra partners into your bedroom regularly and enough to consider trying to have a romantic relationship with new partners.

A lot of people who cheat on their partners are probably polyamorous and in denial. People who practice polyamory are honest about what they do and have agreements with their partners that permit them to get emotionally or sexually involved with other people. Not all poly people are bisexual, but many are. (For more poly lingo, see Chapter 1.)

QUIZ: AM I POLY?

1. In the past, I've had trouble staying faithful to people. T/F
2. I don't get jealous often. T/F
3. I've enjoyed each threesome/orgy I've had. T/F
4. I don't have many relationships. T/F
5. When I'm in a relationship with just a man or just a woman, I feel like something is missing. T/F
6. It's possible to be in love with more than one person at a time. T/F
7. I've never been a serial monogamist. T/F
8. Relationships feel smothering to me. T/F
9. Being involved with more than one person at a time is exhausting. T/F
10. Watching my partner with someone else turns me on. T/F

If you scored three or fewer "trues," chill out. You probably just have intimacy issues.

If you scored five or more "trues," solitary commitments aren't for you

If you scored eight or more "trues," you have poly tendencies.

DOES POLYAMORY = PROMISCUITY?

ABSOLUTELY NOT. PROMISCUITY IMPLIES someone who is indiscriminate, has low standards, and will sleep with almost anyone. Polyamorous individuals are often very discriminating, carefully choosing someone whom they want to welcome into their relationship as a third partner or a play partner. Polyamorous people have no problem saying no to partners whom they do not want to become involved with, and likewise have little to no problem being told no if someone does not want to start a relationship with them.

POLYAMORY TIPS

SO YOU AND YOUR partner want to go poly, eh? Well, here's a tip from a seasoned bi guy that you should heed: if you're in a relationship, you'd better be secure in your relationship. Your relationship will change. And not always in a predictable way. "Opportunities also bring risks," he warns. "It's quite possible to find yourself getting into a situation you just wish you hadn't." New relationships bring new obligations to whatever outsider you bring into your current relationship, and s/he could make demands on you that you never anticipated—regardless of the expectations the third party promised to have.

Sometimes you bring a third guy or gal into your bedroom who's sworn no strings attached, and—ta-da—that person falls in love with you. Or your partner falls in love with him/her and leaves you. Or you love the person, and your partner grows to hate him/her. See what we mean? Spicing things up is not always as simple as it seems. So how, you may ask, do my partner and I experiment with the poly lifestyle without screwing everything up?

A good rule of thumb is to communicate extensively with your partner beforehand, then communicate some more. Just when you think you've talked things through enough, talk some more. Make as many rules as you can to make each other feel comfortable. One rule might be that you or your partner does not see someone else without the consent of the other. Whatever you decide, rules like these will be crucial if/when things go awry with your new lover.

Also, polyamory can bring you and your lover closer because (if done responsibly) it promotes healthy communication. Having the freedom to tell your partner when you're attracted to another individual frees you from typical relationship guilt and possible cheating.

One bisexual interviewed said that he would recommend getting involved only with someone who already has a primary partner so that emotional expectations won't exist. Another recommendation from a bi person who knows is that it works best if you have sex with someone because you are friends and not someone who is your friend because you have sex. The intimacy and past history can sometimes be an advantage.

One final rule: there are no hard-and-fast rules.

DANGERS OF GOING POLY

EMOTIONAL

No one can predict how their relationship will change or whether he or she will want more intimacy than a couple will be willing to offer. For this reason, going poly can bring a lot of unpleasant emotions to the surface that no one involved expected to experience. But if bringing in a new partner breaks your relationship, stop calling yourself poly. Poly people can handle the complexities of multiple relationships.

MEDICAL

You must practice ultrasafe sex unless you have a death wish. (Pick up a copy of *The Ethical Slut* if you're unclear on this.) Sexually transmitted infections, including HIV, are no fun, and if you're going to play with multiple partners, you're exposing yourself to multiple STDs (unless you screen your partners beforehand, and even then they might have herpes or HPV [human papillomavirus] and not know it). Be careful!

JEALOUSY ISSUES

Face it: if you're a jealous person, you know it. One twenty-five-year-old bi friend of ours admitted that though she's had many threesomes, she's never had one with her boyfriend because she just couldn't handle it. She would be sick with jealousy, despite her own ability to be the guest star in other people's threesomes.

If you know you're a jealous person, for the love of god, don't have a threesome or group sex or anything that involves another person's penis or breasts dangerously near your partner. You're just not comfortable with it. And you know what? That's OK! Don't feel bad. It doesn't mean you're insecure or should push yourself into doing something that makes you feel uncomfortable. Accept your limitations.

On the other hand, Alt.com says, "Jealousy is neither a proof of love (and this is where polyamory differs from possessive or insecure monogamy) nor a moral failing (and this is where polyamory differs from emotionally manipulating one's partner into relationships for which they are not ready)." So jealousy can mean that you're unevolved, insecure, or perfectly normal. You choose.

Some people don't realize they're jealous people until they witness their partner moaning under the touch of another, and then they freak out. They end everything midorgy or, worse, bite their lip until after you've orgasmed to punish you for having such a damn good time with someone else. Unlike an unjealous lover, who gets turned on by your pleasure despite who's delivering it, a jealous lover feels as if he or she is watching their relationship disintegrate because their partner can experience pleasure from someone else.

POST-DAMAGE-CONTROL STRATEGIES

SO YOU SUCCEEDED IN having a sexual encounter with more than one other person in your bed. Congratulations! Too bad your partner freaked out and ruined everything. Here are some strategies on how to put out the fire.

- → send the guest star home with an apology (and, if they didn't get a chance to get off, your vibrator)
- → give your partner a Valium or a bong load until he/she calms down
- → draw your partner a bath and say you love him or her (if you do)
- → talk about why s/he freaked out and try to be sympathetic
- → if you decide to "try again," then create eight million rules beforehand
- → if your partner never wants to try again, say that's OK

MARRIED BISEXUALS

WHEN YOU ENTER INTO a monogamous marriage, be it heterosexual or not, the promise is not that you won't be attracted to other people; it's natural to be attracted to many people during your lifetime. The promise is that you won't act on it. If a married bisexual goes behind his or her partner's back to cheat, that's just as equally wrong as if a married nonbisexual cheats. Cheating is cheating. "I don't think extramarital relationships are something that bisexuals need any more than heterosexuals," said one committed bi friend of ours. "I know lots of monogamous married bisexuals." Another bisexual we know who is in an open relationship said that he absolutely believes that bisexuals need to have extramarital relationships to fulfill both sides of their nature. Like many things bisexual, there are two schools of thought on this subject.

Monogamy is popular for a reason: it simplifies things.

Concerning yourself primarily with one person's needs and desires is enough for many people. For many people, having concurrent relationships with more than one person at a time is exhausting and time consuming.

Open relationships are popular for a reason: you can act on your attractions without worrying too much about messing up your current relationship or hurting someone else. As long as you and your partner keep the honest communication flowing and your jealousy in check, you can maintain a life filled with sexual and emotional variety.

But what sort of bisexual are you? Poly or mono? There's only one way to find out. Take the quiz above.

I mean, I'm definitely gay in spirit and I probably could be bisexual. . . . [I]f I wouldn't have found Courtney, I probably would have carried on with a bisexual lifestyle.

—KURT COBAIN, *Advocate*, February 1992

THE CELIBATE BISEXUAL

IN ORDER FOR BISEXUALS in a monogamous marriage to be fulfilled, they must learn how to reconcile their desire for the gender they can no longer have. Bisexuals in these types of marriages must create ways to find sexual fulfillment with their partners through fantasies or role-playing (whatever floats their boats). Some get their kicks from watching gay movies or television, while others use kinky sex toys. They really have to play it by ear, but, most important, they have to respect their possibly straight or gay partner's request to have a purely monogamous relationship. Hey, all relationships require sacrifice!

Inevitably, there are many people who would say they are bisexual if they understood that you don't have to prove your bisexuality at every turn. You can still acknowledge being attracted to the opposite sex if you're in a gay relationship and vice versa. Many married people at some bi rap groups have said they know they're bi but have had sex only with the opposite sex.

THE BI CONTRACT

OK, YOU'VE FOUND SOMEONE willing to have a relationship with you, despite your bisexuality. Your partner has agreed to allow you the "freedom" to see other people. You've agreed to safe sex at all times. Now, let's hash out the specifics. We've designed a contract for you and your partner to fill out in order to outline the boundaries of your new privilege.

DEFINING THE PERSON YOU CAN SEE

Your partner permits you to go out with others, but what exactly are the parameters? Check one.

— If in a primary hetero relationship, you can see only one same-sex person on the side.
— If in a primarily homo relationship, you can only see one opposite sex person on the side.
— You can see anyone, anywhere, but only one time.
— You can't see anyone prettier/more handsome than the primary partner.
— Whatever.

FREQUENCY

You may spend _____ (1, 5, infinite) days/nights with the person per _____ (week, month, year). Now check all that apply below:

— You cannot miss important anniversaries/birthdays/family functions/dinners/kids' plays and so forth to

spend time with the outside relationship.
— The day/date must be specified in advance and not altered without prior approval.
— You can't have sex with him/her more often than with your primary partner.

INTIMACY

Just because you're allowed to go out doesn't mean you're allowed to go all the way. Make sure you're clear with your primary partner about what "dating" outside the relationship means to both of you. Check all that apply:

— You can go beyond first base, but no tongue.
— You can't see the other person naked, except via the Internet.
— You can go only to sex clubs/swingers groups that usually discourage long-term relationships and ensure safe-sex practices.
— You can do whatever you want, but you can't stay overnight or actually sleep in the other person's bed.
— If you stay over, you have to be home by breakfast the next morning.
— You can do whatever you want, but you must keep one foot firmly planted on the ground at all times (known as the "vertical rule" for bisexuals).

KNOWLEDGE

This is important to know before going out on the town. Check one:

— The primary partner wants to know NOTHING about the date or person.
— He/she wants to know where you went and what you did, but no sexual details.

— He/she wants to know EVERYTHING about the date
and the person, including what pleased you and especially
what displeased you.

Now check all that apply:

— You tell the third party that you'll never leave your
primary relationship.
— You are never allowed to bitch about the primary partner
to this third party.
— You are not allowed to have a key to the third party's
place.
— You are never to leave a toothbrush over at the other
person's bathroom.
— You are never to kiss the person hello or squeeze their
tush during chance meetings when out with your primary
partner.

MEETING THE OTHER

Make sure you know what your primary partner really wants to
know before you start gushing about your date.

— He/she wants to know absolutely nothing about the
other person, not even his or her name or gender. Refer
to the other person as "it" and your dates as "going to see a
man about a dog."
— He/she wants to know the gender, but only a fake name
or pseudonym just in case your primary partner has
hooked up with him or her too.
— He/she wants to have formal approval before you two get
intimate.
— He/she wants to "try the person out" first before you two
are allowed to get intimate. (This may mean only getting
medical tests in advance or obtaining measurements.)

— He/she is considering allowing the third party to move in or become a regular part of your relationship, putting the third party on more of an equal footing.

— The third party is allowed over to the house, but is to be referred to as "Uncle Bob" or "Crazy Aunt Sarah."

JUGGLING TWO LOVERS (BY MIKE)

IT'S NOT EASY TO be in love with a gal and a guy at the same time, even if you're honest with both, but there are ways to handle it. I had a yearlong experience dating both a guy and a girl; we all three worked at the same office, and even sat a few desks apart from each other. He was out as gay, she was very straight, and I wasn't out as anything. But he confronted me with my sexuality once—over beers at the nearby Veteran's bar—and I coyly admitted my curiosity. We became lovers, discreetly, although I was sure I still was heterosexual.

So, although I was sneaking off to his place to spend every other night there, when a new woman joined our staff, I was intrigued and asked her out. I remember when she first walked in for an interview, he and I both turned our heads. On our first date, she told me that she had an eight-year relationship with a woman and that now she was willing to give men a serious try. She identified wholly as hetero. I didn't say anything about my gay past. And so things developed sexually, and things got complicated. I told both of them about seeing the other. He said it was fine, because he was sure that I was only fooling myself by being with her. She was fine with it too, saying that she wasn't ready to commit to a serious relationship anyway. She figured that I would eventually want to settle for a "normal" relationship. They became fast friends, and I felt like there was sometimes a tug-of-war among us about whom I'd spend my free time with on weekends.

And then it got even more complicated. I found out that they were having sex with each other behind my back. He said he was surprised that he enjoyed it so much, and she was just as surprised. They still liked me, and just wanted to be casual about the whole thing. At first I was mad, but then a bit delighted. I thought that this might result in the three-way I'd always dreamed of: two people whom I loved so much sharing our lives together. That three-way never happened sexually, but in a spiritual way we were very much together.

We worked out a rather elaborate dating schedule: She and I had Friday nights together, he and she had Saturdays, and he and I went out to the gay bars on Sundays. And so Saturdays I stayed home alone (often thankful for a night of rest), wondering what the heck they were up to. I'd spend a lot of my Friday night's date asking her where he was going to take her the next night. Then I'd spend a lot of Sunday pumping him for info about whether he had slept with her the night before. Then they made the rule that we couldn't talk about the Missing Party during our dates.

We were a hip, progressive triad, even though it was among those wild Me-Decade days of the late '80s. We went to company functions together, the three of us; we danced together; we went on vacations together. Our mutual friends kept asking us how we could keep it going. We didn't have an answer; we just did. It felt right, no one was taking advantage of the others, and we communicated openly and honestly at all times—at least we tried to anyway.

We were all having safe sex with each other—that wasn't an issue—but on one of our joint outings, we all went to get our HIV tests together just to be sure. She, by the way, never had one of those tests before, and she had been the most unsafe of all of us in her past sexual activity.

I remember one time when the three of us walked through the woods all holding hands, and I was thinking that this was the best situation a bisexual could ever be in—hand in hand with two very cool, very smart, very creative lovers who just happened to be both a girl and a guy. I savored it, as complicated and odd as it seemed to the outside world.

Sadly, we never all three slept together. Well, we slept in tents on camping trips and big beds in hotel rooms and crashed altogether after drinking binges, but we never had sex together, no matter how much I encouraged it.

"Too weird," she'd say.

"Couldn't do it," he'd say.

Ultimately, each said they would feel left out in a sexual tryst. He's now in a very committed gay relationship, she's been married to a man for more than a decade, and I'm in a committed relationship with another bi guy. And ultimately, though, the two of them decided they didn't want me in the picture anymore, and they dumped me—the bisexual.

You have now completed Chapter 9. Remember that breathing technique we taught you at the end of Chapter 1? You might want to give that a shot right about now. We know it's unbearably anxiety provoking to ponder all these possibilities and how they might impact your ability to settle down. But just remember, you're not obligated to date multiple genders. You're just expected to. Don't ruin our good name.

CHAPTER 10

THE BEST OF BOTH WORLDS

CONGRATULATIONS! YOU'VE REACHED THE final chapter, and let us say, you have become one helluva bisexual. A model bisexual, in fact. Aside from surviving all of our sardonic quips, you've mastered the art of the flip-flop and now flow smoothly between gay and straight phases like a hyperevolved chameleon.

You've learned every failed acronym for our kind and mapped your own personal sexuality on the Klein grid. You've felt equally encouraged by the vast number of bisexual species in the animal kingdom and equally discouraged by the depressing bi stats about humankind. You understand why the bi community is nonexistent and have possibly pondered being as pissed off about that as we are.

You've come out to someone who (we hope) responded with consideration and have determined through honing your bidar the numbers of bisexuals in your midst. You've enhanced your collection of queer cinema and music, and possibly asked someone out successfully—all the while anticipating their possible aversion to your superior sexual orientation.

Heck, maybe you've even managed to squeeze in a fun little

threesome or a spanking—who knows? Bottom line: you know your tastes a little bit better. Here are a few bi slogans to add to your arsenal or your bumper.

BI SLOGANS

GIVEN THAT WE'RE PUSHING you out into that cruel, cold monosexual world, we thought we'd send you off with a few handy bi slogans to help you fend off ignorant comments from unknowing queers and breeders. But use with caution. Depending on the circumstances, some of them can get you either beat up or laid.

- I'm Bisexual, and I Don't Want to Sleep with You
- Been Either, Done Both!
- Two Roads Diverged in a Yellow Wood, and I Took Both
- Have Your Cake and Eat It Too
- Equal-Opportunity Lover
- I'll Be Your BiFriend
- VisiBIlity, PossiBIlity, What's in the Middle?
- Bi-Some, Double Your Pleasure
- Bisexuals Choose Love over Gender
- Ambi Am Me!
- Don't Fence Me In
- I Love Myself
- I'm Bi—Try to Change Me!
- Nurture Bi Nature
- Parts Is Parts
- There Are No Innocent Bi-Standers
- More than Curious
- We Don't BIte!
- Bilingual and Then Some!
- It's Just Not about, It's A Way of Life
- Mysexual
- Kiss Me Twice, I'm Bisexual

→ I'm Bisexual—You're Confused
→ My Mom Is Straight, but She Don't Hate
→ My Son Is Bi, I Don't Ask Why

SUCCESSFUL AND DUBIOUS MOMENTS IN BI HISTORY

BUCKLE UP, KIDS! YOU won't learn this in social studies. Though few in number, these political, inspiring, disappointing, and sometimes sexy moments in history constitute the closest thing we've got to a past. Here's a final history lesson to make sure you know where we've been and where we're headed . . .

7000 B.C. A horned bisexual African goddess is drawn on caves during the Neolithic period.

580 B.C. Sappho (yeah, yeah, we know she's the famous lesbo poet) has myriad love affairs with women, then falls for a ferryman named Phaon. The dude broke her heart and she leaped off a cliff to get over him. Talk about dyke drama.

338 B.C. Greece falls to the predominantly bisexual Macedonian society, led by fence-sitters Philip and Alexander the Great who divided and conquered the bi societies they ruled in more ways than one.

221 B.C. The Han dynasty features a succession of bisexual emperors who are persuaded and manipulated by female and male lovers seeking to gain favor.

6 B.C. Wall etchings from ancient Greece reveal an older man passing semen anally into a young boy to prepare him for procreation with a woman. There is a word for that practice in American culture today—*illegal.*

245 Philostratus the Younger writes a series of rhetorical love letters—half addressed to boys, half to girls. (They were never answered.)

900s (OR SO) Men declare their love for one another in

ancient Greece and Japan, and no one lifts an eyebrow, except, of course, the men.

994-1064 Muslim author and poet Ibn Hazm writes sultry tales of men pursuing saucy slave girls, sneaking in the occasional story about man-on-man love.

1020 Lady Murasaki writes *The Tale of Genji*, in which the bisexual Prince Genji is met with a chilly reception from a thirteen-year-old girl and thus falls for her brother instead. If only middle school love had been that easy.

1190 Philip II of France and Richard the Lion-Hearted of England share some hot and heavy nights together, despite their queens . . . oh, wait, maybe they were the queens.

1500-1571 Benvenuto Cellini, a violent artist and womanizer, shows his softer side (or some might say harder side) to adolescent male youths.

1600S The Japanese text *Great Mirror* by Saikaku features bisexual men demonstrating same-sex affection.

1603-1837 High-ranking samurai and shoguns frequently have same-sex affairs. Guess that whole "Don't ask, don't tell" policy wasn't in effect.

1611-1680 Li Yu, a Chinese erotic fiction author, writes two books—*The Golden Lotus* and *The Prayer Mat of Flesh*—featuring womanizing male leads who also seduce the male servants. That's why ancient linguists called them "the help."

1650 Bisexual king William III, ruler of the United Netherlands, is born. We know he was bisexual because one hostile critic fantasized about hanging him for his sexual activities or at least having Vice President Cheney "accidentally" shoot him.

1680 The second earl of Rochester, John Wilmot, dies, and his bisexual poem "The Disabled Debauchee" was published, but in life he was quite able-bodied.

1689 Aphra Behn, an English bisexual writer and erotic poet, died and was buried in Westminster Abbey. Her poems featured male and female subjects with kinky titles (well, kinky at the time) such as "To the Fair Clarinda, whom made love to me, imagin'd more than Woman." Yeah . . . a man.

1694-1778 François-Marie Arouet (a.k.a. Voltaire) writes King Frederick a hot love poem, dropping lines about Julius Caesar's bisexual conquests to try to get some action. But did he get laid?

1713-1784 Denis Diderot, bisexual encyclopedist and no stranger to bathhouses, depicts an erotic bisexual fantasy—a biblical scene in which Christ glances at a bridesmaid's bosom and Saint John's butt, but stays faithful to an apostle nonetheless. That Christ, quite the romantic.

1860 Abraham Lincoln sends romantic love letters to his alleged lover of four years, Joshua Speed, before tying the knot with wife Mary Todd and having four kids. Four score!

1905 Sigmund Freud calls bisexuality a "disposition" common to all humans in his *Three Essays on the Theory of Sexuality*. Freud says everyone has a masculine and a feminine side and that each side is heterosexually attracted to members of the opposite sex, but most people repress one side or the other. Duh!

1906 French novelist Sidonie-Gabrielle Colette kisses her cross-dressing girlfriend and mimics copulation with her, scandalizing the Moulin Rouge. Bravo.

1921 The Bloomsbury group, a collective of bisexual braniacs and artists, forms. Members such as Virginia Woolf, E. M. Forster, and surrealist painter Dora Carrington swap spouses and enjoy bisexual relationships.

1929 Anaïs Nin, an erotic writer, begins a heated love triangle with Henry Miller and his wife, June. Mexican painter

Frida Kahlo marries Diego Rivera and cheats on him with both men and women (he deserved it!). Movie star Greta Garbo leaves her male fiancé at the altar, undoubtedly remembering all those hot nights with socialite Mercedes de Acosta Reynal and actress Louise Brooks.

1932 Eleanor Roosevelt falls for Associated Press reporter Lorena Hickok, who penned the first lady love letters that surfaced in 1978.

1948 Sex researcher Alfred Kinsey develops a seven-point scale showing various degrees of sexuality and conceals his own bisexuality along the way. Wimp.

1950 Formation of the first gay organization, the Mattachine Society. Members include bisexual men and women.

1968 Bisexuals are depicted as "swingers" on television's *Laugh-In* and in *Mad* magazine and other mainstream media. Fortunately, Alfred E. Newman remained in the closet.

1975 First bi newsletter, the *Bisexual Expression*, is published in New York, to little fanfare.

1976 San Francisco Bisexual Center is co-founded by Maggi Rubenstein and Harriet Levy. It closes in 1984 as a result of the AIDS epidemic and bi- and homophobia. (Notice how we ran out of jokes?)

1980 Dr. Fritz Klein publishes the Klein Sexual Orientation Grid, which improves upon Kinsey's scale by adding fantasy, desires, and behavior to help confused bisexuals figure out who the hell they are.

1984 Bisexual men are officially recognized in AIDS statistics, forcing health-care providers to admit that they exist, if not solely to spread disease. 1987 *Newsweek* calls bisexuals "ultimate pariahs" for spreading AIDS, and the then-biggest National March on Washington for Lesbian and Gay Rights in history attracts a nationwide bisexual contingent. Seventy-five people turn up. The first Jack-and-Jill-Off Party with bisexual safe sex is thrown in San Francisco by Dolores Bishop and Janet Taylor —Bi political group BiPOL forms in San Francisco, spawning BiCEP in Boston and BiPAC in Manhattan in 1989. Er, we get the first acronym, but really what were they flexing out in Boston? And BiPAC . . . was that some reference to college sports?

1988 Gary North of Long Beach, California, publishes the first national bi newsletter, *Bisexuality: News, Views and Networking,* and sets up a twenty-four-hour hotline. Was it ever.

1989 Openly bisexual Army vet Cliff Arnesen, who was dishonorably discharged because of his sexuality, becomes the first nonhetero veteran to testify before the U.S. Congress Subcommittee on GLB Veteran Health Issues. His discharge was subsequently changed to "honorable" and he later became the president of the New England Gay and Lesbian Veterans. Drop and give us twenty!

1990 First U.S. National Bisexual Conference takes place in San Francisco with eighty workshops and 465 attendees from 20 states and five countries, sparking regional and national conferences to remind bisexuals (or at least hotel bellboys) everywhere that we do exist. The network that formed here became BiNet USA within two years.

1991 The First International Conference on Bisexuality attracts about 250 people from nine countries at Vrije University in Amsterdam, establishing a biannual tradition spurred either by the potent bubblegum weed or by the red-light district.

1992 Sheela Lambert writes, produces, and hosts the first television series by and for the bi community. *Bisexual Network* successfully airs for thirteen weeks on a New York City public-access station.

1993 Lani Ka'ahumanu is the only bi person to speak at the National March on Washington for Lesbian, Gay and Bisexual Equal Rights and Liberation. She was also the last person to speak, and her allotted five-minute time period was cut short.

1995 Social critic, author, and teacher Camille Paglia announces, "Bisexuality should be the universal norm."

1996 *Newsweek* once again puts bisexuality on its cover— this time managing not to offend bisexuals everywhere. Representative Bob Dornan reacts, saying bisexuals are "a direct frontal assault upon every moral code in this country" and are "groping around like alley cats at any drug infested party [they] can go to." Yeah, we wish.

1999 Fritz Klein creates the American Institute of Bisexuality, a.k.a. the Bisexual Foundation, a.k.a. Bisexuality's Jedi Council.

2002 BiNet USA makes an attempt to raise money to get a jump start on its overseeing organization and fund-raising. When goals aren't met, activists try to decide whether to keep the organization going. No decision is made, except the realization that organizing bisexuals is about as fun as herding cats.

2003 Headlines in London scream "Is Prince Charles Bisexual?" as a quickly quieted rumor erupts about his trysts with the help. (He must have taken those Li Yu novels to heart.)

2004 As the Michael Jackson molestation charges develop, bi activists cross their fingers and pray that he won't describe himself as "bisexual."

2005 The *New York Times* publishes "Straight, Gay or Lying? Bisexuality Revisited," the largest work of fiction since reporter Jayson Blair was outed for plagiarism. Oh, wait, where did he work again?

2006 Bi activists try to get the media to call the cowboys "bisexual" rather than gay in *Brokeback Mountain*, and in a short time frame, scramble to find real-life bi cowboys as examples for Oscar day. They didn't find any, but managed to persuade some members of the media to call the two main characters bisexual.

Don't be alarmed if it looks like little progress has been made, because you're right. Though we've enjoyed some trendy moments in the press, we can't help but wonder whether we'll grab headlines merely in waves. Allegedly, we're experiencing a bisexual moment right now, but then again, that might just be because we're writing a book. But some argue that between Generation Y finally coming of age and fully accepting queerdom to the point of ditching labels altogether and Massachusetts legalizing gay marriage, an upswing has begun. Hey, we're bound to establish our existence universally eventually and finally gain the recognition we've desired. But do we really need that acknowledgment and approval in order to love whom we love? Nah, we don't think so either.

BI-NAL EXAM

1. Bisexuals are . . .
   a. really straight
   b. really gay
   c. always confused
   d. more evolved than straight and gay people

2. Bisexuality can be defined as . . .
   a. always being equally attracted to both sexes
   b. promiscuity
   c. whatever the hell I want to define it as
   d. having two penises

3. Polymorphous perversity is . . .
   a. a new gay play about bi's with a lot of nudity
   b. what Jerry Falwell's followers call the bi movement
   c. something Freud came up with to justify bisexuality
   d. a social club where you should be afraid to shake each other's hands

4. A great way to fulfill the bi stereotype is to . . .
   a. deny that you're gay, then actually be gay
   b. have unsafe sex with everybody and give your friends herpes
   c. cheat on your spouse
   d. all of the above

5. The most popular bisexual slur is . . .
   a. fence-sitter
   b. switch-hitter
   c. AC/DC
   d. Who bothers shouting slurs at bisexuals? They don't exist.

6. If you want to turn off lesbians . . .
   a. tell them how much you like riding stick
   b. tell them you can't wait to get married . . . to a guy
   c. tell them you're bisexual
   d. tell them you hate cats

7. Bisexuals have . . .
   a. one virginity
   b. two virginities
   c. three virginities
   d. bisexuals are never virgins

8. A good argument to use when trying to prove the existence of bisexuality is . . .
    a. the Kinsey scale
    b. the "Sex Difference in Sexual Arousal" study
    c. Andy Dick
    d. you're going to need to use every argument you can think of; people are stupid

9. You're not allowed to be bisexual if . . .
    a. you're into designer drugs
    b. you have breast implants
    c. you're a Republican who has breast implants
    d. all of the above

10. According to a 2004 federal study, this many men are bisexual . . .
    a. 1 million
    b. 10 million
    c. 6 million
    d. none

11. The grossest bisexual creature is . . .
    a. yeast
    b. bedbugs
    c. seagulls
    d. gee, those are all pretty nasty

12. Bisexuality has been documented historically since . . .
    a. 7000 BC
    b. 1776
    c. 1969
    d. the existence of *Newsweek*

13. The professional bisexual . . .
    a. is someone who makes money for being bisexual
    b. is your best friend in a fight with a dumb straight/gay person
    c. makes up too many words
    d. all of the above

14. "Support-group backlash" occurs after . . .
    a. you make the mistake of riding in a car with bisexuals
    b. you get creeped out by the nut case talking about his penis
    c. you know what a "boi" is
    d. you get into S&M

15. At bisexual conferences you will find . . .
    a. men in dresses
    b. women with facial hair
    c. cool workshops
    d. all of the above

16. The bisexual actress who said "I always play women I would date" was . . .
    a. Drew Barrymore
    b. Angelina Jolie
    c. Greta Garbo
    d. Mia Kirshner

17. The oldest bisexual movie you are expected to have seen is . . .
    a. *The Rocky Horror Picture Show*
    b. *Jules and Jim*
    c. *Henry and June*
    d. *Chasing Amy*

18. The following straight actress who should never play bisexual again is . . .
    a. Jennifer Lopez
    b. Sarah Michelle Gellar
    c. Rebecca Romijn
    d. actually, none of these actresses should ever play bi again

19. The character of C. J. from _____ initiated the historic first same-sex kiss on network television.
    a. *Roseanne*
    b. *Sex and the City*
    c. *L.A. Law*
    d. *Ally McBeal*

20. What pop star is closeted in the U.S., but out in the U.K.?
    a. Britney Spears
    b. Pink
    c. Christina Aguilera
    d. Hillary Duff

21. The most well-known bisexual president was . . .
    a. George Washington
    b. Richard Nixon
    c. Abraham Lincoln
    d. Bill Clinton

22. The easiest way for bi women to meet other women at a club is to . . .
    a. bring a group of friends
    b. hang at the bar
    c. smoke outside the club
    d. grind on the dance floor

23. A guest star in a threesome situation should always be . . .
    a. attractive
    b. emotionally mature
    c. a good communicator
    d. all of the above

24. The safest material to use to tie up your lover is . . .
    a. ankle/wrist cuffs
    b. scarves
    c. handcuffs
    d. rope

25. Polyamory can be defined as . . .
    a. promiscuity
    b. what Mormons in Utah do
    c. loving more than one in an emotional or sexual way
    d. only for bisexuals

26. Married bisexuals . . .
    a. are shit out of luck
    b. are bored
    c. are cheaters
    d. often explore their bi side with permission from their partners

27. The only openly bi actor(s) on *The L Word* is . . .
    a. Kate Moennig
    b. Laurel Holloman
    c. Daniela Sea
    d. Both A and B
    e. Both A and C

28. Threesomes usually backfire because . . .
    a. ground rules aren't set beforehand
    b. the guest star wants a relationship
    c. someone gets jealous
    d. all of the above

29. The worst thing to be at a S&M party is . . .
    a. obnoxious
    b. horny
    c. an energy vampire
    d. a virgin

30. If you're capable of being in love with more than one
    person at a time that makes you . . .
    a. bisexual
    b. dysfunctional
    c. polyamorous
    d. a human being

ANSWER KEY

1. D	2. C	3. C	4. D	5. A
6. C	7. B	8. D	9. D	10. C
11. D	12. A	13. D	14. B	15. D
16. B	17. B	18. D	19. C	20. C
21. C	22. A	23. D	24. A	25. C
26. D	27. B	28. D	29. C (or D)	30. D

WELCOME TO THE CLUB

CONGRATULATIONS! YOU ARE NOW as officially bisexual as you
were when you first picked up this book. Even if you've chosen
not to adopt the B-word, at least now you have the confidence of
knowing you've mastered something crucial— the ins and outs
of the most complex sexual orientation on the planet, OK, the
universe.

Not to wax philosophical, but bisexuality is the only sexual identity that requires complete self-identification. If we didn't open our mouths, no one would know we exist. We would truly look invisible. Whether you use the B-word or not, people are probably not going to get it. And because it's a word that most people don't use, if you do comfortably use the B-word to label yourself, you're a distinct minority within the gay community and society at large. If everyone truly is bisexual, then bisexuals are the only group that's considered a minority but in actuality is a silent majority.

There are no blood tests, urine samples, IQ quizzes, or talent contests that can test for it, and you get no special cards, embossed certificates, or decorative trophies that show you've joined. There are no identifying haircuts, clothing, tattoos, special handshakes, or even agreed-upon colors or symbols that denote a member.

It is one of the most vilified, misunderstood, and misappropriated terms. It's a word that sets people's teeth on edge, or elicits giggles or, at the very minimum, a raised eyebrow.

And so, since you've made it through this book, we're breaking through all the hogwash and gobbledygook and misunderstandings and declaring you a "100 Percent Certified Bisexual." It doesn't even matter if you didn't read the whole book, and yes, that even includes you who are just flipping through it at the bookstore, or you who happened to sneak it off a friend's shelf. You're all "100 Percent Certified Bisexuals" too.

See how easy it is? It doesn't require years of angst. It doesn't require trying one sex and then the other and comparison shopping. It doesn't require therapy or Prozac. Actually, all it requires is understanding. By now, if you haven't fled the store or burned the book, you've acquired some understanding, and thus have passed our test.

Bisexuality isn't a lifestyle. It's not a code word for a secret society. It's not even a way to be cool anymore. It's an identity, and until we're OK to claim the identity with whatever language or lingo we deem fit, we will remain invisible. So try it out—come on, say it: "Bi-sex-u-al, Bi-sex-u-al." Feel how it rolls off the tongue. (Yeah, we know, the second syllable is sometimes hard to get out.) But now try it louder: "Bi-sex-u-al, Bi-sex-u-al!" Shout it out—come on, SHOUT IT! "Bi-sex-u-al, Bi-sex-u-al!"

So what if you sound like a cult member doing a voodoo sex ritual? So what if you've come out to the old lady next door who just heard you yelling through those paper-thin walls, or your dog, who perked up his ears for a moment? Well, it's a start anyway.

Welcome to the club.

RESOURCES

WEB SITES

THE BISEXUAL'S GUIDE TO THE UNIVERSE
www.guidebi.com; www.myspace.com/bisexualsguide
More about the book, signings, and more rants from
Nicole and Mike

BI SQUISH
www.bisquish.com
Daily news about bi issues

BICAFE
www.bicafe.com
For personal ads, interactions, chats and resources

BIMAGAZINE
www.bimagazine.org
Articles, interviews, fiction, poetry, reviews, and more

BINET USA
www.binetusa.org
The national bi activist umbrella organization

BISEXUAL.ORG

www.bisexual.org

For meeting up, chats, information and articles, founded by the American Institute of Bisexuality and the late Dr. Fritz Klein

BISEXUAL RESOURCE CENTER

www.biresource.org

For articles, email lists, movies, publications, groups, research surveys

GAY AND LESBIAN ALLIANCE AGAINST DEFAMATION (GLAAD)

www.glaad.org

Dedicated for promoting and ensuring fair, accurate, and inclusive representation of LGBT people

GAY, LESBIAN AND STRAIGHT EDUCATION NETWORK (GLSEN)

www.glsen.org

National education organization focused on ensuring safe schools for all students

NATIONAL GAY AND LESBIAN TASK FORCE

www.thetaskforce.org

The first LGBT civil rights and advocacy organization, direct and grassroots lobbying

THE NEW YORK AREA BISEXUAL NETWORK (NYABN)

www.nyabn.org

Also see their companion site, www.bialogue.org, for resource and media guides and info packets

PARENTS, FAMILY AND FRIENDS OF LESBIANS AND GAYS (PFLAG)

www.pflag.org

MUSIC

ANI DIFRANCO
www.righteousbabe.com

BI RADIO
radio.bisexual.com

SKOTT FREEDMAN
www.skottfreedman.com

MAGDALEN HSU-LI
www.magdalenhsuli.com

NICOLE KRISTAL
www.nicolekristal.com

PEACHES
www.peachesrocks.com

TOM ROBINSON
www.tomrobinson.com

BOOKS

Bi America, by Bill Burleson. Haworth Press, 2005

Bi Any Other Name, edited by Loraine Hutchins and Lani Kaahumanu. Alyson Books, 1991

Bisexual and Gay Husbands: Their Stories, Their Words, edited by Fritz Klein, Thomas Schwartz. Haworth Press, 2002

Bisexual Characters in Film: From Anaïs to Zee, by Wayne Bryant. Haworth Press, 1997

The Bisexual Option, by Fritz Klein. Haworth Press, 1993

Bisexuality and HIV/AIDS: A Global Perspective, edited by Rob Tielman, Manuel Carballo, Aart Hendriks. Prometheus Books, 1991

Bisexuality and the Challenge to Lesbian Politics: Sex, Loyalty, and Revolution, by Paula Rust. New York University Press, 1995

Bisexuality in the Lives of Men, edited by Brett Beemyn, Erich W. Steinman. Harrington Park Press, 2000

Bisexuality in the United States, by Paula C. Rodriguez Rust. Columbia University Press, 1999

Blessed Bi Spirit: Bisexual People of Faith, edited by Debra Ruth Kolodny. Continuum International, 2000

Box Lunch: The Layperson's Guide to Cunnilingus, by Diana Cage. Alyson Books, 2004

Current Research on Bisexuality, by Ronald C. Fox. Harrington Park Press, 2004

Dual Attraction: Understanding Bisexuality, by Martin Weinberg, Collin J. Williams, Douglas W. Pryor. Oxford University Press, 1999

The Ethical Slut: A Guide to Infinite Sexual Possibilities, by Dossie Easton and Catherine A. Liszt. Greenery Press, 1998

Exhibitionism for the Shy: Show Off, Dress Up and Talk Hot, by

Carol Queen. Down There Press, 1995

Freaks Talk Back: Tabloid Talk Shows and Sexual Nonconformity, by Joshua Gamson. University of Chicago Press, May 1998

Genderflex: Sexy Stories on the Edge and In Between, edited by Celia Tan. Circlet Press, 1996

Getting Bi: Voices of Bisexuals Around the World. Edited by Robyn Ochs and Sarah Rowley. Bisexual Resources Center, 2005

Going Down: The Instinct Guide to Oral Sex, by Ben R. Rogers and Joel Perry. Alyson, 2002

Hollywood Hardcore Diaries: Erotic Tales from a Porn Reporter, by Mickey Skee. Companion Press, 1999

Life, Sex, and the Pursuit of Happiness, by Fritz Klein. Harrington Park Press, 2005

The Other Side of the Closet: The Coming-Out Crisis for Straight Spouses and Families, by Amity Pierce Buxton. Wiley, 1994

Sleeping Under the Stars, by Geoffrey Karen Dior. Beside Press, 2002

The Straight Girl's Guide to Sleeping with Chicks, by Jen Sincero. Fireside, 2005

Vice Versa: Bisexuality and the Eroticism of Everyday Life, by Marjorie Garber. Simon & Schuster, 1996

A Woman Like That: Lesbian and Bisexual Writers Tell Their Coming Out Stories, edited by Joan Larkin. Harper, 2000

NOTES

CHAPTER 1

p. 10. The B-word. From Nicole's article "Bi Ourselves," *Flux* (spring 1998).

p. 10. "Attraction to both sexes." Online Etymology Dictionary, s.v. "bisexuality." http://www.etymonline.com/index. php?l=b&p=10.

p. 10. "By nature." Sarah Harrison, Skye Tyler, Andy Duncan, David Diehl, and Gwynne Watkins, "From Zeus to Mischa Barton: A Bisexual Timeline," Nerve.com, 2005. http://www.nerve.com/ regulars/quickies/bitimeline/.

p. 10. . . . ever since. Online Etymology Dictionary, s.v. "bisexuality."

p. 11. "Blithering idiot." Ibid.

p. 11–12. "Bisexual by definition." Senator Don Nickles, ENDA debate in U.S. Senate, September 10, 1996, http://www. religioustolerance.org.

CHAPTER 3

p. 25. Zogby poll. "Gay Survey Returns Surprising Results," UPI, February 6, 2006.

p. 25. 2006 study. Dr. Richard Lippa, "California State University Study," Psychological Science, February 2006.

p. 25. 33 percent. Ronald C. Fox, Coming Out Bisexual: Identity,

Behavior, and Sexual Orientation Self-Disclosure, California Institute of Integral Studies, November 1992.

p. 29. *Genre* gay survey. Ronald Mark Kraft, "Carnal Knowledge: The Sex Survey Results Are In!" *Genre*, October 24, 2001, 78.

p. 62. Robert A. Wallace, *How They Do It* (New York: William Morrow, 1980).

CHAPTER 5

p. 64. Adams. Interview by Mike for *IN LA*, Le Meridien Hotel, Beverly Hills, April 1997.

p. 64–65. Ibid.

p. 64. Fell in love. Ross Alexander and James Spada, *Bette Davis: More than a Woman* (New York: Time Warner, 2005).

p. 64. Araki. Interview by Mike for Knight-Ridder/Tribune Syndicate, Four Seasons Hotel, Toronto, September 10, 2005.

p. 64. Baldwin. Interview by Mike for *US Magazine*, Directors Guild of America, Hollywood, April 29, 1993.

p. 65. Bardem. Interview by Mike for Zap2it.com, Beverly Regent Hotel, December 13, 2004.

p. 65. Beals. *Advocate*, January 31, 2006.

p. 65. Bernhard. "Call Her Sandy: An Interview with Sandra Bernhard," *Advocate*, December 15, 1992; Bernhard, interview by Mike for PlanetOut, Sheraton Hotel, Toronto, September 11, 1997.

p. 65. Bon Jovi. Interview by Mike, "Psssst!," *Real People*, Continental Hotel, Toronto, September 6, 1996.

p. 67. Burrows. *Scotsman*, August 2000.

p. 67. Campbell. Interview by Mike for Knight-Ridder/Tribune Syndicate, Continental Hotel, Toronto, September 9, 2005.

p. 67. "I've never had." Mike Szymanski, "Laughing Out Load with the 'Notorious C.H.O.'—Funny Girl, Margaret Cho," June 28, 2002, Zap2it.com.

p. 67. Clooney. http://www.findarticles.com/p/articles/mi_m1589/is_2005_Dec_20/ai_n15980378.

p. 67. Collins. Interview by Mike for *Genre*, Los Angeles City Hall, June 1993.

p. 67. Cuaron. Interview by Mike for Hollywood.com, MPRM, Los Angeles, March 2006.

p. 67. Christopher Stone. "Alan Cumming: Unlikely, but Willing Bisexual Sex Symbol," AfterElton.com, July 6, 2005, http://www.afterelton.com/people/2005/7/alancumming.html; Cumming, interview by Mike for Zap2it.com, Pasadena, February 16, 2005.

p. 69. James Dean. See Paul Alexander, *Boulevard of Broken Dreams: The Life, the Times and the Legend of James Dean* (New York: Viking Press, 1997).

p. 69. De Matteo. *British Sport Daily*, February 2002.

p. 70. Dietrich. http://www.crazy4cinema.com/Actress/Marlene.html and http://www.glbtq.com/arts/dietrich_m.html.

p. 70. See "Reintroducing Robert Downey Jr.," *Detour*, February 1999.

p. 70. DuVall. Interview by Mike for *IN*, Four Seasons Hotel, Toronto, September 6, 1999.

p. 71. Electra. *Loaded* (London), February 2006; Electra, *Bunte* (Germany), March 30, 2004.

p. 71. Etheridge. "Deep Dish," *FAB* (West Hollywood), December 23, 1999.

p. 71. Farrell. Mike Szymanski, "Colin Talks about Playing Bisexual," *Advocate*, September 14, 2004.

p. 71. Boze Hadleigh, Errol Flynn. *The Vinyl Closet* (New York: Les Hombres Press, 1991).

p. 72. "Some People." See Gerald Clarke, *Get Happy: The Life of Judy Garland* (New York: Dell, 2000).

p. 72. Boy George. *Details*, June 1997.

p. 72. "Dykon," Alonso Duralde, "Simply Irresistible: Gina Gershon," *Advocate*, September 30, 2003.

p. 72. Cary Grant. See Boze Hadleigh, *Hollywood Gays*, (Fort Lee, N.J.: Barricade Books, 1996).

p. 72. "I want to represent." "L Is for Leisha," *Advocate*, February 2004.

p. 73. Hayek. Interview by Mike for Zap2it.com, Four Seasons, Toronto, September 7, 2002.

p. 73. Heche. Interview by Mike for Zap2it.com, Four Seasons, Beverly Hills, February 22, 2002. See also http://en.wikipedia.org/Anne_Heche

p. 73. "Really bisexual." Jeff Yarbrough, "Hugh Hefner," *Advocate*, March 8, 1994.

p. 73. Paris Hilton. See Wikipedia, s.v. "Paris Hilton," http://en.wikipedia.org/wiki/Paris_Hilton. Http://www.callingparis.com contains the cell phone photos.

p.74. Iggy Pop. See Jane Rocca, "Age Won't Wear Iggy," *The Age* (Sydney), November 5, 2003.

p. X. Iman. Interview by Mike for *US Magazine*, Melrose Art Gallery, Los Angeles, November 1996.

p. 74. Irvin. Interview by Mike for *Frontiers*, Ma Maison, February 21, 2004.

p. 74. Lane Janger. Szymanski, "Wanting to Try It 'Just One Time,'" interview by Mike for Zap2it.com, Santa Monica, California, April 1, 2001.

p 75–76.. Angelina Jolie. The *Jane* and *Elle* quotes came from the article "Angelina, Saint vs. Sinner," by Julian Kesner and Michelle Megna, *New York Daily News*, February 2, 2006; interview by Mike for *Entertainment Weekly*, Screen Actors Guild Awards, April 1999; interview by Mike for Knight-Ridder/Tribune Syndicate, Century Plaza Hotel, Century City, California, April 1999. Also see http://www.afterellen.com/People/Jolie.html.

p. 76 . Jordan. Interviewed by Mike at the Toronto Film Festival, September 12, 2005.

p. 76 . Kidder. Interviewed by Mike for *Entertainment Weekly*, Hotel Nikko, Beverly Hills, November 17, 1997.

p. 76. Mia Kirsher. NancyAmazon, The L Word online, "Frequently Asked Questions," http://www.thelwordonline.com/l_faq.html.

p. 76. "I swing both ways." Boze Hadleigh, "Interview with Miss Hathaway," *Gay & Lesbian Times Desert*, February 1989.

p. 77. "I have dated." Tim Nassen, "Kristanna Loken Headlines Dyke-Friendly New Film, *BloodRayne*," *Curve*, February 2006.

p. 77. "I'm all for anything." Szymanski, "Having It Both Ways," *Los Angeles Times*, July 20, 1997.

p. 77. Madonna. Interviewed by Mike for *Genre*, Ritz Plaza, New York City, May 1993.

p. 77. Malone. Interviewed by Mike for Zap2it.com, Four Seasons Hotel, Beverly Hills, May 17, 2004.

p. 78. McDormand. Interviewed by Mike for Zap2it.com, Toronto, September 13, 2003.

p. 78. McDowell. Interviewed by Mike for the *Los Angeles Times*, Hollywood Galaxy Theatre premiere, July 2, 1993.

p. 78. "Don't wear a dress." Boze Hadleigh, *Conversations with My Elders*, excerpted in *FAB!* November 2002.

p. 78. Morrissey, *OUT*, November 8, 2005.

p. 79. Mullally, *Advocate*, November 23, 1999.

p. 79. Ndegeocello, *Los Angeles Weekly*, September 18, 1999.

p. 79. Spoto. *Sir Laurence Olivier.* (Cooper Square Press, 2001).

p. 79. Perkins. http://www.reference.com/browse/wiki/Anthony_Perkins.

p. 78. Phoenix. Interview by Mike in Toronto for *Genre*, February 1994; Friend, "River with Love and Anger," *Esquire*, March 1994.

p. 80. Pink, *Q Magazine*, February 2004.

p. 80. Victoria Price, *Vincent Price: A Daughter's Biography* (New York: St. Martin's Press, 2000).

p. 80. Cherry. Interviewed by Mike for Hollywood.com, Outfest, Directors Guild of America, Hollywood, June 12, 2005.

p. 80. Queen Latifah. Interviewed by Mike for SciFi.com, Four Seasons Hotel, Beverly Hills, March 22, 2006.

p. 80. Queen Penn. Dmitri Ehrlich, "Hard Rhymes for Hard Times," interview, February 1998.

p. 80-81. Reeves. Interviewed by Mike for PopcornQ, July 22, 1997. http://aolhometown.planetout.com/popcornq/movienews/97/08/22/new_bi_hits_hollywood.html.

p. 81. "I like men." "Olé! Gabriel," *Advocate*, March 27, 2001.

p. 81. "Yes, I have done that." "Roseanne Bares All," *Advocate*, March 12, 1991.

p. 81. Sarandon. Interviewed by Mike for Zap2it.com, Park Hyatt Hotel, Toronto.

p. 81. Schickner. Interviewed by Mike for the *Los Angeles Times*, July 8, 1993.

p. 81. Sevigny. Interviewed at Oscars for PlanetOut.com, http://www.planetout.com/people/columns/szymanski/archive/20000420.html.

p. 82. Springfield. http://www.dustyspringfield.co.uk.

p. 82. Sting. Interviewed by Mike for *Real People Magazine*, Park Hyatt Hotel, Toronto, September 1995.

p. 82. Stipe. Interviewed for Zap2it.com, Four Seasons Hotel, Beverly Hills, May 17, 2004, .

p. 82. Stole. Interviewed for Zap2it.com, Mondrian Hotel, West Hollywood, August 16, 2005.

p. 82. Tilly. Interviewed by Mike for Mr. Showbiz.com, June 1996.

p. 82. "It's hard to label." Owen Keehnen, "A Broadway Tune: A Halloween Visit with Tommy Tune," March 1997, http://www.glbtq.com/sfeatures/interviewttune.html.

p. 83. Rudolph Valentino. See GLBTQ Culture, http://www.glbtq.com/arts/valentino_r.html.

p. 83. Wilson, *Howard Stern Radio Show*, July 26, 2005.

p. 83. Lawless. Telephone interview by Mike for SciFi.com, March 11, 2006.

p. 83. York. Interviewed by Mike for Zap2it.com, Four Seasons Hotel, Beverly Hills, July 12, 2002.

p. 97. Parker. Interviewed by Mike at his office, West Hollywood, October 3, 1997.

p. 97. "We should all support." Eighth GLAAD Media Awards, Century Plaza Hotel, Century City, California, February 4, 1997.

CHAPTER 8

p. 180. Jen Sincero, *The Straight Girl's Guide to Sleeping with Chicks* (New York: Fireside, 2005).

p. 181. Jamie Goddard and Kurt Brungardt, *Lesbian Sex Secrets for Men: What Every Man Wants to Know about Making Love to a Woman and Never Asks* (New York: Plume, 2000).

p. 181. Dan Anderson and Maggie Berman, *Sex Tips for Straight Women from a Gay Man* (New York: HarperCollins, 1997).

p. 181. Dossie Easton and Catherine A. Liszt, *The Ethical Slut: A Guide to Infinite Sexual Possibilities* (Oakland: Greenery Press, 1998).

p. 181. Diana Cage, *Box Lunch: The Layperson's Guide to Cunnilingus* (Los Angeles: Alyson Books, 2004).

p. 181. Ben R. Rogers and Joel Perry, *Going Down: The Instinct Guide to Oral Sex* (Los Angeles: Alyson Books, 2002).

p. 182. Carol Queen, *Exhibitionism for the Shy: Show Off, Dress Up, and Talk Hot* (San Francisco: Down There Press, 1995).

p. 182. Dossie Easton and Catherine A. Lizst, *The Bottoming Book: How to Get Terrible Things Done to You by Wonderful People* and *The Topping Book; or, Getting Good at Being Bad* (Oakland: Greenery Press, 1998).

p. 183. "A honed bisexual." Mickey Skee, *Bad Boys on Video*, vols. 1-3 (Los Angeles: Companion Press, 2003).

CHAPTER 10

p. 225. The Mystica: An Online Encyclopedia of the Occult, Mysticism, and Magic, s.v. "The Goddess—I, Introduction and History," http://www.themystica.com/mystica/articles/g/goddess_1_intro_and_history.html.

p. 225. Sappho. Harrison et al., "From Zeus to Barton."

p. 225. Green falls. Louis Crompton, *Homosexuality and Civilization* (Cambridge, Mass.: Belknap Press, 2006), 150.

p. 225. The Han Dynasty. Ibid., 217–18.

p. 226. Muslim author. Ibid., 164.

p. 226. Lady Murasaki. Ibid., 415.

p. 226. Phillip II. Harrison et al., "From Zeus to Barton."

p. 226. Benvenuto Celliini. Crompton, *Homosexuality and Civilization*, 281.

p. 226. The Japanese text. Ibid., 438.

p. 226. High-ranking samurai. Ibid., 439.

p. 226. Li-Yu. Ibid., 231.

p. 226. The second earl of Rochester. Ibid., 396.

p. 227. Aphra Behn. Ibid., 401.

p. 227. François-Marie Arouet. Ibid., 505.

p. 227 Denis Diderot. Ibid., 522.

p. 227. Abraham Lincoln. Tripp, *Intimate World of Lincoln*, 19, 209–25.

p. 227. Sigmund Feud. Harrison et al., "From Zeus to Barton."

p. 227. French novelist Colette. Ibid.

p. 227. Bloomsbury group. Ibid.

p. 227–28. Anaïs Nin. Ibid.

p. 228. Eleanor Roosevelt. Ibid.

p. 229 . Mattachine Society. Ibid.

p. 228. Bisexual men are officially recognized." GLBTQ: An Encyclopedia of Gay, Lesbian, Bisexual, Transgender & Queer Culture, s.v. "Bisexual Movements," http://www.glbtq.com/social-sciences/bisex_movements.html.

p. 230. Social critic, author. Harrison et al., "From Zeus to Barton."

p. 230. "Bisexuality should be."

p. 230. "Straight, Gay or Lying? Bisexuality Revisited," The *New York Times*, July 5, 2005, http://www.nytimes.com/2005/07/05/health/05sex.html?ex=1278216000&en=5a82f18cadf2ad83&ei=5088&partner=rssnyt&emc=rss.

ABOUT THE
AUTHORS

NICOLE KRISTAL graduated with a degree in journalism from the University of Oregon where she first learned that organizing bisexuals was similar to herding cats. Since then, she has written for *Newsweek*, *Premiere* magazine, *Back Stage West* newspaper, and Web sites such as BiCafe and Ostrich Ink. In 2003, she decided to pursue her career as a singer-songwriter full-time, performing her bi tunes at respected venues across Los Angeles and at the North American Bisexual Conference in 2004. While struggling to pay the bills, Nicole fell into illicit academic term-paper writing for rich Hollywood kids and later exposed the practice and her experiences on the *CBS Evening News*, WPHT talk radio in Philadelphia, and the Lesley Primeau radio show in Canada. She's currently paying the bills staff-writing for a weekly newspaper in Los Angeles and is in the process of recording a new album.

MIKE SZYMANSKI has been a bi activist since the early 1980s when he was a gay writer who came out as bi in a cover story and then went on the *Donahue Show* to talk about it. He has been on more than forty talk shows, and has written for *E! Online*,

Knight-Ridder Tribune, Atlanta Constitution, Entertainment Weekly, US, and many national magazines and now writes for the *Los Angeles Times, Science Fiction Weekly, WordMag,* and Hollywood.com. Mike has also written popular columns on PlanetOut.com, BiFocus.com, BiCafe.com, and Cybersocket. com. He was previously media coordinator for BiNet USA, and now teaches journalism at UCLA. His current partner found him by reading an article Mike wrote about bisexuality and came out as bi after being married to a woman. They are now raising a child his partner fathered with Mike's sister and have been together for a decade.